D0205968

To Make the Punishment
Fit the Crime

To Make the Punishment Fit the Crime

Essays in the Theory of Criminal Justice

Michael Davis

Westview Press

BOULDER • SAN FRANCISCO • OXFORD

BOWLING GREEN STATE
UNIVERSITY LIBRARIES
LIBRARY
DISCARDED

All rights reserved. No part of this publication may be reproduced or transmitted in any form or by any means, electronic or mechanical, including photocopy, recording, or any information storage and retrieval system, without permission in writing from the publisher.

Copyright © 1992 by Westview Press, Inc.

Published in 1992 in the United States of America by Westview Press, Inc., 5500 Central Avenue, Boulder, Colorado 80301-2847, and in the United Kingdom by Westview Press, 36 Lonsdale Road, Summertown, Oxford OX2 7EW

Library of Congress Cataloging-in-Publication Data
Davis, Michael.
    To make the punishment fit the crime : essays in the theory of criminal justice / by Michael Davis.
        p.   cm.
    Includes bibliographical references and index.
    ISBN 0-8133-1434-8
    1. Punishment.   I. Title.
K5103.D38   1992
345′.077—dc20
[342.577]   92-16916
                                                                          CIP

Printed and bound in the United States of America

(∞)   The paper used in this publication meets the requirements
       of the American National Standard for Permanence of Paper
       for Printed Library Materials Z39.48-1984.

10   9   8   7   6   5   4   3   2   1

For my cellmates, Washtenaw County Jail,
November 1969

Contents

Preface

The ten essays published here have a single theme: Retribution, *properly understood*, provides a practical framework for justifying the institution of criminal law, for deciding statutory penalties, and for sentencing particular criminals.

These essays form the main body of my work on retribution. I have culled them from a larger store, arranged them in a logical (rather than chronological) order, edited out passages that proximity to kin made unnecessary, corrected minor errors, and updated some endnotes. The result is more than a collection of essays.

Part One begins with a survey of punishment theory today, placing in context the topics discussed later. The remainder of Part One explains the relationship between punishment theory, morality, and political theory, distinguishes my approach to retributivism from others (and from utilitarian theories), and offers a justification of what I have come to call "the fairness theory of criminal desert."

Part Two applies the theory to some hard problems. Three chapters are concerned with setting statutory penalties for (respectively) attempts, recidivism, and crimes of strict liability. Another chapter concerns disparity in sentencing. The problems discussed in this part, while each interesting in itself, interest me primarily because they offer opportunities to show my approach to punishment superior to its competitors, both retributive and utilitarian.

Part Three responds to critics, especially Hyman Gross and Andrew von Hirsch. It also exhibits the underlying strength of my approach, both by offering new arguments for it and by contrasting it with competitors.

Those looking for major changes in my position will be disappointed. I have found little to take back (nothing really, except for a few sentences making "protective associations" sound more important than they are). Perhaps I too should be disappointed. Such consistency could mean only that I have learned little since I first began writing about punishment fifteen years ago. But I am not disappointed, merely surprised at how well my writing has stood up. Serious errors there must be. The history of philosophy allows no other conclusion. But, as far as I can tell, these errors remain undiscovered. Gathering these ten essays in one convenient place should help those in search of errors to find them. They have my blessing.

An author's preface should acknowledge debts without swelling into a catalogue about which even the author could not care. I have used endnotes liberally to give credit where I thought it due (and not obvious from the text). I shall not recount those debts here. I shall limit myself to debts not paid elsewhere.

One debt not paid elsewhere is owed to Feinberg-and-Gross, not the philosopher and the lawyer who are duly acknowledged as individuals, but their anthology from which I was teaching during the Winter Semester 1977-78 when, in the middle of discussing von Hirsch's argument for the mutual deducibility of desert from deterrence and deterrence from desert, I realized the deduction only went one way, from desert to deterrence. That realization, together with others that seemed to jump from other readings in the anthology as they bumped against one another, sent me to my desk where, by summer's end, I had a draft of "How to Make the Punishment Fit the Crime." That was the first time I used Feinberg-and-Gross. Though I had taught philosophy of law before, using other anthologies, I had always ended the semester less interested in the law's problems than I began. Feinberg-and-Gross made me a philosopher of law, an accomplishment for which I remain grateful.

I hope my students felt as good about the class as I did. However that may be, I owe them, and those who followed — not only at Illinois State University but also at the University of Illinois at Chicago and the Illinois Institute of Technology — much for seeming to enjoy learning along with me, for generally approving of my writings when I assigned them, and for telling me when they thought I had strayed too far from common sense. Scholarly works generally don't give students the credit they deserve, perhaps because the student contribution is so pervasive as to be at once certain and invisible.

Last, I must thank Rebecca Newton for turning a confusing pile of offprints, typescripts, and penciled notes into a text almost camera-ready; La Verne Hepburn for completing that job; Sohair ElBaz for getting the bibliography together; Don Scheid, for helping me decide what to leave out; and Spencer Carr for holding my hand through all the difficulties preceding publication.

To my seven-year-old son who is still trying to figure out what his father does, and to my lawyer wife who knows all too well, I offer this book as a hunter might offer his family the day's kill, or as a togaed Roman might pour off some of his drink to honor the gods.

There remains only the required acknowledgment of journals for granting permission to reprint.

Three articles are reprinted here without significant change: Chapter Two, "The Relative Independence of Punishment Theory," which originally appeared in *Law and Philosophy* 7 (December 1988): 321-350, reprinted by permission of Kluwer Academic Publishers; Chapter Eight, "Sentencing:

Must Justice Be Even-Handed?," which originally appeared in *Law and Philosophy* 1 (April 1982): 77-117, reprinted by permission of Kluwer Academic Publishers; and Chapter Ten, which originally appeared in *Iyyun* 39 (July 1990): 295-319, under the somewhat shorter title "Using the Market to Measure Deserved Punishment."

The other seven articles are reprinted with significant excisions: Chapter One, "Recent Work in Punishment Theory," which originally appeared in *Public Affairs Quarterly* 4 (July 1990): 217-233; Chapter Three, "Harm and Retribution," which originally appeared in *Philosophy and Public Affairs* 15 (Summer 1986): 236-266; Chapter Four, "How to Make the Punishment Fit the Crime," which originally appeared in *Ethics* 93 (July 1983): 726-752, ©1983 by The University of Chicago Press, all rights reserved; Chapter Five, "Why Attempts Deserve Less Punishment Than Complete Crimes," which originally appeared in *Law and Philosophy* 5 (April 1986): 1-32, reprinted by permission of Kluwer Academic Publishers; Chapter Six, "Just Deserts for Recidivists," which originally appeared in *Criminal Justice Ethics* 4 (Summer/Fall 1985): 29-50; Chapter Seven, "Strict Liability: Deserved Punishment for Faultless Conduct," which originally appeared in *Wayne Law Review* 33 (Summer 1987): 1363-1393; and Chapter Nine, "Criminal Desert, Harm, and Fairness," which originally appeared in the *Israel Law Review* 25 (Summer/Autumn 1991): 581-594.

Michael Davis

PART ONE

Theory

1

Recent Work in Punishment Theory

We do not have a good history of punishment *theory* in this century. Indeed, we do not even have a good history of punishment.[1] Perhaps we don't because it is still too early—so much has happened so recently. We can, however, already identify some large trends and notable events. Because these form the background against which the rest of this book must be understood, this chapter is a sketch for a part of that history, an attempt to put in order recent work in punishment theory.

Where to Start?

Choosing a starting point is easy. What is most striking about punishment theory in this century is the break in it beginning with the Second World War. What Auden called "a low dishonest decade" ended with publication of J. D. Mabbott's "Punishment" (1939). Almost fifteen years passed before anything comparable occurred again.[2] For example, Anthony Flew's influential paper, "The Justification of Punishment," appeared only in 1954; John Rawls' famous "Two Concepts of Rules," the following year.

The war no doubt had something to do with this break. But the war cannot explain it all. Legal theory recovered much more quickly. Hans Kelsen published *The General Theory of Law and State* in 1945. The analytic jurisprudence of the criminal law recovered almost as fast. Jerome Hall's *General Principles of Criminal Law* came out in 1947.

The break in punishment theory also cannot be explained by any lack of issues to consider. The punishment of war crimes raised difficult questions for the theory of punishment, as it did for legal theory generally. What, for example, was the function of trying, convicting, and hanging under retroactive laws those who used the Nazi state to murder millions of helpless civilians? Execution is not reform. Nor can punishment for violating retroactive laws deter lawbreaking. Yet, while the war seemed to have shaken legal theory to its foundations, it did not do the same for punishment theory.[3]

3

Explaining the break in punishment theory as a mere byproduct of the general movement of philosophy away from both grand theory and practical applications is tempting. The decade after the Second World War was the summertime of language analysis. In ethics, the hot topics were meta-ethical: Do ethical terms mean anything at all? Can argument concerning substantive ethical questions be more than an irrational appeal to emotions? Since punishment theory is in part at least a species of applied ethics, it would not have done well in such a climate.

Yet, the state of philosophy is not enough to explain that long vacation from important work. Political theory did not cease in the same way that punishment theory did. Political theorists just became more common in political science departments as they became less common in philosophy departments. When the break in punishment theory did end, it ended more or less simultaneously in its two traditional homes, law schools and philosophy departments. It was as though punishment theorists had gone to sleep in 1939 and not awakened until fifteen years later.[4]

This Rip-van-Winkle hypothesis is preposterous, of course. Yet, more evidence supports it. When punishment theory began to revive in the mid-fifties, it began about where it ended in 1939. We can distinguish two rather different debates.

One is between deterrent theorists and retributivists over whether deterrence or retribution is "*the* purpose of punishment." Though retributivists might have been expected to challenge deterrent theorists to make sense of the war crime trials, they seldom referred to those trials at all, and when they did, the reference was fleeting.[5] Deterrent theorists clearly had the advantage—just as they had in 1939.

The other debate is between deterrent theorists and reform theorists over whether crime should be reconceived as a social disease and punishment replaced by treatment. Here the deterrent theorists seem to be the underdogs. Indeed, their opponents often confused them with retributivists.[6] And that was exactly how things were in 1939. Neither a great war nor a decade of peace had noticeably advanced punishment theory or even changed its terms.

Some Big Trends

Explaining why that was is probably best left to historians. Our concern here is what has happened since the fifties. The last three decades seem to be the richest period in punishment theory since its first three decades as a subject distinct from political theory, the golden age that began with Beccaria's *Crimes and Punishments* (1764), included Bentham's *Introduction to the Principles of Morals and Legislation* (1789), and ended with Kant's *Metaphysical Elements of Justice* (1797).

We may observe two decisive trends since 1955. The first is the collapse of reform as an alternative to traditional punishment. The fifties and sixties were a period of reformist experiments in statutory penalties, sentencing policy, prison regimes, and parole. How strange that Karl Menninger's *The Crime of Punishment* appeared only in 1969. By then, the reformist experiments were coming to an end. The results were appalling. Reform had not reduced the crime rate or even slowed its long rise. Reform had not even changed the recidivism rate. Recidivism remained so constant across prison regimes that even those who opposed reform on principle were surprised.[7] More surprising yet, reform did not seem to have made prison more humane or to have shortened the time criminals served behind bars. Reform seemed instead to have increased the time served even for minor crimes, to have contributed to prison overcrowding, and so to have set the stage for the great prison riots that began the 1970's.

We might have expected the decline of reform to mean the ascension of deterrence. That is not what happened. After a confused period in the early seventies in which deterrence, incapacitation, social education, and other preventive theories competed for dominance, *retribution* – under the new title of "just deserts" – suddenly pushed them all aside.[8] Two works of what might be called "applied theory" seem to have contributed substantially to this sudden change: first, *Fair and Certain Punishment*, the report of the Twentieth Century Fund Task Force on Criminal Sentencing; and second, Andrew von Hirsch's *Doing Justice: The Choice of Punishment*. Since both were published in 1976, we may date a new era from their publication. It is the era in which we still live.

The new era is not, of course, one in which deterrent theorists are as rare as unicorns. Indeed, even reform theorists are not that rare. But deterrent theorists are far fewer than they used to be and they no longer dismiss retribution with a few words. Even the titles of important deterrentist works suggest the change. Compare, for example, Herbert Packer's confident *Limits of the Criminal Sanction* (1968) with Hyman Gross's more ambiguous *Theory of Criminal Justice* (1979), and both these with C. L. Ten's defensive *Crime, Guilt, and Punishment* (1987).[9] There are at least two reasons for this historic reversal in the relative appeal of the various theories of punishment.

One reason is that while deterrence claims to provide an empirical approach to the justification of punishment, criminologists have been unable to give it much empirical content. The rate of crime certainly does not respond to every change in statutory penalty or even always inversely to severity of statutory penalty. Predicting the effect of any statutory penalty remains at least as risky as predicting next year's stock prices.

Another reason deterrence is on the defensive is that the terms of debate have changed. The debate between reform and deterrence was primarily over which was a more effective approach to *controlling* objectionable behavior. Criminal punishment was thought of primarily as a means of social control. While criminal punishment was thought of in that way, retributive theories would necessarily seem hopelessly out of place. Retributive theories are primarily theories of justice, not social control.

The failure of reform experiments together with an inability to give much empirical content to deterrence undermined the appeal of thinking of criminal punishment as a means of social control. Of course, no one denied that criminal punishment does help to control objectionable behavior to a certain degree. But the appeal of theories is more a matter of motivation than mere fact. The question was: Why think of punishment as having deterrence as its (primary) purpose, function, rationale, or justification when thinking of it in that way tells little or nothing about *how* to set statutory penalties or sentence individual criminals? Deterrence theorists have yet to work out a convincing answer to that question.

The contrast with retributive theories could not be greater. Thinking of criminal punishment primarily as a means of doing justice (to use von Hirsch's apt phrase) at least seems to allow us to put aside the many empirical questions to which we have no answers anyway and get down to the business of revising the penalty provisions of statutes, restricting judicial discretion, abolishing parole, and otherwise trying to make sentences both just and determinate.

So, today, the theory of punishment is largely retributive theory. We might therefore suppose theorizing about punishment to be more or less over. What can one punishment theorist say to another if both are retributivists? Interestingly, the answer is: a great deal.

H.L.A. Hart argued long ago that punishment theory should be conceived as answering several distinct questions. We may usefully distinguish at least five here:

1. Why establish any institution of punishment at all?
2. Why establish this institution with its special concepts, principles of legislation, adjudicative procedures, and permissible penalties rather than some other?
3. What should the penalty be for violation of this statute?
4. Why punish this criminal for this violation of the statute (or, if he is to be let go, why do that)?
5. How much should this criminal be punished (if she is to be)?

Hart also argued that no answer to any one of these questions need determine the answer to any other, that there may be great opportunity for mixing and matching answers, and that any particular configuration of answers may require a complex justification drawing on such utilitarian considerations as deterrence as well as on such non-utilitarian considerations as justice. Though most effort seems to have gone into answering the first of these questions – Why establish any institution of punishment at all? – significant work has recently been done on all five. Let's look at some of the high points, taking the questions in order.

Justifying Punishment as an Institution

Punishment theory has always been primarily concerned with punishment by law, especially by the criminal law. Yet, the concept of punishment includes much more than criminal punishment. Stormy seas punish the shore; owners punish their pets; parents punish their children; adults punish their peers by small slights; gods punish mortals; and so on. Punishment theorists often draw on such related practices for insight into criminal punishment. Whether this is wise is at least open to question. Criminal punishment is an institution quite unlike these others in scale, formality, and clientele. Insofar as these others nonetheless resemble criminal punishment, the question becomes which we should treat as the standard or central case of punishment and which as nonstandard or peripheral. *Our* terms for punishment, both "punishment" and "penalty," are – like "crime," "justice," and even "condemnation" – originally legal terms, not terms deriving from domestic or ordinary social life. So, etymology at least warns us not to make too much of punishment outside the criminal law.

Retributivists, however, have generally tried to offer an analysis of criminal punishment that would fit it into a general theory of punishment. There seem to be two longterm trends in such attempts – and one undercurrent that has only recently itself become a trend. One longterm trend consists of what have been called "moral education," "penitential," or "paternalistic" theories; the second, of "reprobative," "expressive," or "condemnatory" theories. Theories in the undercurrent have been called "benefits-and-burdens," "reciprocity," or "restoration" theories.

Paternalistic theories hold that all justified punishment, or at least all punishment of rational agents, must aim at a certain good for those punished. This good may be subjective "penance" (Morris, Hampton, Duff) or an objective "connection with correct values" (Nozick).[10]

While paternalistic theories focus on the person punished, *condemnatory* theories focus on the person or community *doing* the punishing. For such theories, punishment is primarily a suitably emphatic denunciation of the wrongdoer for her wrongdoing (von Hirsch, Kadish, Primoratz).[11] Punishment need not imply any intention to bring about penance or some other good state in the person punished; its primary function is simply "expressive," for example, to reaffirm the wrongness of what has been done.

Paternalistic theories superficially resemble traditional *reform* theories; condemnatory theories, traditional *deterrence* theories; yet, both are fundamentally different from these varieties of preventive theory. According to the paternalistic theory (in its pure form, at least), punishment would be justified even if wrongdoers never repented what they did or changed their ways as a result of punishment. What is important—important because it respects the moral personality of the wrongdoer—is that punishment be imposed with the intention of helping the wrongdoer rationally appreciate the wrongness of what he has done. In much the same way, according to the condemnatory theory (in its pure form), punishment would be justified even if the emphatic condemnation of wrongdoers had no effect at all on the rate of wrongdoing. Reaffirming the wrongness of an act is good in itself, good enough to justify punishment, all else equal.

That brings us to restoration theory, what was described earlier as an undercurrent in the justification of punishment as an institution. Restoration is not a theory of punishment in general but of criminal punishment (and its analogues) in particular. It holds that the purpose of criminal punishment as an institution is to maintain the just distribution of benefits and burdens the law itself creates. A relatively just society is to be thought of as a cooperative enterprise, or social contract, from which each benefits if others generally do their part and in which doing one's part will sometimes be burdensome. According to restoration theory (in its pure form), the institution of punishment is justified whenever a practice of punishment will keep the subjects of the law from gaining an unfair advantage over one another by lawbreaking.

We described the restoration theory as, until recently, an undercurrent in retributive theorizing about the institution of punishment. The reason for so describing it is that defenders of the theory were surprisingly scarce until the eighties. Herbert Morris (1968) is generally cited as its first modern defender, but he never discussed the purpose, function, rationale, or justification of punishment in the paper in which he is supposed to have given that defense. He simply assumed a society having a cooperative *structure* and then appealed to that structure in explaining how a criminal could have a right to punishment.[12] When he finally did suggest a (partial) "justification" for the institution of punishment more than a decade later, what he suggested was a paternalistic theory, doing so without any suggestion that he had changed his mind about anything.[13]

John Finnis seems to have been the first to endorse the view that maintaining a fair balance between burdens and benefits is "the most specific and essential aim of punishment" as an institution.[14] Though Finnis did this in a well-known paper in *Analysis* (1972), no one seems to have given him the credit. Perhaps the reason no one has is that he himself claims only to be clarifying a view he attributes to Jeffrie Murphy.

Except for Morris, Murphy is the only writer commonly cited as a defender of the theory. Yet, he is not. While he did in fact do much to develop the theory, he originally attributed it to Kant[15] and soon argued that it could *not* apply in any society much like ours.[16] Having denied the theory any practical employment, he eventually decided that Kant held no theory of punishment whatever.[17] So, as far as Murphy is concerned, the restoration theory is a defenseless orphan.

A few writers have listed me among the theory's defenders.[18] We shall see later why they might think that. But, for now, it will be enough to point out that my present view, one held since I began writing about punishment, is that there are so many good reasons for the institution of punishment that debate over something properly called "the" purpose, function, rationale, or justification simply obscures the obvious.[19]

Though Finnis seems to be the first writer explicitly to endorse the restoration theory, he is not the only one to have done so. Among the others are Alan Gewirth (1978), David Hoekema (1980), Wojciech Sadurski (1985), and George Sher (1987).[20] Perhaps these endorsements have generally been overlooked because they occur deep within large works concerned with moral theory or social justice.

Justifying This or That Institution of Punishment

We come then to our second question: why establish this particular institution of criminal punishment rather than some other? A particular institution of criminal punishment can, of course, be quite complex, including police, lawyers, courts, prisons, probation officers, professional schools of various kinds, constitutional principles, and a whole range of interconnecting policies and practices. Wholesale comparison of one institution of criminal punishment with another, say, Illinois' with England's, is almost too large to undertake. Retail comparisons, say of Illinois' policy on probation for juveniles with England's, risks missing the context in which the policy works and, with that, features essential to making sense of it. So, the justification of a particular institution of criminal punishment, or even of a substantial part of it, by comparison with others, is relatively rare. And so, retributive attempts are even rarer. They are, however, not unknown. George Fletcher's *Rethinking Criminal Law* (1978) is probably the best example of what can be done.

More common than this comparative approach are attempts to justify a particular institution, or an important part of it, by an argument from first principles. We can identify at least two major debates of this sort over the last thirty years: one concerning the legislation of morality (what began as the Hart-Devlin debate); the other concerning capital punishment. Though both debates have involved a good deal of retributive rhetoric, they seem in fact to have had little to do with theories about the purpose of punishment.

Consider the Hart-Devlin debate. Devlin insisted that punishing immoral conduct was justified, in part at least, as an emphatic denunciation of its "sinfulness." Devlin would then seem to hold a condemnatory theory of punishment. Yet, as Devlin made clear, he wanted to denounce wrongdoing by punishment in order to maintain social order. For him, the ultimate justification of the criminal law is its contribution to social order, its educational *effect*, not its appropriateness for denouncing wrongdoing. The condemnatory theory actually had no part in his argument.[21]

The same seems to be true of the debate over capital punishment. For example, Jeffrey Reiman recently based a novel argument against the death penalty in part on what he called "the retributive principle." A form of *lex talionis*, it reads: "The equality and rationality of persons implies that an offender deserves and his victim has the right to impose suffering on the offender equal to that which he imposed on the victim."[22] Whatever the merits of this principle as a measure of deserved punishment, it is altogether silent about the purpose of punishment as an institution, its function, or rationale. Its only contribution to the justification of punishment is to identify a right to respond to an offender in a certain way. It leaves open the question of setting up a system of criminal punishment to support that right.

Recently several writers have claimed that punishment theory in general or the justification of a system of criminal justice in particular must rest on a political theory.[23] The guiding idea seems to be that political theory should determine the purpose, function, rationale, or justification of punishment and, by doing that, the organization of a particular system of criminal justice. The claim is plausible enough for the theory of criminal legislation. Socialism, for example, is likely to make criminal some activity liberalism would not (and vice versa). The claim is, however, not so plausible for other aspects of criminal justice (for example, how much to punish), perhaps because these are largely determined by moral rather than political considerations, as I shall argue in Chapter Two. So far, the arguments made for the importance of political theory fail to distinguish between moral and political theory. Discussion of the relation of political theory to punishment theory seems likely to continue.

What I have said so far may suggest that theories about the purpose, function, rationale, or justification of punishment as an institution can make no contribution to theorizing about the choice between institutions of criminal punishment (apart from the obvious contribution to the theory of legislation). That is not so. But there are surprisingly few examples of theories actually contributing much. Perhaps the best of these is R. A. Duff's *Trials and Punishments*. Duff's version of paternalistic theory led him to analyze the trial as a structure to encourage penance in the criminal. Whatever the merits of paternalism as a theory of punishment generally, Duff does show paternalism to have much to say about how trials should be conducted.

That is enough about choosing between institutions of criminal punishment. We may turn now to setting statutory penalties.

Statutory Penalties

While one might expect different views about the purpose of instituting punishment to produce important differences in the penalties available, that does not seem to be so. Except for capital punishment, the range of penalties seems to be uncontroversial. Imprisonment is the most severe penalty available, unless capital punishment is; fine, suspended sentence, and probation are the least severe. The upper limit seems to be set by considerations of humane treatment rather than by considerations of purpose.

Theories about the purpose of punishment do, nonetheless, have some part here. Considerations of crime control, at least in lawless times like these, seem to assure that the actual penalty scale will often reach the upper limit set by considerations of humane treatment. Considerations of crime control also seem to assure that the penalty scale will not go too low. Why have a penalty people would not want to avoid? So, two points for deterrent theorists.

Any points for retributivists? Though von Hirsch in particular has claimed otherwise,[24] retributive considerations do not *seem* to have much to do with setting the end points of the penalty scale. Would we keep capital punishment or even life imprisonment if we had decisive proof that lowering the upper limit of the penalty scale to, say, five years imprisonment, would not increase the crime rate at all?

Since neither the penalties available nor their ranking seems to present any problem for punishment theorists generally, the only retributivist problem of setting statutory penalties is finding a procedure to connect statutory crimes to statutory penalties in a just way. The heart of this problem is finding a principled way to rank crimes. Here the condemnatory theory has dominated until now. Why?

If justified punishment condemns the wrongdoer for his wrongdoing in a suitably emphatic way, then the suitability of a particular statutory penalty should (it seems) be determinable using ordinary standards of condemnation. Perhaps the appeal of the condemnatory theory is due to its apparent usefulness in setting penalties. Certainly, the primary interest of those who now accept the theory is in setting statutory penalties (or individual sentences), not in the philosophical debate over the purpose of punishment. If the paternalistic theory is the preserve of academic philosophers (as it more or less seems to be), the condemnatory theory is largely the preserve of lawyers (like Kadish) and criminologists (like von Hirsch).

But perhaps the period in which condemnatory theory dominates the setting of penalties is almost over. Just as deterrent theory had trouble giving empirical content to its key notion, so (it now seems) does condemnatory theory. Condemnatory theory's preferred approach to ranking crimes was once the sociological survey of "seriousness." That proved something of an embarrassment. Since the pioneering work of Sellin and Wolfgang,[25] this approach, while generally ranking crimes in ways not too different from the criminal law as we know it, has regularly produced striking anomalies. The anomalies occur so frequently and are so serious that the sociological survey has in fact had little effect on practice. (For examples of these anomalies, see Chapter Three.)

Von Hirsch has recently argued for another method.[26] Assuming that moral condemnation must rest on judgments concerning how much harm a crime does and the criminal's culpability (her state of mind at the time of the crime), he has suggested that a just penalty can be determined by forcing a sentencing commission, legislature, or judge to rate crimes explicitly taking those considerations into account while working out a statutory scheme. They are forced to compare one crime with another in a systematic way. The results of this process would then be compared with the results of the sociological survey. Where the results diverge, the sentencing commission would have to reconsider what it has done, making explicit its rationale for choosing one result over the other.

Von Hirsch's forced choice is far from a formal procedure. He has, however, had success in Minnesota and Washington getting agreement among those assigned the job of working out sentencing guidelines. Whether such agreement is a function of condemnation (as he asserts), of some other theory of punishment (as I think), or of no one theory is anyone's guess. Von Hirsch has yet to show that his method works because (and only because) the condemnatory theory is true. The sociological evidence of widespread agreement independent of following any method suggests that von Hirsch will have trouble showing any connection between his method and condemnatory theory.

The only other approach to giving empirical content to condemnatory theories now available is to rely on the legislator's, sentencing commissioner's, or judge's intuition. But, given the frequent anomalies in survey results, this intuitive approach seems to ignore the problem rather than solve it. Still, if there were no alternative, it would doubtless continue in use for some time, in part perhaps just because it ignores the underlying problem.

There is, however, now an alternative, one I developed over the last decade. It uses the value of the unfair advantage the criminal necessarily takes by her crime to determine the ranking of crimes. My emphasis on the value of unfair advantage has led several writers to suppose that I accept a restoration theory. But, as indicated earlier, I do not. What I do accept (and shall defend in later chapters) is much less controversial. I call it the "fairness theory of criminal desert" to distinguish it from the restoration theory. It offers relatively rigorous arguments where others only appeal to intuition or generate results strikingly at odds with practice. The only trouble with it seems to be that it draws on economics rather than sociology and so, is foreign to most people now interested in setting statutory penalties. Perhaps the experts will retool once they see the advantage of doing so.

Punishing Individuals

We come then to the reasons for punishing this criminal for this crime, especially questions of justifications or excuse. Here again, while condemnatory theories have considerable popularity, in fact they cannot explain why we should *punish* this criminal for what he did. Punitive condemnation is supposed to be for moral *blameworthiness*. But blameworthiness, as such, seems to deserve blame, not punishment, that is to say, judgments or hard words, not loss of life, liberty, or property. Condemnable acts are not, as such, punishable. Crimes, on the other hand, do seem to be punishable as such — at least within a relatively just legal system. So, for example, suppose that someone has broken the law of a relatively just legal system and that punishment is the prescribed response. That the law of such a legal system so provides seems to be good reason (all else equal) to do as the law provides. In such a legal system, the crime itself gives us good reason (all else equal) to punish.[27]

Condemnatory theory seems to become useful only once we agree that, all else equal, this criminal deserves to be punished as the law provides. For example, the moral *praiseworthiness* of what he has done does seem good reason not to punish a person for what he did even if he did thereby violate the law. Whether it should always provide a legal justification (or always excuse completely) is harder to say. But that it must seems unlikely. For example, suppose a woman steals a car to get her injured child to the hospital in time. Suppose too that stealing the car was in fact the only way to get the child to the hospital in time. While perhaps everyone would agree that the theft is in some respects morally praiseworthy, would all agree as well that the thief should be found "not guilty" rather than, say, convicted and given a suspended sentence?

Similarly, moral blame*less*ness — for example, owing to mental illness or necessity — also seems a good reason *not* to punish the criminal for the resulting crime. But whether blamelessness must always be sufficient to excuse from punishment again seems doubtful. Condemnation seems at best to provide only a partial theory of justification and excuse. This comes out well both in Sanford Kadish's "Excusing Crime" (1987) and in Kathleen Moore's *Pardons* (1989).

Conclusions

We come then to our last question: *how much* should we punish this criminal for this crime? So long as we consider the *maximum* punishment the criminal can legally deserve for the crime in question, the fairness theory seems (for reasons given earlier) to be the only option. The advantages and disadvantages of the various approaches to deciding statutory penalties reappear in deciding how much to punish. So, for example, the condemnatory theory would have to explain why a judge *must* measure legal desert *solely* by moral blameworthiness. But, once the judge determines the maximum legal punishment, the fairness theory has nothing further to say. We are left to consider whether facts about the criminal such as his character or facts about our society such as the state of our prisons or the effect of punishment on third-parties, may permit (or forbid) mitigating the otherwise deserved punishment. Here moral blameworthiness or its opposite may have a place: Though this woman has committed a serious crime, her otherwise good life gives us reason to blame her less than we would otherwise and so gives us reason to be merciful.[28] Here too perhaps is the place for such utilitarian considerations as reform, incapacitation, compensating victims, and community satisfaction — or, at least, here such considerations *could* have a place if claims on their behalf have sufficient empirical backing. Though mitigation deserves more attention, we cannot give it here. Our subject is recent work in punishment theory. Sentencing has not yet had the attention it deserves (though we will devote Chapter Eight to it).[29] With that, we have reached the boundary of what has been done. Though much has been accomplished in the last two decades, the surprise is how much remains to do. Let us now see what can be accomplished.

Notes

A draft of this chapter was presented to the Philosophy Colloquium, Illinois Institute of Technology, October 20, 1988, and at a gathering sponsored by the Center for Ethics in Society, Western Michigan University, October 27, 1988. I should like to thank those present — as well as Patrick McAnany, R. A. Duff, Igor Primoratz, and Wojciech Sadurski — for many helpful suggestions. I should also like to thank John Kleinig, Don Scheid, and Andrew von Hirsch for corresponding with me on a number of the questions discussed here. I hope they will not be too unhappy with the result.

1. Since first writing this, I have found the more extreme observation that we lack even a good history of punishment theory before this century. Hugo, Bedau, *Death Is Different* (Boston: Northeastern University Press, 1987), p.

257 n. 11. Bedau does, however, temper that observation with the citation of some useful work on the eighteenth and nineteenth century.

2. John Kleinig, *Punishment and Desert* (The Hague: Marinus Nijhoff, 1973), pp. 134-154, includes a thorough temporally ordered bibliography of works more or less concerned with punishment. Though it does include almost two pages of references for the years 1940-1953, the most important to punishment theory is probably Sheldon Glueck's reformist *Crime and Justice* (1945). The most important work on the list, Charles L. Stevenson's *Ethics and Language* (1944), has only a few pages on punishment and these seem to have had no effect on punishment theory. My claim then is not that nothing was published on punishment theory during that period, but that nothing of importance was. The fact that a good deal was in fact published on the subject during those years only adds to the mystery.

3. Think, for example, of the debate between Hart and Fuller concerning the relation of law and morality. H.L.A. Hart, "Positivism and the Separation of Law and Morals," *Harvard Law Review* 71 (February 1958): 593-629; and Lon Fuller, "Positivism and Fidelity to Law — A Reply to Professor Hart," *Harvard Law Review* 71 (February 1958): 630-672).

4. Note, for example, how little Mabbott's 1955 response to Flew differs from his 1939 paper. J. D. Mabbott, "Professor Flew on Punishment," *Philosophy* 30 (July 1955): 256-265.

5. Note, for example, Walter Bern's extended challenge to opponents of the death penalty to explain punishing the Nazis without appealing to the same retributive considerations that would (he claims) justify the death penalty for ordinary murderers. *For Capital Punishment: Crime and the Morality of the Death Penalty* (New York: Basic Books, 1979). Note, too, Primoratz's similar use of our intuitions about punishing war criminals. Igor Primoratz, "Punishment as Language," *Philosophy* 64 (April 1989): 187-205. Compare these with the corresponding passages (p. 109-110) of so late a work as H. J. McCloskey, "Utilitarian and Retributive Punishment," *Journal of Philosophy* 66 (February 16, 1967): 91-110.

6. The explanation for this tendency is, of course, that retributivism and deterrentism agree that criminals are more or less rational (capable of following rules, capable as well of choosing to obey or not on the basis of good reasons, and so on). That assumption is exactly what reform theories generally deny.

7. But see R. Martinson, "New Findings, New Views: A Note of Caution Regarding Sentencing Reform," *Hofstra Law Review* 7 (Winter 1979): 243-258, for some reasons to think that while most attempts at reform have failed, a few have had some success. For a recent attempt to revive reform as a general theory of crime control rather than "punishment", see R. D. Ellis and C. S. Ellis, *Theories of Criminal Justice* (Wolfeboro, New Hampshire: Longwood Academic Press, 1989).

8. For a detailed (and perceptive) review of the literature of the fifties and early sixties, see Patrick McAnany, "Punishment: Current Survey of Philosophy and Law," *Saint Louis University Law Journal* 11 (Summer 1967): 491-535.

9. C. L. Ten, *Crime, Guilt, and Punishment* (Oxford: Clarendon Press, 1987), claims to be arguing for a "third way" or "mixed view" much as Hart did. Yet, while Hart was opening up punishment theory to *some* retributive considerations (beyond the purely formal ones allowed by Rawls' 1955 paper), Ten seems to be trying to find some room for *utilitarian* considerations. He is therefore classed here as part of the utilitarian rearguard (though, for other purposes he might well be put in another category).

10. Herbert Morris, "A Paternalistic Theory of Punishment," *American Philosophical Quarterly* 18 (October 1981): 263-271; Jean Hampton, "The Moral Education Theory of Punishment," *Philosophy and Public Affairs* 13 (Summer 1984): 208-338; R. A. Duff, *Trials and Punishments* (Cambridge: Cambridge University Press, 1985); and Robert Nozick, *Philophical Explanations* (Cambridge, Mass.: Harvard University Press, 1981), especially, pp. 370-384.

11. Andred von Hirsch, *Past or Future Crimes* (New Brunswick, New Jersey: Rutgers University Press, 1985); Sanford Kadish, "Complicity, Cause, and Blame: A Study in the Interpretation of Doctrine," *California Law Review* 73 (1985): 257-289; and Igor Primoratz, "Punishment as Language." Though Joel Feinberg, "The Expressive Theory of Punishment," *Monist* 49 (July 1965): 397-423, is often linked to the condemnatory form of retributivism, that seems to be wrong logically (even though right historically). Feinberg's expressionism is ultimately descriptive or utilitarian, not retributive. For a defense of this controversial claim, see Primoratz.

12. Herbert Morris, "Persons and Punishment," *Monist* 52 (October 1968): 475-501, has been so useful as an example of the restoration theory for so long that one must read carefully not to read too much in. So, for example, just because Morris says that it would be "just" to do such-and-such, we are not entitled to conclude he means "justified," only that one consideration relevant to justification is satisfied.

13. Morris, "Paternalistic Theory of Punishment."

14. P. 135 in John Finnis, "The Restoration of Retribution," *Analysis* 32 (March 1972): 131-135.

15. Jeffrie Murphy, "Kant's Theory of Criminal Punishment," in L. W. Beck, *Proceedings of the Third International Kant Congress* (Dordrect: D. Reidel, 1971), pp. 434-441.

16. Jeffrie Murphy, "Marxism and Retribution," *Philosophy and Public Affairs* 2 (Spring 1973): 217-243.

17. Jeffrie Murphy, "Does Kant Have a Theory of Punishment," *Columbia Law Review* 87 (April 1987): 509-432.

18. Michael Philips, "The Justification of Punishment and the Justification of Political Authority," *Law and Philosophy* 5 (December 1985): 393-416; Andrew von Hirsch, "Allocating Penalties: From 'Why Punish?' to 'How Much?'" Unpublished paper prepared for the Conference on Justice in Punishment, Jerusalem, Israel, March 1988; and Kathleen Moore, *Pardons* (New York: Oxford University Press, 1989).

19. See Chapter Four.

20. Alan Gewirth, *Reason and Morality* (Chicago: University of Chicago Press, 1978), pp. 294-299; David Hoekema, "The Right to Punish and the Right to be Punished," in H. G. Blocker and E. H. Smith, *John Rawls' Theory of Social Justice: An Introduction* (Athens, Ohio: Ohio University Press, 1980), pp. 239-269; Wojciech Sadurski, *Giving Desert Its Due* (Dordrecht: D. Reidel, 1985): 221-158; and George Scher, *Desert* (Princeton, New Jersey: Princeton University Press, 1987), pp. 69-88.

21. Patrick Devlin, "Morals and the Criminal Law," in Patrick Devlin, *The Enforcement of Morals* (London: Oxford University Press, 1965), pp. 1-25.

22. Jeffrey Reiman, "Justice, Civilization, and the Death Penalty: Answering van den Haag," *Philosophy and Public Affairs* 14 (Spring 1985), p. 125.

23. Philips, "The Justification of Punishment and the Justification of Political Authority"; Ted Honderich, "Punishment, the New Retributivism, and Political Philosophy," in A. Philips Griffiths, *Philosophy and Practice* (Cambridge: Cambridge University Press, 1985; Nicola Lacey, *State Punishment* (London: Routledge, 1988); Wojciech Sadurski, "Theory of Punishment, Social Justice, and Liberal Neutrality," *Law and Philosophy* 7 (December 1989): 351-374; and perhaps J. Braithwaite and P. Pettit, *Not Just Deserts: A Republican Theory of Criminal Justice* (Oxford: Clarendon Press, 1990).

24. Von Hirsch, *Past and Future Crimes*.

25. Thorsten Sellin and Marvin E. Wolfgang, *The Measurement of Delinquency* (New York: Wiley, 1964).

26. Von Hirsch, *Past or Future Crimes*, pp. 74-76.

27. This view is, of course, close to the "arid legalism" of Mabbott's "Punishment," *Mind* 48 (April 1939): 152-167. It differs, however, in presupposing a relatively just legal system. So, while Mabbott's legalism is "arid" in the sense of ignoring considerations of justice (apart from the procedural considerations built into the concept of law itself), mine is not. Insofar as retributivism is primarily a theory of just punishment, Mabbott is *not* a retributivist.

28. Claudia Card, "On Mercy," *Philosophical Review* 81 (April 1972): 182-207.

29. Compare von Hirsch, "Punishments in the Community and the Principles of Desert" *Rutgers Law Review* 20 (Spring 1989): 595-618.

2

The Relative Independence
of Punishment Theory

Punishment theory today goes on more or less independently of political theory. Should it? Michael Philips (among others) has recently argued that it should *not*.[1] Any theory of punishment complete enough to be useful must, according to Philips, presuppose a justification of the state that puts substantial limits on what punishment can be. We ignore those limits at our peril. So, for example, retributivism cannot find a plausible political theory to undergird it unless it recognizes deterrence as a legitimate function of punishment (p. 404).

Philips' thesis is, I think, potentially important. How important may be judged by putting it in context. Beccaria's *Crimes and Punishments* (1764) seems to be the *first* work ever written the primary subject of which is the justification and practice of punishment. Today such works take up a long shelf in any good academic library. Before Beccaria the theory of punishment was a mere outpost of political theory. Hobbes was unusual in giving it two chapters of *Leviathan*.[2] Most political philosophers (for example, Locke in *The Second Treatise* or Rousseau in *The Social Contract*) said much less, and what they said was perfunctory. After Beccaria, philosophers (and others) wrote whole books on punishment, but what they wrote was no longer (explicitly) political theory.

I don't know why this happened. I am not even sure that it did happen. Perhaps there is a forgotten literature on punishment a good historian could uncover. But, whatever history may turn out to be, Philips has raised fundamental questions about an assumption punishment theorists seem to accept without even being aware of doing so.

Philips argues that the assumption of independence should be abandoned. I shall argue that it should not. What Philips takes to be political theory are in fact *pre*conditions *both* of any plausible political theory *and* of any plausible theory of punishment. Understanding the relation of these preconditions to punishment theory will help us to understand better the logic of justifying punishment. It will also allow us to dispose of a common objection to the fairness version of retributivism. Nothing below relies on the history I have outlined. A philosopher's history is no more reliable than a historian's philosophy.

Some Preliminaries

Because certain terms in Philips' argument are obscure and certain premises unnecessarily question-begging, I must begin with these.

Philips' subject is not punishment in general, or even legal punishment in the sense that includes such oddities as punitive damages in tort or incarceration for contempt of court. It is *criminal punishment* strictly so called — or, as he says, "the conditions under which and the reason for which the state may legitimately inflict pain, impose fines, or restrict the liberty of its citizens [for violating] its laws" (p. 393).

The reference to "the state" in Philips' definition is unfortunate. It builds political theory into the very concept of criminal punishment. Criminal punishment outside the state becomes logically impossible. A theory of the state would be necessary even to know what criminal punishment is. In short, his definition seems to steal the prize he wants to win. Since most standard definitions of criminal punishment refer not to "the state" but to some "authority," "mechanism," or "procedure,"[4] I shall generally not use the term "state" (or "political authority") in what follows even where Philips would.[5] This change in terms should save Philips from any appearance of impropriety without unduly weakening his argument.

Philips seems to recognize three senses of "justifying (criminal) punishment": (1) justifying the criminal law as an *institution*, (2) justifying individual *statutory* penalties, and (3) justifying individual *sentences*. So, for example, he seems to intend justification in the first sense when he says that "punishment is one part of the criminal justice system, and both the legitimate functions and the moral justification of punishment must be understood in relation to that system" (p. 398). In contrast, he seems to intend justification in the second and third senses when he asserts, "if it is true that the very reasons that justify attaching penalties to a type of action also justify attempting to suppress tokens of that type, then any sound theory of state authority must acknowledge that punishment has a legitimate deterrent function" (p. 397).

For Philips, justifying punishment in any one of our three senses is (in part at least) a matter of showing that punishment serves some *function* (for example, deterrence). Yet, he never tells us what he means by "function." Is "function" equivalent to "effect" so that if punishment has a deterrent *effect* it has a deterrent *function*? Or is it equivalent to "intent" (or "purpose") so that, whatever the effect, punishment would have a deterrent function if the person doing the punishing intends the punishment as a deterrent? Or does "function" have its biological meaning, presupposing a self-regulating system, so that saying punishment has a deterrent function is equivalent to describing the criminal law as a system tending to readjust punishments whenever deterrence is threatened (whatever the system's actual effect or the intentions of those who instituted it or now operate it)? Or does "function" have some other meaning?

Though Philips often uses "intent" or "effect" where he could use "function," he seems, on the whole, to understand "function" as more or less equivalent to "intent." So, for example, he claims, "To say that punishment has a legitimate retributive function . . . is to say that other things equal the state has a right to punish . . . in a manner intended to impose suffering on wrongdoers that they deserve, because they deserve it" (p. 408). I shall hereafter understand "function" in this way (though without assuming that "the state" is what must have the necessary intention).

Philips devotes much time to trying to show that deterrence is relevant to the justification of the criminal law (at least in part) because punishment "deters." His devotion seems misplaced. Though Philips never tells us what he means by "deter," I assume he intends *prevention* of wrongdoing in some suitably general sense rather than merely *frightening* potential criminals into doing what they should.[6] Except perhaps for Kant, I know of no retributivist who thinks deterring wrongdoing in this wide sense is irrelevant to the justification of the criminal law.[7] Controversies in the theory of punishment seem to concern either a) the relation of deterrence to other relevant considerations in the justification of punishment as an institution (whether, for example, deterrence is either necessary or sufficient to justify a system of criminal law) or b) what part, if any, deterrence should have in the justification of statutory penalties or individual sentences.[8] Recalling that should keep us from wasting time with straw men.

Philips distinguishes between the justification of punishment proper and justification taking into account (what we might call) "side constraints." He does not require a theory of punishment to state necessary and sufficient conditions for justified acts of punishment. He thinks it enough if such a theory provides "reasons to punish, other things equal" (p. 399). But, for Philips, such a theory is radically incomplete. It will not settle any question until the "other things equal" is replaced by a set of specific principles. What these principles are will, Philips asserts, depend on our theory of "state authority" (and, he adds parenthetically, "perhaps, on certain additional moral views as well") (p. 399). From this assertion, it is only a short step to his conclusion that punishment theory presupposes political theory.

This distinction between incomplete theories of punishment and side constraints is tendentious. Philips would, it seems, have to say that the theory of (criminal) legislation is part of the theory of (criminal) punishment proper because it tells us what acts (all else equal) should be made punishable (though not what acts *are* punishable) (p. 405). The theory of excuse (or clemency), however, is *not* part of the theory of punishment proper because it only tells us what crimes or criminals should *not* be punished (or, in other words, when all else is not equal). The theory of excuse works like a side constraint. For much the same reason, Philips would, it seems, have to say that a theory setting the *minimum* punishment a criminal should receive would be part of the theory of punishments, since it tells how much we should punish, while a theory setting the *maximum* would not be, since it limits how much we should punish. I am not sure what Philips would say about the theory of justification. Is it a side constraint, like the theory of excuse, because it limits what can be punished? Or is it, like the theory of legislation, part of the theory of punishment proper because it is the logical complement of any theory telling us what to punish?

Philips' distinction between (incomplete) theories of punishment and mere side constraints seems so at odds with ordinary usage that I shall drop it. While there are important side constraints on any plausible theory of punishment (about which I shall say more later), a "theory of punishment" having nothing to say about excuse, justification, maximum punishment, or clemency would not deserve the name. The theory of punishment is, I think, chiefly about the logical effect of such institutional side constraints.

Dropping Philips' distinction between punishment theory proper and side constraints leaves us with a question: what should we do about the theory of criminal legislation? Philips thinks the theory obviously part of the theory of punishment. His reason is that the theory of legislation tells us what should be made punishable. So, for example, he claims that "in order to tell us what acts are rightly punished and what acts are not the retributivist must tell us what laws the state may legitimately pass to begin with . . . [and] to do this he needs a theory of the moral justification of state authority" (p. 405).

This argument is hardly decisive. The argument for having a system of criminal law seems (more or less) independent of any particular theory of legislation. We must, of course, assume that no legal punishment would be justified unless some law made an act punishable. We must assume a principle of legality. But we need not assume any more relation between the theory of punishment and the theory of legislation to explain why we should want a system of criminal law. Whatever plausible political theory we adopt, the resulting social order will be much the same (that is, it will have police, courts, laws against murder, robbery, and tax evasion, and so on).

Once we turn from the institution of punishment to setting statutory penalties, we have even less reason to concern ourselves with the theory of legislation. Having (justifiably) made an act a crime, we need only consider how bad the act is. We need not *assume* that the amount of punishment *must* be determined by the reasons for adopting the statute (whatever those might have been). However political our reasons for making a type of act criminal, we could have other reasons sufficient to choose the statutory penalty (for example, deterrence or moral desert). The same would ordinarily be true at sentencing.

Of course, if the law has mistakenly made an act a crime and left us no legal way to excuse it, treat it as justified, or give it a trivial penalty, we may have to refuse to dirty our hands, or compromise our principles by choosing the lowest penalty we can. But we would not then suppose ourselves engaged in ordinary punishment, the subject to which the theory of punishment principally applies. Nor need we appeal to political principles to decide what to do. The crisis a bad law creates is (in part) a moral crisis, whatever our political theory has to say about.

That, I think, is reason enough to doubt that the theory of legislation is properly part of the theory of punishment. There is another reason as well. Most political theories, for example, democracy or depotism, clearly have important things to say about which acts should be made crimes (and which should not). The theory of legislation seems to have a natural home in political theory in a way it does not in the theory of punishment. Defining the theory of punishment so that it *must* include the theory of legislation thus seems to beg the very question Philips wants to purchase by argument.

So, I shall hereafter suppose the theory of legislation to be outside even a complete theory of punishment. For our purposes, a complete theory need answer only three questions: (1) when (and why) would we be justified in having a system of criminal law? (2) when (and why) would we be justified in assigning a certain penalty to a type of act once it has been made a crime? and (3) when (and why) would we be justified in imposing a particular punishment upon a particular criminal? Since Philips has much to say about theories as far as they answer all these questions, excluding the theory of legislation from the theory of punishment should not do his argument any injustice.

Why Punishment Theory Is Relatively Independent

I can now briefly state the argument for punishment theory's independence of political theory. Both *any* plausible political theory and *any* plausible theory of punishment must implicitly or explicitly assume the following (whatever else they assume):

(a) rational agents much like us, beings able to plan taking into account distant consequences and able as well to act according to plan;

(b) acts of these agents which, though likely to be desired by the agent, should nonetheless be prohibited (as well as acts these agents generally would not want to do that should nonetheless be required);

(c) the need for some conventional procedure to connect undesirable consequences to the prohibited acts often enough to keep prohibited acts within tolerable limits (for example, a system of tort liability or criminal punishment);

(d) such other facts as that no large society has the resources to keep the number of prohibited acts within tolerable limits without the voluntary cooperation of most members;

(e) moral principles permitting institution of a system of criminal punishment (for example, a principle allowing people to cooperate whenever doing so interferes with no morally permissible act) — subject to certain constraints;

(f) a set of moral constraints on what may be prohibited or allowed (that is, a partial theory of criminal legislation and justification);

(g) a set of moral constraints on when agents may be held responsible for what they have done and how much responsibility they may have (that is, a partial theory of excuse);

(h) a set of moral constraints on what may be done to a rational agent in response to what he has done when he is responsible for what he has done (for example, the principle that no one should be treated worse than he deserves) — that is, a partial theory of humane treatment;

(i) the rest of ordinary morality, including the principle of fairness; and

(j) a conception of (social) justice a logical consequence of which (perhaps in conjunction with assumptions a-i) is that each rational agent subject to the criminal law has good reason to want the others to do as the laws require even when doing so is burdensome to them.

Assumptions a-j are, I claim, preconditions of any plausible political theory today. I intend very little by that claim. I do not, for example, claim that we cannot *imagine* a political theory inconsistent with one or more of those assumptions. I claim only that such a theory would be implausible. Nor do I claim that all *plausible* political theories must understand assumption a-j in exactly the same way. Variation is possible. Neither ordinary facts nor moral principles are ever quite fixed. I claim only that the range of variation is small. So, for example, any political theory that attributed *all* criminal acts to irrational impulses would today be inconsistent with assumption (d). The only factual question open is how much crime is attributable to rational choice, not whether any is. Similarly, any political theory that allowed no principle of fairness would seem to most people to suffer a serious moral defect. Fairness must have a place in any plausible conception of (social) justice.

Assumptions a-j are, I think, part of the "deep structure" that political theories tend to share rather than part of the "surface structure" that distinguishes them. For this reason, perhaps, criminal punishment tends to differ far less from one political system to another than the political systems to which it belongs. And, for this reason too, offering a justification of punishment more or less independent of political theory is easy. Assumptions a-i are about matters of fact or morality, not about when government is legitimate, the rightful powers of (legitimate or illegitimate) government, when laws should be adopted, or anything else uniquely political. Even a controversy over the principle of fairness is a moral controversy, whatever its importance for political theory.

That any theory of punishment can rest on assumptions a-i without resting on political theory seems to me so obvious as to need no further argument. But that is not true of assumption (j). It refers to a conception of justice connected with law, clearly a political conception in some reasonably straightforward sense. Even so, *assumption* (j) is itself *not* political in the same sense. What assumption (j) requires is *not* a particular conception of the purpose, function, or nature of justice, only a conception allowing a certain inference. This requirement is, I believe, consistent with any plausible political theory. To see why, consider how a political theory could be *in*consistent with assumption (j).

To be inconsistent with assumption (j), a political theory would have to omit any justification of the criminal law or offer a justification that leaves open the question whether rational members of the society would find the justification convincing and so, leave open as well the question whether they should want each other to obey the law. A political theory that just omitted any justification of the criminal law would probably be implausible in consequence. A political theory that left open the question whether rational members of the society should find the justification convincing (or allowed the conclusion that they would not) would be strikingly implausible.

The plausibility of a theory is (in part) a function of the audience it addresses. Political theories (for example, theories of legislation or legitimacy) are typically addressed (at least in part) to members of the society they are about. They are guides to conduct, not mere scientific descriptions. To be plausible, a political theory must make assumptions about what constitutes good reasons in the society in question (for example, that serving each subject's interests is a good reason for a legal order). If the theory justifies the proposed social order, it must offer members of a society in question reasons to want the laws generally obeyed (whether or not it gives each any reason to obey the law himself). If the theory offers such reasons, it offers as well reasons for each subject to want the criminal law in particular obeyed. These reasons should satisfy assumption (j). Assumption (j) is simply a methodological precondition of any plausible political theory.

Assumptions a-j and the Justification of Retributivism

So far I have only *claimed* that punishment theory is independent of political theory because a plausible theory of punishment can rest entirely on *nonpolitical* assumptions. I have not actually shown that that is so. I shall now try to do that in three steps, beginning with the justification of criminal punishment as an institution and ending with the justification of particular sentences. (I shall omit discussion of clemency only because Philips does.[9]) What follows is not meant to *prove* the version of retributivism it develops, only to sketch a possible proof. All I claim for the sketch is that it allows us to see how a retributive theory might be both plausible and independent of political theory.[10]

The Criminal Law as an Institution. Any theory of criminal punishment must be about an institution having (something like) the following features:

(1) a body of rules capable of guiding ordinary conduct, what we may call "primary rules";

(2) rational agents, that is, beings capable of following these rules or not as they choose, capable of choosing on the basis of reasons, and capable of treating the prospect of a specific undesirable consequence as a reason against doing an act (to be weighed with other reasons for and against);

(3) secondary rules connecting failure to follow primary rules with "penalties," that is, specific undesirable consequences.

(4) conventional procedures for imposing penalties upon rational agents in accordance with the secondary rules as such;

(5) a justified presumption that both primary and secondary rules are generally known to those subject to them; and

(6) a practice of justifying imposition of a penalty (in part at least) by the fact that the individual upon whom it is to be imposed failed to follow the appropriate primary rule when he could have.[11]

Any institution having these six features will be a relatively clear example of a system of criminal punishment (whether or not it is a system of criminal law, that is, whether or not its rules constitute a legal system strictly so called). Criminal punishment so defined, though a means of social control, does not seem to presuppose a state. We can easily imagine a society we would normally describe as "stateless," for example, one without legislatures, taxes, standing armies, police, or organized executive. Such a society could nonetheless have an institution satisfying our definition — and clearly recognizable as a system of criminal punishment. Ordinary morality or custom could provide the primary rules. Custom could also establish who should hear a case, the procedures to be followed, and what penalties should be imposed. The society might itself administer the penalty (for example, outlawry or stoning) or instead leave its administration to certain individuals (for example, the victim or her family).[12]

Any institution satisfying our definition of criminal punishment is obviously consistent with assumptions (a)-(d). Since such an institution presupposes no state, its justification will depend on ordinary moral principles (assumption e), not on any political theory. What might this justification be? Criminal punishment would, it seems, be justified as an institution (*all else equal*) if it serves the interests of rational agents in the society in question better than does any alternative (and would be justified *all things considered* if it is also consistent with the moral principles of assumptions f-h). How might criminal punishment serve the interests of rational agents?

The primary rules order certain important social relations. The secondary rules allow each rational agent subject to them to know what he must do to be free from the interference of those procedures the society has in place to support the primary rules and what interference he should expect if he does not do as the primary rules require. Criminal punishment treats rational agents as beings capable of benefiting from such information, as beings capable of planning on the basis of it and acting according to plan. Whatever the content of the primary rules, the relative predictability of criminal punishment makes it preferable (all else equal) to institutions of social control that are less predictable.[13]

This point may be put another way. Criminal punishment assumes just those agents who can treat the prospect of a penalty as a reason against doing an act they would otherwise do. Or, in other words, criminal punishment assumes that its penalties can have a deterrent effect. Does it follow from this assumption that what I am sketching is in part a deterrence theory? I have, of course, recognized moral limits on the theory (assumptions f-h). But any deterrentists could do the same. The crucial question is whether (as Philips would have it) my assumptions commit me to recognizing that the institution of criminal punishment has a deterrent *function*. They do not.

To say that the institution of criminal punishment has a deterrent function means (according to Philips) that society institutes criminal punishment (in part at least) *in order* to prevent crime. Admitting (as I have) that criminal punishment must have some deterrent effect is consistent with denying any such intention. Rational agents can have an interest in instituting punishment other than the control of crime, an interest sufficient (all else equal) to justify what they do. They may, for example, want to denounce wrongdoing with what they consider suitable emphasis; to make wrongdoers understand the seriousness of what they have done; to help preserve a just order by establishing useful practices (the primary rules) and using penalties to make sure would-be freeloaders pay for trying to ride free; or to accomplish some combination of these or similar ends. Since each of these ends seems sufficient (all else equal) to motivate some rational persons to support punishment as an institution, we must, I think, admit that each provides a plausible justification (even if, on balance, an inadequate one).[14]

For a deterrentist, however, that plausibility will be mysterious. Isn't deterrence of overriding importance? Perhaps I can dispel the mystery. I have claimed only that criminal punishment can be justified even if the society instituting it does not *intend* to prevent crime. I have not claimed that deterrence is *entirely* irrelevant to justification. I do not claim that. What I do claim is that deterrence may plausibly be treated as a mere *side constraint* on the institution of criminal punishment. So, for example, any system of criminal punishment that set penalties so low as to threaten the desired level of social order would be disqualified — just as would any system that set penalties so high as to violate the principle of humane treatment. The system, though justified insofar as it does what it was intended to do (say, denounce wrongdoing), would not be justified all things considered. Deterrence (like humane treatment or any other side constraint) can be of overriding importance even if it is *not* what justifies the institution.

This conclusion is one consequence of connecting "function" with "intention" in the way Philips does. I shall now point out another. I have been assuming that the society in question *has* an intention. There is no reason to assume that. The members of a particular society might well agree to institute a system of criminal law without agreeing on why it should be instituted. Each could (justifiably) support the same institution because overall it serves her purposes better than any alternative (even though none of her purposes is shared by every other member of the society). In such circumstances — which seem to me to be *our* circumstances — the institution of punishment would have no function in Philips' sense (except the trivial one of satisfying the motley interests of those subject to it). The institution would nonetheless be justified because it served the interests of those subject to it better than any alternative (and did so without violating any side constraint).

Though I have put this argument in terms of "society," I think it applies to states as well. That a state maintains a system of criminal punishment — and is justified in doing so — is consistent with its having *no* intention whatever. States, like societies, are moved by the intentions of individuals, not by any distinct "group mind." So, even state-instituted punishment might have no function at all (even while serving various purposes of various subjects of the state).

This conclusion is so contrary to Philips' thesis as to suggest that equating "function" with "intention" is a mistake, either Philips' or mine. I don't think it is my mistake. I have cited Philips' own words for this way of understanding "function." In addition, to equate "function" with either "effect" or "tendency of a self-regulating system" would leave his position so diminished that perhaps even Kant could accept it. So, it seems, Philips (and other deterrentists as well) owe us an explanation of what they mean by "deterrent function."[15]

I have, I think, now said enough about justifying the *institution* of punishment.

Setting Statutory Penalties. Whatever plausible justification we give for instituting criminal punishment, the institution itself will have the six features listed above and satisfy assumptions a-j. The institution will have a complex structure of conceptual, moral, and factual presuppositions. Though punishment theorists have devoted most of their effort to trying to show that the institution of criminal punishment must or should have this or that function (often to the exclusion of all others), little of practical important turns on such a showing. The structure of punishment as an institution, not its teleology, largely determines such practical matters as what penalties the statutes should provide.

I have noted two side constraints on the institution of punishment: first, the penalties provided must not be so mild that they cannot discourage crime enough; and second, the penalties must not be so severe that they are inhumane. The institution of punishment thus brings with it a range of permissible penalties. We might suppose that radically different justifications of the institution would generate radically different lists of permissible penalties. That does not seem to be so. There are both utilitarians and retributivists on each side of the debate over the death penalty.[16] There is, as far as I can tell, little debate over the permissibility of any other penalty (except in a few odd places like Iran). Apparently, here too plausibility allows for little variation. Penalties will range from death or long imprisonment to small fine, small loss of liberty (probation), or the like still significant burden.

Given a list of permissible penalties, all a theory of statutory penalties need do is connect penalties with crimes in a way consistent with the presuppositions of criminal punishment. For retributivists, the crucial presupposition is the principle of humane treatment that prohibits treating people worse than they deserve (and so, prohibits a schedule of penalties that commits us to treat criminals worse than they deserve). Retributivists disagree here only about how to measure criminal desert. Many argue that criminal desert should be measured by the *crime's* moral blameworthiness all things considered (or even by the *criminal's* moral blameworthiness all things considered). Others, however, argue instead that it should only be measured by the unfair advantage the crime as such takes. That is my view. I shall now explain why, beginning with my reasons for rejecting the alternative.

Anyone wishing to measure criminal desert by moral blameworthiness must explain how acts themselves morally indifferent can be morally blameworthy just because they are illegal. How, for example, can carrying an unlicensed firearm or possessing a controlled substance be morally blameworthy? Anyone who cannot answer such questions must either give up moral blameworthiness as the measure of criminal desert or take the implausible position that all acts themselves morally indifferent deserve the same punishment.

The obvious way to explain the moral blameworthiness of disobeying laws themselves morally indifferent is, of course, to claim that disobeying the law is, as such, morally blameworthy. Unfortunately, that explanation begs the question *unless* followed by an explanation of what makes disobeying the law as such morally blameworthy. And, even if such an explanation follows, we might still have no measure of blameworthiness. All laws being equally law, all lawbreaking is, as such, morally equal too. An explanation of the moral blameworthiness of lawbreaking is useless here unless it yields a ranking of crimes morally indifferent in themselves.

These considerations ensure that all plausible versions of retributivism will explain the moral blameworthiness of illegal acts themselves morally indifferent in exactly the same way. They will appeal to the principle of fairness, the one moral principle relevant to virtually every violation of law in any relatively just system of criminal law. Though the exact terms of the principle of fairness remain in dispute, the following formulation should be good enough for our purposes:[17]

Do your part in any morally-permissible practice from which you benefit if:

(a) you would want the practice to continue even if you could not avoid doing your part,

(b) the benefits you receive depend (in part at least) on others doing their part even when what they must do is burdensome to them;

(c) what is true of you is true of other participants generally; and

(d) participants do their part at least partly because they expect most others to do the same.

Any appeal to this principle to measure the moral blameworthiness of lawbreaking must assume that laws create practices. That, of course, is true of laws generally (though not of laws fallen into desuetude or not yet in force). The practice created is, however, no ordinary practice. It is cooperative. Each person serves others and is served in return. The benefit each receives depends in part on what others do. Each must see this interdependence to see the point of doing his part. The principle of fairness thus applies to any subject of the law having reason both to want the law in force generally and to want to escape the responsibility the law imposes on her in particular. The principle applies just when there is unfair advantage to be taken.

We might then explain why breaking a law like that against carrying an unlicensed firearm is morally blameworthy, even though carrying an unlicensed firearm is as such morally indifferent, in this way: General obedience to this law has an effect everyone wants (for example, increasing without undue cost one's own safety and the safety of those for whom one cares). One could, of course, be even safer if he disobeyed the law while others obeyed. He could have the advantage of the law-created safety without the disadvantage of the law-created vulnerability that comes from going without a gun. But as others took the same advantage, the benefit the law provides would diminish and, if disobedience became common enough, disappear altogether. So, if our potential lawbreaker would rather give up carrying an unlicensed firearm than live in a society without the practice in question, illegally carrying an unlicensed gun is morally blameworthy. The crime would take unfair advantage of the law-created practice.

This explanation does not apply only to crimes like possessing an unlicensed firearm. It applies as well to criminal laws that merely restate ordinary moral requirements. We have good reason to want our fellow subjects to abstain from murder, robbery, arson, assault, and the like, as well as from carrying unlicensed firearms. We also have reason to believe that the criminal law makes such immoral acts less likely than they would otherwise be, that each of us abstains from such immoral acts at least partly because the law gives us some assurance that others will do the same; and so on. We have only to think of assumptions (b) and (c) — and of Hobbes's state of nature — to see the force of this reasoning.

I have made my case at the level of particular statutes. I have explained why violating a particular statute is morally blameworthy by pointing to the cooperative practice the particular statute creates. But nothing in the explanation requires remaining at that level. *Insofar* as we are entitled to think of the criminal law as a system (that is, as a complex practice), we are entitled to generalize the explanation to the criminal law as a whole (whatever plausible theory of justice we accept). Assumption (j) assures that the criminal law as a whole is a practice to which the principle of fairness would normally apply. Only in a relatively unjust legal system — for example, that of Nazi Germany — would we *not* be able to show that each subject benefits from the criminal law, has reason to want others to obey it, and so on. So, only in a relatively unjust system would we have to examine the relevant statute to determine whether some morally indifferent act is morally blameworthy because the statute makes it a crime.[18]

Though we began by trying to use moral blameworthiness rather than fairness to measure deserved punishment, we have ended by bringing in fairness anyway. But fairness, like lawbreaking, does not come in degrees. An act is fair or it is not. Have we reached a dead end? No. While fairness does not come in degrees, something connected with fairness clearly does: the *value* of the advantage unfairly taken. We can easily gauge this value for crimes by imagining a fair market in which licenses to commit crimes are sold.[19] The ranking that results is surprisingly close to the criminal law as we know it.[20] But why (it may be asked) should we measure criminal desert only by the unfair advantage a crime takes? Why not include as well all factors that go into moral blameworthiness?

There are, I think, at least two reasons to assign *statutory* penalties to crimes taking into account only the unfair advantage the crime itself takes. One reason is practical. We have no reliable procedure to do anything else.[21] The other reason is theoretical, a byproduct of justifying the criminal law as an institution.

Using unfair advantage to measure deserved punishment connects criminal punishment with the criminal law's *special* contribution to the moral order. The criminal law creates a cooperative practice of which the crime takes unfair advantage (whatever else it does). Criminal punishment cancels that unfair advantage (though civil damages, public apology, private repentance, or the like may still be necessary to rectify completely the wrong done).[22] Measuring criminal desert by moral-blameworthiness-all-things-considered means that imposing criminal penalties must take account of *all* morally relevant considerations, not just those relevant to what a criminal law made the act.

We have, I think, good reason to want statutory penalties to reflect only the criminal desert unfair advantage measures. Statutes incorporating all relevant circumstances would make punishment far harder to predict than it would otherwise be (if for no other reason than that an all-things-considered judgment requires consideration of many more things than does an estimate of mere unfair advantage). We might prefer predictability to absolute justice. We might also prefer to maintain control over how much of our moral circumstances we must reveal in court. The more closely the statute proportions penalties to moral desert all things considered, the more the judge must consider to determine what a crime deserves. The more a judge *must* consider, the more she must *pry* to do even minimum justice.

How persuasive are these reasons for preferring unfair advantage to moral-blameworthiness-all-things-considered as the measure of criminal desert? They are, I think, far more persuasive for the maximum statutory penalty than for the minimum. For anyone adverse to risk, for example, a flexible maximum must (all else equal) seriously threaten the very predictability that makes the institution of criminal law attractive in the first place. A flexible minimum, however, only opens the prospect that the actual punishment may not be as bad as feared. If, in addition, the defendant must raise a subject to have it considered as a defense or in mitigation, he would retain some control over what the judge must consider.

Of course, whether such reasons persuade depends on whether we view ourselves as potential criminals or instead as angels, perfectly law-abiding citizens, or the like. For most of us, I think, the view to take is that of the potential criminal. We know ourselves to be capable of breaking the law under easily realizable circumstances. Indeed, many of us have already committed crimes (driving over the speed limit, for example, or possessing an illegal substance). That most of us know ourselves to be at least potentially a criminal may explain why legal systems generally set relatively rigid maximums but otherwise grant prosecutors, judges, or the executive much discretion.

That, I think, is enough for now of the argument for measuring (statutory) criminal desert by unfair advantage rather than by moral blameworthiness more generally. Contrary to what Philips claims, the argument does not assume that legislators do or should set penalties *in order* to match the unfair advantage each crime takes. I have assumed throughout only that unfair advantage *constrains* what legislatures may do, not that it is (even part of) what they do or should intend. The legislator whose only purpose is to deter more those crimes he fears more is constrained in exactly the same way as one whose only purpose is to denounce crime in accordance with its moral depravity. A retributive method of setting statutory penalties need not depend on any particular theory of legislation (that is, on any particular theory of the purpose of criminal laws).

Setting Individual Sentences. The retributivism so far developed lacks one feature generally thought to define retributivism. It requires neither that punishment be instituted nor that statutory penalties be adopted in order (in Philips' words) "to impose suffering on wrongdoers that they deserve, because they deserve it" (p. 408). I have been altogether silent about (what Philips calls) "retributive intent" (p. 408). This, of course, is no accident. Indeed, I have stressed the problems inherent in claims concerning "the state's intention" in instituting punishment or "the legislature's intention" in adopting this or that statutory penalty. I have, I think, also shown that we can avoid such claims while justifying punishment as an institution or even while justifying statutory penalties.

That, I think, is reason enough to avoid talk of intention until now. But I have another reason. The claim that punishment should be imposed "because" it is deserved seems out of place in legislatures (or constitutional conventions). Such bodies do not impose punishment. They make policy. For them, justice is properly a mere side constraint. Courts, however, are different. Not only do they actually impose punishments, they are supposed to be (as we say) "courts of justice" as well as "courts of law." As often noted, retributivist talk of desert seems at home in court in a way it does not in a legislature. Whatever a retributivist might claim about instituting punishment or adopting statutory penalties, he must claim that *judges* should impose only such punishment on criminals as is deserved and should do so (at least in part) for the reason that the criminal deserves it. The judge who imposes more suffering than the criminal deserves does an injustice. But the judge who, though imposing the right sentence, does so only to discourage other criminals, or only to satisfy the victim, or only for some combination of these or other practical reasons would, it seems, have misunderstood her job. For judges, justice is no mere side constraint.[23]

Consider the sixth feature in our definition of criminal punishment. Criminal punishment must include a "practice of *justifying* imposition of a penalty (at least in part) by the fact that the individual [committed the appropriate crime]." The judge's role in the practice of punishment is (in part at least) to justify the imposition of punishment by showing that the crime is connected to the punishment in the appropriate way. Because (according to retributivists) desert is at least an important part of what connects penalty to crime in the appropriate way (though only a side constraint on legislation), desert must be part of any adequate justification of what the judge does. And because one can only justify her own action by reasons she herself accepts (as opposed, say, to "merely going through the motions" of giving a justification), the judge's sentence will be justifiable only if she actually intends to impose the punishment (at least in part) because it is deserved.[24]

When the practice of punishment is a legal practice, the judge's justification must begin with legal desert. She will try to convict only those who are legally guilty, to punish only those who have been legally convicted, and to impose only those punishments the law provides. The judge will refuse to punish anyone she finds to be legally justified in what he did or to be legally excused. Those she finds to be only partially excused by law, she will try to punish only for what is legally unexcused. While justifications generally bar conviction, excuses sometimes bar conviction (for example, "not guilty by reason of insanity"), sometimes allow conviction but bar punishment (for example, "guilty but insane"), and sometimes leave the judge to decide what is deserved (for example, "diminished responsibility"). The judge will try to proceed accordingly.

A legal justification or excuse is one recognized in the law as such, whether by statute, precedent, or legal principle. The judge cannot justifiably ignore a legal justification or excuse. But she may justifiably recognize a justification, excuse, or other relevant factor even if the law does not. She may, for example, treat as justified any illegal act that, while taking advantage, did not do so unfairly (that is, in a way the law abiding would mind). A judge may treat as excused an illegal act when, for example, the criminal in question is not morally responsible or the act is morally good all things considered. When a judge recognizes a justification or excuse that the law does not, she must do so as a moral agent who is also a judge, not as a judge as such. She must, that is, explain her action as a consequence of moral side constraints, not as a part of her official intention. Insofar as the law prevents a judge from considering a morally required justification or excuse, the law is morally objectionable.

We may then conceive the judge's justified choice of sentence as proceeding in two stages. In the first, the judge tries to match *legal* punishment to *legal* desert. If (as I have argued) unfair advantage is the measure of legal desert, the judge should try to make her initial sentence match the unfair advantage the criminal took by his crime as such (including aggravating and mitigating circumstances). The match thus identified will be the maximum sentence the criminal can legally receive (constituting, as it does, exactly what the criminal deserves for what he *did against the law*, his criminal desert).

The second stage allows the judge to take into account other factors, including those the law or morality requires (or at least does not exclude). Among such factors might be the time the criminal sat in jail waiting trial, the harm his punishment would do innocent third-parties, or the probability that a severe sentence would reform him. These factors are not relevant to *criminal* desert as such, even if the law *requires* them to be taken into account. They do not concern the crime, only what should be done with the criminal. They may weigh for or against mitigating the initial sentence but cannot justify enhancing it. To impose a sentence greater than the initial one would be to impose more legal suffering than the crime can justify—or, in other words, more than the criminal can legally deserve.[25]

One Objection Considered

Among Philips' objections to the fairness version of retributivism[26] is one others have made as well, that "one may break the law of a just state without taking unfair advantage of one's fellow citizens" (p. 407).[27] We are now ready to exhibit the value of the foregoing sketch by quickly disposing of this objection. We have already given a general argument for the claim that every crime takes unfair advantage. Philips challenges that argument by offering as counter-examples four situations that appear to him to include lawbreaking without including unfair advantage. If our intuitions concerning these examples can be shown to follow from the theory I have sketched, or if the theory leads us to revise our intuitions, nothing would remain of the objection.

The first of these examples is "running a stop sign at a deserted country intersection with clear visibility in all directions" (p. 407). Why does Philips think this an example of taking no unfair advantage? Presumably because no one would suffer if Philips ran the stop sign or even be put in danger. But if that is why Philips thinks this an example of taking no unfair advantage, the example is simply a morally indifferent act like carrying an unlicensed firearm. We can show it to take unfair advantage by showing that it fits into a cooperative practice, whether the particular traffic law or the criminal law as a whole. Because showing a *statute* to satisfy the principle of fairness is harder than showing the criminal law as a whole to do so, let us consider only the statute. The crucial question would then be: Do we want individuals deciding whether this country road is deserted enough and visibility is good enough to justify stopping?

The answer is plainly no (unless the stop sign was put up by mistake or has outlived its usefulness). We put up stop signs where we think we will be safer if people stop whether they think it necessary or not. All things considered, we are better off if people obey those signs *even* when they firmly believe they can disobey them safely. People are just too prone to misjudge such matters. If (as seems likely) Philips wants the advantage of other people obeying the statute even when *they* think it safe to run the stop sign, Philips would be taking unfair advantage if he ran the stop sign just because *he* thought the road deserted enough and visibility clear enough to justify doing so. Running the stop sign under the conditions Philips specifies does, contrary to what he claims, take unfair advantage. That no one is in fact harmed or put in danger is irrelevant.[28]

Philips' second example of breaking a law without taking unfair advantage is "stealing a car in order to rush a badly wounded person to the hospital" (p. 407). Here the unfair advantage is clear. We don't want private individuals deciding when to take our property for what they consider good reason even though we of course would love to be able to take other people's property when we have what we consider good reason. Whatever appeal this second example has is, I think, due to the reason for the theft. All else equal, stealing a car to save a life is morally good *even* if it takes unfair advantage. So, we are not inclined to punish the thief (all else equal). But nothing I have said is inconsistent with that. I have already explained how an act might both take unfair advantage and be justifiably excused.

Philips' third example of breaking a law without taking unfair advantage is "breaking into a male neighbor's house in order to come to the aid of a woman who is screaming in terror and crying out for help" (p. 407). This example differs from the second in only one respect. In this example, the "victim" (the male neighbor) is himself engaged in a serious crime. He is not, like the owner of the stolen car, an innocent bystander. This difference is important. So long as we are right about what is happening in our neighbor's house (our neighbor is not, for example, simply playing his TV too loudly), we would, I think, be *justified* in breaking in. The law against breaking and entering was not meant to create a practice allowing felons to commit their crimes without interruption. Our break-in would only break the law in the technical sense that any justified violation of the law does. That justified violations of the law fail to take unfair advantage is not surprising. That failure explains why they do not deserve legal punishment.

Philips' last example of breaking a law without taking unfair advantage is "helping a terminally ill friend in great agony to end his life" (p. 407). This example differs from the first, I think, only in our having doubts about the relevant law (presumably, a statute that forbids knowingly aiding a suicide). So, we must begin by asking how we might benefit from the practice (even taking account of its considerable *cost* in suffering). The answer is obvious. The statute *might* make us all safer by protecting us from being "helped" into suicide when the suicide is not in our interests (when, for example, temporarily depressed, we are helped by a person whose only motive is benefiting from our death). Suppose for a moment this benefit is worth the costs the statute imposes. If people do in fact generally abstain from helping suicides in part because the law forbids such helping, then they bear a burden the person would not who illegally helped a suicide. The unfair advantage is clear.

The appeal of this example is, I think, that we doubt that the statute's benefits can compensate for the suffering imposed on all those for whom suicide is the rational choice. We are therefore inclined to see no unfairness in the advantage we would take by doing what the statute forbids. But this inclination is consistent with our theory. The principle of fairness applies only to practices that we "would want . . . to continue even if [we] could not avoid doing [our] part." If the benefits of this statute seem so slight that we would happily give them up to avoid the burdens, the practice it creates is not itself cooperative and taking advantage of it not as such unfair.

Admitting this is, however, still consistent with claiming that the act in question takes unfair advantage. Helping with a suicide may take unfair advantage because (except under special circumstances) breaking any law (in a relatively just legal system) does that. Claiming that the act takes unfair advantage in this way is, however, still consistent with admitting (as I would) that the act should not be punished. Helping in a suicide under the conditions Philips specifies may be excusable (as in Philips' second example). Nothing I have said is inconsistent with that. So, even this last example is consistent with the theory presented here.

Conclusion

While there are many other objections I could consider, I have, I think, said enough to make clear what I might say in response to many of them. And even if I have not, the purpose of this chapter is not to respond to such objections but to establish that punishment theory is (more or less) independent of political theory. I have, I think, now established that.

Notes

1. Michael Philips, "The Justification of Punishment and the Justification of Political Authority," *Law and Philosophy* 5 (December 1986): 393-416. To keep footnotes to a minimum, I shall hereafter give all page references to this paper within parentheses in the text. Others who have defended similar views now include Ted Honderich, "Punishment, the New Retributivism, and Political Philosophy," in A. Philips Griffiths, *Philosophy and Practice* (Cambridge: Cambridge University Press, 1985; Nicola Lacey, *State Punishment* (London: Routledge, 1988); and Wojciech Sadurski, "Theory of

Punishment, Social Justice, and Liberal Neutrality," *Law and Philosophy* 7 (December 1989): 351-374.

2. Two other notable exceptions are Plato's *Laws* (Book IX) and Montesquieu's *Spirit of Laws* (Book VI).

3. Though both Kant's *Metaphysical Foundations of Justice* (1797) and Hegel's *Philosophy of Right* (1821) resemble earlier political works in taking up punishment in the course of a systematic treatment of law and government, they do not seem to be merely filling in an outline in the pre-Beccarian manner. They seem instead to treat punishment as worthy of serious attention in its own right.

4. See, for example, Anthony Flew, "The Justification of Punishment," *Philosophy* 29 (October 1954): 291-307 ("authority"); Herbert Morris, "Persons and Punishment," *Monist* 52 (October 1968): 475-501 ("mechanism"); or Michael Davis, "How to Make the Punishment Fit the Crime," *Ethics* 93 (July 1983): 726-752 ("procedure").

5. Philips' use of "state" has a disconcertingly nineteenth century ring to it. Does Philips have a Hegelian or Marxist agenda?

6. This assumption seems safe. Note, for example, that Philips tries to show that deterrence is relevant to setting statutory penalties by asking "if the resumption of the death penalty does nothing to reduce the rate of increase in the homicide rate *anywhere* in the country, then [is that] not good evidence that the death penalty has no greater deterrent value than non-capital penalties ... ?" (p. 410n). Since this question is addressed to me, I should perhaps also say out that it misses the point it purports to address. The statistics cannot tell us that resumption of the death penalty "*did* nothing" (a complex theoretical matter), only that whatever it did did not show up in the statistics. What we make of that will depend a good deal on what else we believe. That the superior deterrent effect of the death penalty was not evident in post-resumption statistics is some sort of evidence against the death-penalty's superior deterrent effect. It is, however, "good evidence" only if, for example, one also believes (as I do not) that the death penalty's deterrent effect must be both large and not subject to countervailing factors (for example, jury nullification). For more on this point, see my "Death, Deterrence, and the Method of Common Sense," *Social Theory and Practice* 7 (Summer 1981): 145-77.

7. See, for example, D. A. Duff, *Trials and Punishments* (Cambridge University Press: Cambridge, 1985). Duff offers a penitential version of retributivism that acknowledges deterrence as a practical necessity. For a much more typical acknowledgement of deterrence in the justification of the institution of punishment, see Andrew von Hirsch, *Past or Future Crimes* (Rutgers University Press: New Brunswick, New Jersey, 1985). For von Hirsch, deterrence and condemnation are severally necessary and only jointly sufficient to justify the institution of punishment.

8. See, for example, von Hirsch, *Past or Future Crimes,* as well as relevant works cited in Chapter Eight.

9. I say a bit more about clemency in Chapters Four and Eight. But the only thorough contemporary treatment of this subject I know of is Katherine Moore's *Pardons* (Oxford University Press: New York, 1989).

10. For proof, see below, especially Chapter Four.

11. This is a slightly revised version of the definition I give in "How to Make the Punishment Fit the Crime," p. 728. Nothing should turn on the revisions, all of which I regard as editorial.

12. Is such a society a mere figment of my imagination? Certainly "stateless societies" are not. What may be is a stateless society that has decision by judge rather than the conceptually simpler mediation by a third-party or direct negotiation between the parties. See, for example, A. R. Radcliffe-Brown, *Structure and Function in Primitive Society* (Free Press: New York, 1952), esp. pp. 217-218.

13. This justification is, I think, now fairly standard. See, for example, H. L. A. Hart, *Punishment and Responsibility: Essays in the Philosophy of Law* (Oxford University Press: New York, 1968), esp. pp. 28-53; Morris, "Persons and Punishment," pp. 477-78; and even Rolf Sartorius, *Individual Conduct and Social Norms* (Dickenson Publishing Co.: Encino, Calif, 1975), pp. 106-109.

14. See, for example, Robert Nozick, *Philosophical Explanations* (Belknap Press: Cambridge, Massachusetts, 1981), pp. 366-93 (a denunciation connecting the criminal with correct values); D. A. Duff, *Trials and Punishments* (penitence); James Sterba, "Is There A Rationale for Punishment?," *American Journal of Jurisprudence* 29 (1984): 29-43 (preventing free-loading); and Herbert Morris, "A Paternalistic Theory of Punishment," *American Philosophical Quarterly* 18 (October 1981): 263-71 (penitence in combination with other unstated purposes). These examples are, of course, good evidence for the plausibility of such theories only if we are willing to say (as I am) that good philosophers do not publicly defend implausible positions — though the positions they do defend often turn out, upon careful inspection, to be mistaken. My own view is that we owe the arguments of those we regard as skilled members of our profession such an inspection (hence this chapter). Note, however, that Philips may be of another opinion. He dismisses without argument several philosophers he regards as "talented" because their claims are "too utterly fantastic . . . to warrant discussion" (p. 406). I think Philips owes us a criterion of plausibility (or, as he also calls it, acceptability).

15. Those who argue that punishment as an institution has a "condemnatory" (or "expressive") function face a similar problem. Punishment is *in effect* a condemnation. How can one describe an act as a crime without thereby condemning it? Whether the state, society, or the legislature intends

such a condemnation is, of course, another matter. And whether the system is structured so as to maintain that condemnation (rather than, say, something related to it like taking back unfair advantage) is yet another matter. These "other matters" have, I think, been largely ignored, beginning with Feinberg's seminal paper "The Expressive Function of Punishment." See Joel Feinberg, *Doing and Deserving* (Princeton University Press: Princeton, New Jersey, 1970), pp. 95-118. Matters are not improved by changing the claim from descriptive to prescriptive. Even if the claim is that punishment *should* have a deterrent or condemnatory function, the question remains what "function" means in that context. There is also the new question of why we should want punishment to have that one function.

16. For example, see my "Death, Deterrence, and the Method of Common Sense," which tries to mediate between utilitarians. See also Jeffrey Reiman's attempt to do much the same for retributivists: "Justice, Civilization, and the Death Penalty: Answering van den Haag," *Philosophy and Public Affairs* 14 (Spring 1985): 115-48.

17. The principle of fairness has been under a cloud since Robert Nozick criticized it in *Anarchy, State, and Utopia* (Basic Books: New York, 1974), esp. pp. 90-95. That cloud need not concern us for two reasons. First, my statement of the principle is (I think) a version of the principle Arneson defended against Nozick's criticisms. See Richard J. Arneson, "The Principle of Fairness and Free-Rider Problems," *Ethics* 92 (July 1982): 616-33. Second, the counter-examples upon which Nozick's criticisms (and those of his successors) rest are in fact irrelevant to what they purport to show. See my "Nozick's Argument *for* the Legitimacy of the Welfare State," *Ethics* 97 (April 1987): 576-94.

18. Compare Philips: "A more plausible and popular position is that people who violate the laws of a *just* state do wrong. But even if this can be established, it remains an open question whether or under what conditions *unjust* states may punish with retributive intent [crimes like rape, murder, and so on] . . . we might expect those in whom the spirit of retributivism flourishes to demand punishment proportional to desert in such cases. What retributivism requires is a theory of the state that permits punishment with retributive intent for any illegal act that is also immoral," (p. 406). I have now explained why such a theory is *not* required.

19. For defense of this claim, see Chapters Four, Five, Six, Seven, and Ten.

20. Moral blameworthiness usually gets analyzed as a complex relation between "harm" and "culpability." For the problems with this approach, see Chapter Three.

21. See note 20 above.

22. It is important to keep in mind the distinction between the advantage one generally gets *simply by breaking the law* from those other advantages that may or may not be a consequence of that act. Harm to an individual,

for example, is contingent — except in crimes like murder or arson in which doing a specific harm is part of the definition of the crime. Civil liability is primarily a function of relations between two (or more) *individuals*. Criminal liability is primarily a function of the relation of any individual to a *practice*. Compare Philips (p. 398 n. 4).

23. Though I will say something about the troublesome relation between moral and legal justice below, I should perhaps make three points here. First, this characterization of the judge's job does not presuppose any political theory. Judges (as noted above) can exist in stateless societies. Second, I must admit that talking about "the judge's job" is equivalent to talking about the judge's function — *provided* "function" has something like its biological sense. Third, I regard this claim about the judge's job as in part conceptual. Institutions in which "judges" are *not* supposed to treat criminal desert as the primary consideration in sentencing will *not* seem to be courts in the ordinary sense, but "kangaroo courts," "revolutionary tribunals," or (at best) "administrative agencies." I do not, however, regard the claim as merely conceptual. I believe, for example, that we could justifiably remove from the bench a judge who plainly ignored criminal desert (even if his sentences turn out to be statistically similar to those of judges who took desert seriously). I don't think we could do the same with a judge who *only* considered criminal desert (unless the law specifically mandated that other considerations be taken into account).

24. Perhaps this is unnecessary, but let me point out an important difference between my retributive judge and a deterrent "judge." A retributive judge may (as a matter of fact) send innocent people to jail. She may even be aware that she must be doing that (though not who in particular is innocent). What she cannot do, without ceasing to be a retributive judge, is *try* to send such a person to jail. Punishing the innocent is logically inconsistent with punishing-according-to-criminal-desert (though not with punishing as such). The same is not true of punishing-according-to-deterrent-effect. One can, at least in principle, deter others by punishing an innocent person. For a deterrentist judge, punishing the innocent is at worst an option barred by side constraints, not something in principle inconsistent with his official intention. I don't think Philips appreciates this difference between retributive and deterrence theories. Compare Philips (pp. 400-401).

25. Compare Chapter Four, esp. pp. 95-96 and Chapter Eight.

26. Actually, Philips claims this sort of theory is *not* retributive because "the purpose of punishment here is to remove an unearned or undeserved benefit *rather than* to impose a deserved disadvantage" (P. 407n). The italics are mine. Since Philips names me (as well as Herbert Morris) as failing this test, I think I must respond. My view (and I think that of Morris as well) is that the judge (when choosing the initial sentence) should seek to remove

undeserved advantage *by* imposing deserved disadvantage. Whatever undeserved advantage cannot be removed in this way is beyond the reach of a judge in a criminal proceeding. On this view, the two concepts, "removing undeserved benefit" and "imposing deserved disadvantage," are conceptually linked, not opposed. I therefore believe my view to satisfy even Philips's definition of retributivism.

27. See, for example, Hyman Gross, "Fringe Liability, Unfair Advantage, and the Price of Crime," *Wayne Law Review* 33 (Summer 1987): 1395-1411, esp. pp. 1401-406; or von Hirsch, *Past or Future Crimes*, esp. pp. 56-60. For further defense of the unfair-advantage approach against the criticism of these two important theorists, see Chapter Nine.

28. This rural stop sign has a surprisingly long history. See, for example, my paper "Smith, Gert, and Obligation to Obey the Law," *Southern Journal of Philosophy* 20 (Summer 1982): 139-52, which criticizes its use two decades ago in M.B.E. Smith, "Is There a Prima Facie Obligation to Obey the Law?," *Yale Law Review* 82 (April 1973): 950-976.

3

Harm and Retribution

Recently, a respected legal theorist, Hugo Bedau, was asked to evaluate a proposed revision of Pennsylvania's penal code. He began by noting: "The classification [of crimes and punishments] . . . has been assumed to be fundamentally retributive, and so its penalty schedule must be based on two basic retributive principles: (1) the severity of the punishment must be proportional to the gravity of the offense, and (2) the gravity of the offense must be a function of fault in the offender and harm caused the victim."[1] These two "basic principles" (or part of them) are often referred to as "*lex talionis*."

What interests me here are two of Bedau's three uses of "must." Because the classification of crimes and punishments is retributive, *it must*, Bedau says, be based on *lex talionis*. And, for the same reason, the penalties provided *must* be a function of fault in the offender and harm done the victim (and, except in special cases, nothing else). My thesis is that there is no "must" about either.

Some retributivists, most notably F. H. Bradley, may seem to have argued something similar.[2] But the upshot of their arguments was that retribution needs a utilitarian principle to proportion punishment to crime. Those retributivists defended a compromised retributivism. I shall not. I shall not because there is, I believe, a better *retributivist* principle for proportioning punishment to crime. That principle proportions punishment to the unfair advantage the criminal takes just by committing his crime. Let us call it "the unfair-advantage principle."

The unfair-advantage principle superficially resembles *lex talionis* enough that, as far as I can tell, no one has clearly distinguished them. Yet the differences are important. Or, at least, that is what I shall try to show. I proceed in this way. First, I distinguish *lex talionis* from the unfair-advantage principle. Second, I show that the unfair-advantage principle can explain a variety of criminal laws better than *lex talionis* can. Third, I show that *lex talionis* is virtually unusable in large areas of criminal law while the unfair-advantage principle should be equally usable everywhere. Last, I consider saving *lex talionis* by leaving the measurement of harm to intuition or empirical survey. I argue that it cannot be saved in that way.

I shall not now explain (or defend) the unfair advantage principle more than necessary to make clear how it differs from *lex talionis*. Further explanation (and defense) must wait till later chapters.

My thesis, if proved, should be important to retributivists in at least three ways. First, it should help to establish that the unfair-advantage approach to punishment is significantly different from other forms of (uncompromised) retributivism (since it gives up *lex talionis* while other forms do not). Second, given the problems of *lex talionis*, the argument here should help to establish the superiority of the unfair-advantage approach over other forms of retributivism. And third, because critics of (uncompromised) retributivism tend to treat *lex talionis* as retributivism's chief weakness,[3] my argument should also help to dissuade such critics from treating it as a weakness of retributivism as such. They would have to treat *lex talionis* merely as a weakness of some forms of retributivism. If they still chose to reject retributivism categorically, they would have to do it for reasons independent of *lex talionis*.

While this chapter is supposed to be a contribution to retributive theory, much of what is said should also be relevant to those "utilitarian" (or "consequentialist") theories of punishment in which desert limits what may be done to the criminal. Such "mixed" theories need not interpret "desert" as requiring proportion between punishment and the harm the criminal did.

But (I should add) this chapter is not supposed to be relevant only to theory. Retributivism is not merely a subject for theorists. As Bedau's commentary on the proposed revision of Pennsylvania's penal code suggests, retributivism is again a principle helping to shape and justify the way punishment is in fact administered. So, what I say here should be useful to legislators, criminologists, and others who are concerned to make punishment as just as possible.

What is *Lex Talionis?*

Lex talionis (or *jus talionis*) may once have referred unequivocally to a certain principle defining or limiting the right of retaliation, but it has long since become equivocal. *Lex talionis* may now refer either to a general principle of corrective justice or to a particular principle of criminal law. As a general principle of corrective justice, *lex* requires the wrongdoer to suffer as much as (but no more than) he has wrongfully made others suffer. This principle is more at home in the mountains of Corsica or in a schoolyard fight than in the criminal law. ("He hit you once, so you should hit him just once in return.")[4] This is not the *lex talionis* that concerns me. My concern is a principle of criminal law, one that is supposed to explain what statutory penalties and judicial sentences must be to be justified as acts of a relatively just legal system. Whatever light that principle sheds on natural justice, poetic justice, divine justice, or the like is, while welcome, gratuitous.

Lex talionis, understood as a principle of criminal law, is still equivocal. It may be understood either "formally" or "materially." Understood formally, it is the first of Bedau's "two basic principles," that is, the principle that punishment should be proportioned to the gravity of the offense or otherwise made to "fit the crime." This *lex talionis* is simply a reminder that criminal justice consists primarily in punishing violations of the criminal law, not in punishing faults of character, deterring antisocial behavior, or doing other sorts of good. Other good may be done as well, of course, but doing it is secondary, not to be achieved by punishment greater than the crime deserves (however desert happens to be measured). Bedau was certainly right to include that principle among the "basic principles" of retributivism. So understood, *lex talionis* is essential to any retributive theory.[6] Differences among retributive theories are largely in how to measure desert, not in whether desert is what punishment should be measured against. For example, some retributivists have held that deserved punishment is determined by the moral wrong the criminal did when he broke the law; others, that it is the special moral wrong involved in breaking a particular criminal law as such.

Lex talionis may also be understood "materially," that is, as a principle requiring punishment to be proportioned (in part at least) to harm done (or, perhaps, to be limited by the harm done). This is Bedau's second "basic principle." Different retributive theories differ concerning what shall count as harm (and how important harm is for determining punishment). But, any theory for which *lex talionis* is not purely formal will have to understand "harm" as existing *independent of a particular criminal statute*. Harm will have to be something a statute can protect against by forbidding (or requiring) certain acts. The loss of an eye is an example of such a harm. For most retributivists, the invasion of a right would be another. What else may be is controversial.

Lex talionis is so often invoked as the principle that requires an eye for an eye, a tooth for a tooth, that it may be worth a moment to point out that even those among its defenders who talk that way, do not mean what they seem to say. For example, Kant states the "law of retribution" as "any undeserved evil that you inflict on someone else among the people is one that you do to yourself."[6] Yet, his examples of retribution include apology followed by solitary confinement as punishment for attacking a social inferior without just cause, penal servitude as punishment for theft, and death as punishment for treason. Accompanying each example is an explanation of how the suggested punishment would satisfy the "spirit," if not the letter, of *lex talionis*.[7] Plainly, even Kant understood *lex talionis* to require an *equivalent* "evil," not the *same* "evil."

Of course, retributivists are divided on whether *lex talionis* requires the punishment to be equivalent or merely specifies equivalence as the most justice will allow. Kant left little room for clemency. For him, justice generally required a certain punishment and the sovereign had no right to do more or less. Most modern retributivists would reject Kant's rigorism. But that need not concern us.

We may now complete our explanation of *lex talionis* by contrasting it with the unfair-advantage principle.

The unfair-advantage principle assumes that each criminal law (or perhaps the criminal law as a whole) creates a system of cooperation. Some people forbear doing what they would otherwise do because the law has given them reasonable assurance that others will do the same (and everyone will be better off if everyone abstains). Such a system imposes burdens insofar as people do forbear doing what they would otherwise do. Anyone who breaks a law does not bear the same burden the rest do. Unless he is punished, he will, in effect, have gotten away with doing less than others. He will have an advantage they do not.

According to the unfair-advantage principle, it is this advantage the criminal law is supposed to take back by punishing the criminal for his crime. The advantage bears no necessary relation to the harm the criminal actually did. For example, he may have done great damage and only committed theft; or no damage at all even though he tried to commit murder. According to the unfair-advantage principle, the damage a criminal actually does is between him and his victim, a private matter to be settled by civil suit (or the moral equivalent). His *crime* consists only in the unfair advantage he necessarily took over the law-abiding by breaking the law in question. The measure of punishment due is the relative value of *that* unfair advantage. The greater the advantage, the greater the punishment should be. The focus of the unfair-advantage principle is on what the *criminal* gained; the focus of *lex talionis*, on what *others* lost.[8]

In one respect, however, the two principles are alike. Neither the unfair advantage principle nor *lex talionis* distinguishes sharply between laying down rules for punishment and applying those rules in particular cases. Under either principle, a legislature has little or no discretion concerning *how much* the crime should be punished (though it may have wide discretion concerning the form of that punishment). That a legislature happens to require a certain penalty for a certain crime does not mean that the criminal deserves it for the crime in question or that it would be just for a judge to impose it even under an otherwise just procedure. The principle of punishment, whether *lex talionis* or unfair-advantage, determines what is just. From the perspective of either principle, there is only one continuous process of proportioning punishment to crime once a legislature has made an act criminal. The judge completes whatever the legislature has left undone.

The rule-act distinction seems to belong to utilitarian, rather than to retributive, theories of punishment. I shall say nothing more about it here. For retributivists, the important distinction seems to be between (a) the legislative decision to make a class of acts criminal, (b) the legislative or judicial decision that a certain crime deserves (no more than) a certain punishment, and (c) the judicial decision that the actual sentence should be such and such (the judge taking into account the criminal as well as his crime to determine whether the sentence should be less than what the crime itself deserves).[9]

Harm, "Harm," and No "Harm"

Harm is the engine of *lex talionis*. To determine how much (or how little) *lex talionis* can help us understand the criminal law, we must consider the place of harm in the criminal law. Is it the right place for *lex talionis* to provide an adequate theory of how much to punish?

I suggest that, while trying to answer that question, we confine ourselves to the criminal law as we know it. This limitation is not meant to foreclose the possibility that a retributive theory might provide a criticism of practice.[10] Rather, it serves to remind us of the practice we are trying to understand. We may wish to criticize some of it, perhaps all of it. But criticism not founded on understanding will hardly convince. So, whether our ultimate aim is understanding or reform, we should begin with the criminal law as it is.

Harm certainly has a significant place in the criminal law even if "harm" is understood strictly as physical injury to some person or physical damage to some thing. Many common crimes do harm in this sense. Murder and mayhem require that some individual suffer physical injury: arson and wanton destruction of property, that some property be damaged.

But many common crimes do not harm — if "harm" is understood that strictly. Kidnapping, robbery, theft, burglary, and perhaps even battery may leave no mark on any person or reduce the value of anything. Such crimes do harm, if they do harm, only in a looser sense of "harm." They invade the *right* of some individual. A kidnapper must deprive his victim of liberty, for example, by carrying the victim off against his will. A robber must deprive her victim of property by force. And so on. The rights in question (liberty, property, or the like) are rights existing independent of the particular criminal statute. They would be enforceable by civil suit whether or not protected by criminal statute. So, extending "harm" to include what such crimes do is certainly consistent with *lex talionis*.[11]

But, extended only in this way, "harm" is still not broad enough for anything like a full theory of deserved punishment. Some serious crimes do not seem to be an invasion of anyone's right but merely a beneficial restraint on commerce. For example, a blackmailer may have a right (that is, a "liberty-right") to publish the information he uses to blackmail and a similar right to accept payment for silence. What right (what "claim-right") could one have (all else equal) to the helpful silence of another if one is not willing to pay for it? What right not to be given an opportunity to pay for it?

The law – civil or criminal – is ordinarily not concerned to prevent publication of the sort of (truthful) information a blackmailer uses, nor is it generally concerned with people receiving money to keep silent. The blackmail statute simply forbids a blackmailer's volunteering his silence for pay. Here, it seems, if we are still to talk of "harm," we must understand "harm" as violating a (preexisting) *interest*, that is, an interest in not having someone force you to choose between paying for his silence and having your reputation blasted, not as violating a (preexisting) right. The point of prohibiting blackmail seems to be to remove a certain temptation to destroy the reputation of others. The law against blackmail may be said to protect an individual from the "harm of lost reputation," but that "harm" is to an interest, not (like the harms discussed earlier) harm that constitutes "breach of the peace" or invades a right.

But extending "harm" to include protecting (some) interests of individuals still does not extend the concept enough to explain punishing all serious crimes. Some serious crimes do not seem to invade the interest of any individual (at least, not in anything like the full-blooded sense of "interest" we have been considering so far). For example, treason seems to be a crime against government, a corporate person, not an individual. The same seems to be true of tax evasion, smuggling, and similar "social crimes." Here it is natural to talk of "harming the interests of society" ("society" referring to the corporate entity, not to any particular individuals). The interests of society may, it seems, be distinct from those of any individual (though still connected with them in certain complex ways). I may, for example, commit treason by giving some rebels a bed for the night and a few crumbs in the morning (if I do it in part to help their cause). I may in this small way help impede the government's efforts to starve the rebellion into submission. Yet, it is hard to see how the interests of any individual would be harmed by my kindness (at least, in the way their interests would be harmed by my blackmailing them). Who in particular would be worse off? One can, of course, imagine situations in which my kindness adversely affected someone (for example, by giving the rebels enough encouragement to persevere until they engaged in some deadly attack on government facilities they would not otherwise have attacked). But those would not be the only cases, or even the most common.

It might, however, be argued that any act of treason, even my seemingly harmless kindness, necessarily harms the interests of some individuals, for example, the interests of those individuals who cooperate to produce the shared good of political stability. What are we to make of this argument? We must, I think, distinguish two forms of it. One form is in fact an appeal to the unfair-advantage principle, not *lex talionis*, and so cannot threaten any claim we may make concerning the infirmity of *lex talionis*; the other, while an appeal to *lex talionis*, is so only supposing a sense of "harm" we have yet to consider.

Let us begin with the first form of the argument. The claim it makes is that I harm those who cooperate to produce political stability by taking *unfair* advantage of that stability while refusing to do my share. The advantage must be "unfair" because we ordinarily do not consider taking fair advantage to deserve punishment. If we now ask how one is to know that the advantage is "unfair," the answer seems to be that the system of cooperation producing that stability is (in part at least) defined by the criminal statute prohibiting treason. My act of kindness to the rebels would not take unfair advantage of anyone if the criminal law allowed such kindness. My kindness is not cooperation because, and it seems simply because, it is prohibited. The harm my kindness does cannot, then, on this analysis, be defined apart from the criminal statute in question. Since *lex talionis* (as we have understood it) is supposed to provide a measure of harm (and so, of deserved punishment) *independent* of the existence of the particular criminal statute in question, this form of the argument cannot be an appeal to *lex talionis*. And indeed, as the explicit reference to "unfair advantage" suggests, it is nothing more than a special form of appeal to the unfair-advantage principle itself.

That brings us to the other form of the argument. The claim is that, treason statute or not, my kindness to the rebels harms the interests of those cooperating to maintain political stability. My kindness does that by at least *risking* that political stability (whether fairly or unfairly). We have already had to adopt a relatively abstract notion of harm, that is, harm as damage to some interest of an individual or society (an individual's rights being among those interests). But this second form of the argument asks us to go further. Or, rather, it asks us to go further in one way (by having "harm" include "risk of harm") so as not to go further in another (by having "harm" include "harm to society"). Since I do not think we can avoid this second extension anyway, I think we may allow those who hope to keep *lex talionis* from becoming unusable to deny that "harm" includes "harm to society" (strictly speaking). There are, after all, many other crimes in which the only plausible harm is a "risk of harm to person or property."

Consider, for example, the crime of reckless driving. If I drive recklessly on an empty highway, I do not in fact invade anyone's interest in safety (since I endanger no one). I also do not invade any interest of government in the way my earlier act of kindness did (since what I do does not endanger the government even to the degree helping rebels does). What I do is *risk endangering* anyone who *might* be on the highway (even though it happens that no one is there). If we are to describe what I am doing in terms of preexisting interest, we shall have to say that I am violating the interest of all those who might have used the highway in not having me risk endangering them, or perhaps society's interest in not having people risk endangering each other. If the interests we have discussed so far may be described as "primary," this is a "secondary interest," that is, an interest in not having a primary interest put at risk (where "risk" refers to the harm reasonably foreseeable given what the actor knows or, perhaps, should know of it, and "danger" refers to the harm reasonably foreseeable given — something like — full information).

Perhaps we can explain punishing attempts in the same way. By definition, an attempt does not do the harm the complete crime would have done. Some attempts violate no primary interest at all. For example, an attempted murder might consist of no more than putting sugar, believed to be poison, in the coffee of one's senile aunt or trying to shoot one's enemy from ambush with an empty gun believed to be loaded. While such crimes do not in fact endanger, they could, like reckless driving, endanger someone under other circumstances and, for all the actor knew, the other circumstances prevailed. So, it seems reasonable to say that attempts violate a secondary interest in not having our safety or control of property risked (whether it is in fact endangered or not).

There are, however, other crimes, some serious, that seem not to harm even a secondary interest. Consider, for example, the crime of conspiracy. A conspiracy may be no more than an agreement to attempt an ordinary crime, for example, robbery or murder. Two would-be criminals can be guilty of such a conspiracy if, having agreed to commit the crime, they buy rope or do some other (ordinarily) lawful act in preparation for carrying out the planned crime. They need not do anything amounting to an attempt. Since two would-be criminals cannot lawfully do some acts one would-be criminal can lawfully do, the "harm" of conspiracy seems to be harm in a sense different from that in which attempt does harm. It is, it seems, an invasion of the interest in not having people join together to undertake a criminal attempt. Perhaps we can call this a "tertiary interest."

If so, we shall have to talk of "fourth-degree interests" too. Consider the crime of solicitation. You commit this crime by (in effect) attempting to commit conspiracy, that is, by going about trying to get others to agree to attempt a crime for you. ("Try," because if you succeed, there is a conspiracy.) The "harm" done by solicitation seems very far from harm strictly so called. Of course, if solicitation of a certain sort were allowed, there might be more successful attempts of the corresponding primary crime. That possibility is something that rightly concerns a legislature. But, more than in conspiracy or attempt, it seems odd to talk about that sensible concern in terms of someone's (fourth-degree) interest a particular criminal harms by a particular solicitation.

We have, it seems, already stretched the concept of harm pretty far. But we have not yet stretched it far enough to cover the whole criminal law. There are some crimes that do not seem to involve harm even in this most extended sense. Consider, for example, recidivism. A recidivist statute may punish as a separate crime being-guilty-of-an-ordinary-crime-when-one-has-previously-been-convicted-of-others. The recidivist commits the same "underlying" crime a first offender would if he did the same act. But the recidivist commits two crimes, the "underlying" crime and recidivism, where the first offender would commit only one.

Because *lex talionis* includes both harm and fault in its calculations of deserved punishment, it might seem that punishment for recidivism can be justified under *lex talionis* by supposing that repeat offenders deserve greater punishment because repetition demonstrates greater fault. In fact, such a justification will work for only one class of recidivist statute, that is, those that treat repetition as an aggravating factor. Most recidivist statutes do not treat repetition that way. Instead they treat repetition as a separate crime. The punishment allowable under the recidivist statute is *in addition to* the maximum punishment for the underlying crime and can be many times that *maximum* (indeed, it can be considerably more than the maximum for all the preceding offenses together). For example, conviction for three thefts might require a mandatory life sentence even though the maximum punishment for each theft would have been ten years imprisonment (and even though the criminal in fact served the maximum each time). Explaining such hugely enhanced punishments as a function merely of increased fault certainly looks *ad hoc* (especially in the absence of any independent measure of fault).

It seems, then, that if we are to explain recidivist statutes under *lex talionis*, we must explain them (at least in large part) as punishing invasion of an interest not invaded by a first offender committing the same "underlying" crime. Such an explanation will require some ingenuity. What interest could potential victims have in suffering a crime at the hands of a first offender *rather than* at the hands of a recidivist? What interest could society have in having a particular crime committed by a first offender rather than by a recidivist?

So, if the recidivist deserves more punishment than a first offender, he must, it seems, deserve it for reasons independent of the harm *he* does. At least two contemporary theorists concerned with criminal desert have drawn that conclusion. Both George Fletcher and Hyman Gross have argued that the "recidivist premium" cannot be explained by the principles of punishment (Gross adding that recidivist statutes are best thought of as "crude counterparts of civil commitment").[12]

To say that it is hard to find the interest an individual recidivist invades by being a recidivist (in addition to the interest he invades by the "underlying" crime) is, of course, not to say that there may not be good reason to punish recidivism in the way we do. Thinking of such reasons is not hard. For example, recidivist statutes may give us a means of incapacitating those criminals most likely to contribute most to the rate of crime. The problem is to turn such a general reason, suitable for justifying criminalization, into a harm (that is, an injury to a preexisting interest) suitable for proportioning punishment to the crime. That is the problem because *lex talionis* proportions punishment (in part at least) to the harm a particular criminal did. Where we cannot find an interest the criminal invaded, we cannot invoke *lex talionis* — except to justify no punishment whatever.

Perhaps, if we thought long and hard, we could discover an interest recidivists invade. "Interest" is an extraordinarily flexible category. But, it seems unlikely that our discovery would have enough intuitive appeal to justify the very substantial penalties with which recidivism is in fact punished. Our concern is not a question far from experience. *Lex talionis* is itself supposed to be common sense. If the interest *lex talionis* requires can be discovered only by much hard thought, it is unlikely to be what a legislator (or judge) would take into account. And if not something actually taken into account, it is unlikely to explain the criminal law as it is. So, even this brief and impressionistic survey of the criminal law seems to have stretched the concept of harm to the breaking point (or beyond).

Recidivist statutes provide a clear example of the superiority of the unfair-advantage principle over *lex talionis*. We may summarize the argument of Chapter Six in this way: The recidivist deserves punishment, if he deserves punishment, because committing another crime after he has been convicted of others takes an advantage a first offender would not take just by committing the same "underlying" crime. It is perhaps analogous to going back for seconds when not everyone has had a first helping. There is nothing unfair about it unless it is against "the rules." But if it is against the rules (that is, there is a recidivist statute), it is unfair to take that advantage and so there is something to deserve punishment. Whether the state should prohibit criminals from "going back for seconds" is (according to the unfair-advantage principle) an independent question. Moreover, it is a question for the theory of legislation (that is, for the theory demarking what should be prohibited from what should not be), not for the theory of punishment.

Here, it seems, *lex talionis* reveals disturbing prelegal roots the unfair-advantage principle does not have. According to *lex talionis*, a law, even if itself not unjust, can*not* make an act punishable unless the act is "punishable" law or no law, that is, unless the act invades a (legitimate) interest existing independent of the criminal law in question. The criminal law cannot make a "harmless" act punishable because without harm there is, according to *lex* *talionis*, nothing to measure deserved punishment against. Since it would be unjust to punish to any degree what cannot deserve punishment to any degree, for *lex talionis* prelegal conditions limit what the law can punish. The law cannot add to what deserves punishment, only select a subset of punishable acts to make punishable at law. *Lex talionis* is, in effect, a theory of legislation as well as a theory of how much to punish.

The unfair-advantage principle is not (or, at least, not to the same degree). The principle is consistent with any theory of what the criminal law should forbid or allow (provided the criminal law is conceived as part of a relatively just legal system). That is so because (ordinarily) any law within a relatively just legal system creates a cooperative scheme most departures from which would take unfair advantage. Of course, a particular departure for special reason may not amount to taking such advantage (for example, as explained in Chapter Two, because the departure constitutes a "mere technical violation" or because enforcing the law in that case would be discriminatory or otherwise unfair). In such cases, the unfair-advantage principle would provide the basis for excuse or justification. Such special cases, while important for any adequate theory of criminal law, present a problem different from the one we are now considering. The category of excuse or justification presupposes that punishment for the crime in question is generally deserved. The problem we have been considering until now is whether *lex talionis* or the unfair-advantage principle better explains how punishment for various *sorts* of crime can be deserved.

Because the unfair-advantage principle is concerned with unfair advantage taken by disobeying the law rather than with harm done against the law, the unfair-advantage principle automatically separates (most) questions of demarcation from those of proportion. Because separating such questions seems more judicious than implicitly supposing that what justifies making an act criminal will also provide the measure of punishment for doing the act once doing it is a crime, I take this difference between the unfair-advantage principle and *lex talionis* to be an advantage of the unfair-advantage principle.[13]

Doing Harm or Failing to Help Prevent Harm?

Lex talionis limits the criminal law to protecting (preexisting) interests. A law which does not protect some such interest cannot be understood as part of the criminal law; what it "punishes" cannot be understood as a crime; and so, what is done to the "criminal" cannot be justified *as punishment* even though what is done is obviously part of the ordinary processes of the criminal law. Given the criminal law as we know it, that is a significant limitation. The point of legislation does not always translate easily into an interest a particular criminal invades by a particular crime. Recidivist statutes provide one example of that, an example of the difficulty of finding an *interest* the criminal invades. I should now like to consider a class of crimes in which the difficulty is not finding an interest but finding an *invasion*. Some crimes consist of no more than an intentional *non*doing, for example, refusing to aid a police officer when asked, "misprison of treason," or failure to report a bribe. Let us consider the last of these examples briefly to see how *lex talionis* may not explain why such a crime deserves punishment.

In Illinois, anyone " . . . connected with any professional or amateur contest, sporting event or exhibition, who fails to report [to an appropriate official] . . . any offer or promise made to him [with the intent, understanding, or agreement that he will not use his best efforts in connection with such contest]" commits the class-A misdemeanor of failing to report a bribe.[14] The point of this statute is plain enough. If more people reported bribe attempts, fewer bribes would be offered and more would-be bribers would be caught. Preventing bribes would, in turn, help to preserve the integrity of contests, sporting events, and the like. It is also plain that the statute helps to protect certain interests. The statute helps to protect our interest in not being misled concerning the nature of the contest or sporting event we might attend, participate in, or bet on (and, if we have such an interest, our interest in not being forced to decide whether or not to take a bribe). But the statute provides that protection by requiring ordinary citizens to report any attempt at a certain sort of solicitation.

How might *lex talionis* apply here? If bribe attempts were never reported but bribes were never accepted, the contests or events the statute is supposed to protect would still be as fair as they could be. So, someone failing to report a bribe does not, as would someone who took a bribe, *increase* the danger that a contest or event will be less fair than it would be if he had not been offered the bribe. He merely does not *increase* the probability that the contest will be fair. He does not aid in apprehending those who make such contests unfair. That is harm only if failure to do good (or prevent harm) can constitute doing harm (or *invading* an interest).

There are cases in which failure to act does harm — or, more accurately, is part of doing harm. For example, if relying on your promise to report any attempt to bribe and hearing nothing of the bribe you were offered, I state publicly that there has been no attempt to bribe, I would suffer loss of credibility when the attempt later became known. And you would be one cause of that loss. I would be harmed, law or no law. And you would have caused that harm.

The ordinary case of failing to report a bribe is, however, not like that. Ordinarily, the expectation that anyone offered a bribe will report it does not exist or, if it exists, exists only because the statute makes failing to report the bribe a crime. Without the statute, there does not seem to be a larger act that could constitute doing harm (unless we are willing to give up the distinction between doing harm and letting it happen). Someone who fails to report the bribe attempt could have helped prevent invasion of certain interests and did not. But he does not seem to have *invaded* any interest at all. He has not done harm, only let it happen.

Because *lex talionis* proportions punishment to the harm the criminal *does*, it seems to forbid punishing someone who has done no harm. That is certainly inconsistent with a significant part of the criminal law as we know it. Statutes imposing duties to act are not, like retroactive criminal statutes or secret laws, mere oddities more often discussed by legal theorists than invoked in a courtroom. Any theory of just punishment that cannot explain such common statutes as part of the criminal law is already substantially less desirable, all else equal, than one that can.

So, it is worth noting that, unlike *lex talionis*, the unfair-advantage principle is immune to such problems. The principle does not require a statute to protect against invasion of an interest for the statute to be part of the criminal law. All the principle requires is that the statute be part of a system of cooperation (and that the statute include criminal penalties). Even a statute the legislature has adopted without good reason may create a system of cooperation. If it does (and if the statute allows criminal penalties), the unfair-advantage principle applies.

Of course, a particularly silly statute may not create a system of cooperation. People may just scoff at the statute (while letting it remain "on the books" out of misplaced piety, disinterest, or who knows what). If the statute is a "dead letter," the unfair-advantage principle would not recognize it as part of the criminal law (except in some sense too extended to justify punishment). One can take no advantage by violating a "dead law" and so, according to the unfair-advantage principle, one cannot deserve punishment even if one does violate it. And that is so even, contrary to what we are now assuming, the statute would prevent invasion of some significant interest if it were obeyed.[15]

It might also happen that a silly statute, though it does not deserve to be enforced, is being enforced and, because it is being enforced, is generally being obeyed. If so, the statute is part of a system of cooperation and, for the unfair-advantage principle, that is all that is necessary for the penalties to apply (supposing the legal system as a whole to be relatively just). People will be shouldering burdens they would not otherwise shoulder. Unless the criminal is a special case, his failure to shoulder the same burden will give him an unfair advantage over others. That advantage is all the unfair-advantage principle requires that punishment be proportioned to.

So, according to that principle, the important distinction is not between doing harm and letting it happen (or between invading an interest and failing to help prevent such an invasion), but between cooperating and not cooperating with the criminal law (by obeying or disobeying it). The criminal law punishes failure to report a bribe for exactly the same reason it punishes reckless driving or recidivism. All are failures to cooperate, failures to abide by the rules of the cooperative scheme constituting the criminal law within a relatively just legal system. The reckless driver fails to drive as the law requires. The recidivist fails to abstain from "taking seconds" the law has forbidden. And the person who does not bother to report a bribe attempt fails to do what the law says he should. Each benefits from the cooperation of others but does not respond as they have. Each makes himself an exception and, according to the unfair-advantage principle, punishment is supposed to undo that exceptional status.

Harm as the Measure of Desert

The last two sections compared *lex talionis* and the unfair-advantage principle as explanations of *what* the criminal law punishes. We learned that *lex talionis* cannot make sense of certain kinds of criminal law the unfair-advantage principle can. We may now inquire which principle is better at helping us understand *how much* punishment a crime deserves. To be fair to *lex talionis*, we must, given the results of the last two sections, limit our inquiry to those crimes for which there is an identifiable harm (or invasion of interest). That, as we saw, is a significant limitation, but one about which we have said enough already.

Does the concept of harm give us insight into how much punishment a criminal deserves for what he did? The answer seems to be that it certainly does—sometimes. For example, it seems only simple good sense to explain why murder deserves more punishment than battery by pointing out that the harm done by killing someone is greater than the harm done by hitting him. The simpler the legal system, the more likely it is that the relation among crimes will be like that, one crime differing from another only in the seriousness of harm done. Perhaps this explanation's good sense has something to do with the enduring appeal of *lex talionis*.

Unfortunately, modern systems of criminal law are not simple. They include many laws differing from one another in more than harm. Consider, for example, whether killing someone through reckless operation of an automobile deserves more or less punishment than grabbing someone with the intention of throwing acid in his face. The automobile driver has, it seems, done more harm strictly speaking. He has caused a death while the would-be acid thrower may not actually have thrown the acid because, say, someone knocked the bottle from his hand just in time. The driver has recklessly violated the primary interest in life; the would-be acid thrower, only a secondary interest in not having acid thrown in one's face and a primary interest in not being grabbed and put in fear of serious injury. So, who deserves the greater penalty, the reckless driver or the would-be acid thrower?

Most defenders of *lex talionis* would, I think, answer that the would-be acid thrower deserves the greater penalty. If that is their answer, they have the support of many systems of criminal law. For example, in Illinois, the reckless driver who kills is guilty of a class-4 felony (one to three years imprisonment) while the would-be acid thrower is guilty of a class-1 felony (four to fifteen years imprisonment).[16] But, of course, giving the "right answer" is not enough. The defenders of *lex talionis* must also be able to get that answer in a way that helps us to understand why the criminal law does what it does (or, occasionally, why it should not do what it does). How would they get their answer?

The defenders of *lex talionis* would, I think, point out that there is more to proportioning punishment to crime than proportioning it to harm. All else equal, they might say, the ranking of harms corresponds to the ranking of deserved punishments. But in the case I have put, all else is not equal. I have, first, mixed different kinds of *"mens rea"* (and so, different kinds of "wickedness," "culpability," or "fault"). The driver was only reckless while the would-be acid thrower committed his crime intentionally. According to (what we may call) "the principle of culpability," a crime done intentionally deserves more punishment, all else equal, than one done recklessly. Second, I have also mixed kinds of harm, a secondary interest in bodily integrity with a primary interest in life. That too affects deserved punishment. All else equal, an injury to a secondary interest deserves less punishment than an injury to the corresponding primary interest but not necessarily less than injury to *any* primary interest.

We must, I think, agree with the defenders of *lex talionis* that all this is so. Having agreed, however, we must add that taking such considerations into account makes using *lex talionis* more difficult than seems desirable. For example, to determine whether the reckless driver or the would-be acid thrower deserves more punishment, we need to take into account not only the harm each did or threatened, but the *mens rea* of each. How are we to do that?

Defenders of *lex talionis* have had surprisingly little to say on this question. Kant simply urges that the criminal be made to suffer "according to the spirit – even if not the letter [of *lex talionis*] . . . " and then gives the examples of that spirit mentioned earlier.[17] The long history of retributism does not, I believe, provide any better explanation of how to apply *lex talionis* to "hard cases" of setting penalties (though much of criminal law consists of such hard cases).[18] If it were impossible to provide a better explanation as part of a theory otherwise at least as satisfactory as *lex talionis*, that failing would be no more unfortunate than our mortality, a misfortune to be lived with if we are to live at all. But, if there is an alternative theory that is otherwise at least as satisfactory and has more to say about scaling penalties than does *lex talionis*, the same failing is a serious weakness. I believe the unfair-advantage principle provides the basis for such an alternative theory (as I shall show in later chapters).

Why have the defenders of *lex talionis* had so little to say about setting particular penalties? The answer is obvious. It is hard to say anything more helpful so long as one depends on *lex talionis*. What we need is some way to weigh a variety of considerations (at least four kinds of interest and several kinds of *mens rea* including purposefulness, intention, recklessness, and negligence). The problem bears an unpleasant likeness to that which a utilitarian theory of punishment faces. We could, for example, think of the weight of a certain secondary interest as equal to the product of the primary interest threatened and the probability of that threat being realized. So, if I attempt a crime with a fifty-fifty chance of success, my attempt would (all else equal) be half as bad as the complete crime. But, thinking in such terms requires cardinal numbers (or something very like them). *Lex talionis* would have to be arithmetic and so, to apply it, we would have to find some way to assign cardinal numbers to the various primary harms. We would, for example, have to be able to say how much worse is being killed than being disfigured by acid. Fifty percent worse? Two hundred percent worse? Or what? And we would have to be able to do the same for kinds of *mens rea* as well. Is intentionally committing a certain crime twice as bad as committing it recklessly?

The absurdity of such questions suggests either a deeper absurdity in any version of retributivism assuming *lex talionis* or a mistake in our understanding of *lex talionis*. My view is that it reveals a deeper absurdity. But, to be fair, let us assume that defenders of *lex talionis* can work out the mathematics necessary to handle comparison of different kinds of interest and different mental states, and then examine *lex talionis* under the most favorable conditions, that is, holding *mens rea* and kind of interest constant. Intentional crime will be compared with intentional crime, complete crime with complete crime, and so on.

Consider two crimes in which *mens rea* and kind of interest seem identical. For example, Illinois distinguishes between (ordinary) involuntary manslaughter and what is often called "vehicular homicide" (though Illinois calls it "reckless homicide"). While vehicular homicide is a class-4 felony (one to three years imprisonment), involuntary manslaughter is a class-3 felony (two to five years imprisonment).[19] Does *lex talionis* help us to understand why these two kinds of manslaughter are punished as they are? It *seems* not. Manslaughter, whether "involuntary" or "vehicular," requires exactly the same *mens rea*, "recklessness," and the same harm, death. So, how can the defenders of *lex talionis* defend against what seems to be a clear counterexample to their version of retributivism?

They have at least three strategies open to them. One is to dismiss the distinction between "involuntary manslaughter" and "vehicular homicide" as an "anomaly," that is, as an indefensible distinction. The second strategy is to show that the two crimes, contrary to all appearances, violate different interests. The third strategy is to show that our example is not as "clean" as it should be, that is, that there is in it another factor *lex talionis* recognizes as relevant.

The first strategy would be tempting if Illinois were alone (or almost alone) in distinguishing between involuntary manslaughter and vehicular homicide. Unfortunately, the distinction has long been part of the criminal law of many jurisdictions, both American and foreign. So, dismissing the distinction as an anomaly would appear *ad hoc* without a powerful argument. That argument cannot (on pain of begging the question) rest on the principle that, all else equal, punishment should be proportioned to harm done. And it is hard to see on what other ground it could rest. So, the strategy of dismissal looks uninviting.

If the first strategy looks uninviting, so does the second. It is hard to guess what interest (ordinary) involuntary manslaughter violates that vehicular homicide would not violate as well. Death by automobile is seldom pretty and is often as painful as death by any means by which involuntary manslaughter is commonly committed. Still, with enough ingenuity, perhaps we could find some way to distinguish the interest harmed by involuntary manslaughter from the interest harmed by vehicular homicide. But the ingenuity required signals another problem with the second strategy. The greater the ingenuity required, the less intuitive what we find is likely to be.

That leaves the third strategy, showing the example not to be as "clean" as it seems. The strategy has some promise. It seems that, as soon as cars became common, juries began to refuse to convict of involuntary manslaughter drivers who recklessly caused death. Legislatures responded by creating a less serious crime of which juries were willing to convict drivers. Whether juries were reluctant to convict drivers of involuntary manslaughter because they thought, "There but for the grace of God go I," or because they considered driving to constitute a partial excuse for manslaughter, a cousin of duress or extreme temptation, or because of some other reason, is open to debate. It is, however, easy to see why juries might have thought driving a partial excuse. Living would be far less convenient if we did not drive, yet driving puts us in circumstances where it is easier to be reckless with life than it is in (ordinary) involuntary manslaughter. Since this is a general feature of conduct, it should be recognized by law as other such excuses are, not left to the discretion of the judge when sentencing.

This third strategy is not as *ad hoc* as it may seem. Legal theorists have long explained the distinction between ("second degree") murder and *voluntary* manslaughter in just this way. Voluntary manslaughter differs from murder neither in the harm caused, death, nor in the intention to kill. An intentional killing is voluntary manslaughter rather than murder if there are certain extenuating circumstances. In Illinois, for example, a killer commits voluntary manslaughter if he kills "under a sudden and intense provocation" or because he "wrongly believes himself to be acting in self-defense."[20]

Though obviously promising, the third strategy is not without problems. One problem is that thinking of voluntary manslaughter as partially excused murder seems more informative than thinking of vehicular homicide as partially excused involuntary manslaughter. "Provocation" or "mistake of fact" sounds more like an excuse than does "driving a vehicle" (or even "the convenience and difficulty of driving"). A more substantial problem is simply an extension of one discussed earlier. It now seems that *lex talionis* cannot be applied without a theory of excuses. Since that is so, we have a new layer of complexity in the setting of statutory penalties. We must weigh not only various kinds of interests and various kinds of *mens rea* but also partial excuses if likely to be widely shared by those doing the harm in question (all this without any guidance on how to weigh such things). The problem would be even more complex for a judge imposing sentence if the legislature left him with full discretion.

Any theory upon which intelligent people have long labored is likely to have the resources to answer almost any objection. The objections made here are probably no exception. But, if each answer is bought at the cost of new complexity, the theory may become too expensive to hold, at least if there is a simpler alternative available. So, it will be useful to contrast the complexity to which *lex talionis* has already driven us here with the *relative* simplicity with which the unfair-advantage principle handles the same examples.

The unfair-advantage principle does not require us to distinguish harm, *mens rea*, and excuse in a statute like that prohibiting vehicular homicide. To find *what*, according to the unfair-advantage principle, we are to proportion punishment to, we need only determine the unfair advantage the criminal would take by violating the statute in question. One way to do that is to formulate a license that would pardon in advance one instance of that crime. Ordinarily, the formula of the license will be a simple paraphrase of the statute itself. Having formulated the license, we can determine *how much* unfair advantage the crime takes by comparing the value of licenses pardoning similar crimes (for example, with the value of a license pardoning involuntary manslaughter). That would place the crime in question (in our case, vehicular homicide) in a ranking of crimes.

But how (it may be asked) are we to compare the advantages such licenses represent without the same arithmetic *lex talionis* requires? The answer is simple. *Lex talionis* requires cardinal numbers because it requires us to agree (at least approximately) on both the degree we would assign each harm, *mens rea*, and excuse and the weight we would assign these factors relative to one another. *Lex talionis* presupposes a single point of view from which all this can be done. The unfair-advantage principle presupposes no such thing. Instead, it provides guidance on how to *construct* such a point of view (or rather, its equivalent). Unfair advantage is, of course, a function of physical act, degree of *mens rea*, and so on just as harm (and fault) are in *lex talionis*. But, under the unfair-advantage principle, these factors can be weighed differently by different people (just as people may have widely different views about the relative value of houses and apartments) and yet provide the basis for agreement on what punishment is deserved (just as people can agree on what "the going rate" for this house or that apartment would be). How much unfair advantage an act takes is primarily a function of the social circumstances in which the act is committed (just as market price is). One way to represent that function, one I shall defend at length later, is as the result of auctioning pardons in advance for the relevant crimes under circumstances otherwise as close as possible to those of the society in question, consistent with getting a reasonable result. The procedure permits comparison (to the degree necessary) of relative seriousness of crimes without use of any numbers beyond those necessary to indicate ordinal rank.[21]

Consider again the problem of explaining why vehicular homicide is punished less than involuntary manslaughter. According to the unfair-advantage principle, we can solve that problem by explaining why a license to commit the crime would be worth less than a license to commit similar crimes ranked above it. So, to explain why vehicular homicide should be punished less than involuntary manslaughter, we need only explain why a license to commit vehicular manslaughter would not be worth as much as a license to commit involuntary manslaughter. The explanation is obvious if we think of vehicular homicide as a special case of involuntary manslaughter (that is, as involuntary manslaughter with the "partial excuse" of "done with a vehicle"). A license to commit involuntary manslaughter would be more valuable than a license to commit vehicular homicide because (and just insofar as) a license to commit involuntary manslaughter in any way whatever is more useful than a license to commit it in only this particular way, by use of a vehicle. The unfair-advantage principle does not need a theory of excuses to reach this result (that is, a theory of what should count as an excuse). Whatever lowers the value of a license is relevant, whether it fits the general category of excuse or not. For example, the requirement that the involuntary manslaughter be done with a vehicle would reduce the value of a license to do involuntary manslaughter because committing involuntary manslaughter with a vehicle is inherently more risky than committing it in the other ways in which it is commonly committed (for example, by failure to provide one's patient with adequate medical attention or by careless use of a rifle). A rational person choosing between various acts of recklessness would, all else equal, prefer to be reckless in some way other than driving. If that is so, licenses for reckless driving would, all else equal, be worth less than licenses to kill by other means (even if a substantial portion of drivers did not share that preference). That being so, vehicular manslaughter would, according to the unfair advantage principle, deserve less punishment than (ordinary) involuntary manslaughter (all else equal).

I have, it should be noticed, framed the problem as one of comparing a general license to commit manslaughter with a special license to commit a certain kind of manslaughter. This frame fits one statutory scheme, that is, the one in which a reckless driver who has killed someone could be charged under either the involuntary manslaughter statute or the vehicular homicide statute. This is not the only statutory scheme. Another scheme expressly excludes vehicular homicide from coverage under the involuntary manslaughter statute. I have not framed the problem to fit that scheme because doing so would have meant an argument more complicated than necessary for my limited purpose here. The argument I have given, whatever its faults, is enough to show how much easier to use than *lex talionis* the unfair-advantage principle can be. The argument also shows that the two principles are quite different in the way they work. We would not, for example, expect *lex talionis* to be as sensitive to the details of a statutory scheme as the unfair-advantage principle here seems to be.

Testing *Lex Talionis* Against Intuition

We have compared the ability of harm and unfair advantage to provide a measure of deserved punishment. While doing that, we implicitly considered whether the measure each provided fit our intuitive notions of justice. Discussion was limited to two crimes, recidivism and failing to report a bribe, but the results are worth recalling. It seemed the legislature could have good reason to make recidivism or failure to report a bribe criminal, good reason even though neither crime seems to constitute invasion of an interest. We did not consider whether punishment for such crimes would be just, and we must admit that there could well be controversy about how much punishment such crimes deserve. But neither example would have raised doubts about the adequacy of *lex talionis* as an explanation of the criminal law if punishing such crimes was clearly unjust. All retributive theories are theories of *just* punishment. They undertake to *explain* the criminal law only as an element of a relatively just legal system. If the crimes in question should not be crimes, we are not likely to be much concerned whether our theory of punishment can find a punishment for them or not. Our concern is more likely to be pointing out the anomaly and calling for repeal of the offending statute.

So, insofar as our earlier discussion succeeded in raising doubts about *lex talionis* as a measure of deserved punishment, it presupposes that punishing recidivism or failure to report a bribe could be just. We could, of course, now reject that presupposition. But, we could not reject it because of a *clear* intuition that punishing such crimes is unjust. If we had a clear intuition of that, we would have rejected those examples as they were presented. Since we did not, whatever reason we may have for rejecting them now, if we want to reject them now, the reason cannot be intuition. So, we must conclude from our earlier discussion that *lex talionis* seems to forbid punishment of some offenses as unjust the punishment of which does not seem unjust to us. *Lex talionis* is, in that respect at least, inconsistent with our intuitive notions of justice.

Of course, recidivism and failing to report a bribe, while not mere oddities, are not paradigms of crime. They cast doubt on the ability of *lex talionis* to help us understand the criminal law as we know it. But they still leave *lex talionis* wide scope. They make it harder to accept *lex talionis* without making it unreasonable. If we are to find anything more decisive, we shall have to find it among crimes constituting the central cases of criminal law. Yet, as we saw, finding appropriate examples there will be troublesome. Because application of *lex talionis* to such crimes is at least complicated, we are not likely to know what punishment *lex talionis* would recommend for such crimes. If we cannot know that, we cannot tell whether our intuitions diverge from what *lex talionis* would recommend. And if we cannot tell that, we cannot test *lex talionis* any more than we have already.

It may seem that this disposes of further testing too quickly. We can (it might be said) work case by case, making comparisons just as we would for the unfair-advantage principle. There would be no decision procedure, but we could know when we had an answer. If our arguments for a particular crime being "worse" than another succeeded in convincing all rational persons concerned, we would know what *lex talionis* required. We could then test that answer against the criminal law as it is, the unfair-advantage principle, or our own sense of justice, as we chose. There might (it would be admitted) be some cases where rational persons disagreed, but surely (it would be added) there are many about which all can agree.

Unfortunately, this approach to using *lex talionis* must be rejected here, though it might serve in another context.[22] Our concern now is to test *lex talionis* (and the unfair-advantage principle) against *our* intuitions. What the suggested approach amounts to is also determining what *lex talionis* says by *our* intuitions. That would be permissible if the relevant intuitions of justice were *not* closely related to our judgments of how bad crimes are. But, since these are virtually the same intuitions, the suggested approach would simply beg the question we wish to answer. For all we would know, the intuitive judgments upon which we had to rely import the whole unfair-advantage principle into *lex talionis*. We could not know what we were testing.

Though this approach seems to beg the question, something much like it might not. I think we could avoid begging the question by using intuitions of gravity of offense other than our own and adopting some mechanical procedure to apply *lex talionis* to these. For example, we might conduct a survey of the general population to determine the ranking of common crimes according to harm (in the extended sense). If we selected common crimes so that all had the same *mens rea* (and none included any recognizable excuse), we could translate that ranking of crimes by harm into a ranking of crimes by criminal desert as *lex talionis* understands it. The ranking would, of course, be incomplete. We would not know how crimes of different *mens rea* or with an excuse would be ranked relative to the crimes already ranked. We would also not know what punishment the crimes actually ranked would deserve. We would only know that what was ranked lower deserved no more than what was ranked above. But, even that would be enough to test *lex talionis*. If the ranking (more or less) fit our intuitions about what crimes deserved more punishment, *lex talionis* would at least be shown to fit our intuitions about what some common crimes deserve in punishment relative to one another. If, however, the ranking did not fit those intuitions, that would leave *lex talionis* with very little support where most of its support should be.

Sociologists can rarely provide the information legal theorists wish for. The technical problems tend to be insurmountable. Rarer is the wish granted before a theorist makes it. Yet, our wish for a survey of the general population concerning the ranking of crimes seems to have been granted several times over. For at least two decades now, sociologists have been conducting such surveys. The results are intriguing. There seems to be surprising agreement among those surveyed concerning the ranking of crimes according to "seriousness." And this agreement itself seems to be principled rather than a mere reflection of what those surveyed happen to hear about existing statutes.[23]

Wishes granted are often like good fish filleted. There is always at least one bone to catch in your throat. The research in question is not all we could wish. Most researchers only asked those surveyed to rank crimes according to "seriousness." None provided a definition of "seriousness." Only one seems to have asked informants to go on to rank penalties according to "severity" or to assign penalties to crimes (and this survey was not intended to produce a ranking of crimes extensive enough for our purposes). No researcher asked informants to rank crimes according to harm done (or according to importance of interest invaded).

So, to use any of these surveys in the way we wish, we must make an assumption. We must assume that those surveyed meant by "seriousness" what we mean by "harm" or "importance of invaded interests" (that is, that they were answering a question about deserved punishment as *lex talionis* understands it). The assumption is not unreasonable. Researchers may be forgiven for not asking informants to rank crimes according to harm done. Asking that might well have led informants to consider only the primary interests invaded or even only the physical harm done. In contrast, "seriousness" seems a fair translation of "importance of invaded interests." Or, at least, it should seem so to one who believes (as defenders of *lex talionis* seem to) that *lex talionis* is common sense and if the crimes to be ranked all have the same *mens rea* (as indeed most do) and include no excusing conditions (as most do not). We have as good a test of *lex talionis* as we are likely to get. What follows?

The survey results do correspond in a rough way to normal statutory schemes and to our intuitions of what crimes deserve most punishment. But there are also striking disparities. And, the more detailed the crime descriptions used in the survey, the greater the disparities. One survey will be enough for our purposes. Consider the highly respected and often cited 1974 study by Rossi, Waite, Bose, and Berk: "Planned killing of a policemen" and "selling heroin" are among the top three crimes. "Assault with a gun on a policemen" and "kidnapping for ransom" are ranked eleventh and twelfth, respectively. Ranked fifteenth is "assassination of a public official," just *below* "killing someone after an argument over a business transaction" and just above "making sexual advances to young children." "Beating up a child" is ranked thirtieth, between "armed holdup of a taxi driver" and "armed robbery of a neighborhood druggist." "Spying for a foreign government" is ranked forty-fifth, just between "armed robbery of an armored truck" and "killing a pedestrian while exceeding the speed limit." "Forcible rape of a former spouse" is sixty-second, just below "neglecting to care for own children" (and substantially below "selling pep pills"). At 103 is "bribing a public official to obtain favors," between "using false identification to obtain goods from a store" and "passing worthless checks involving less than $100."[24]

There are other oddities in this ranking of 140 crimes. But I think these are enough to show that, if this ranking is indeed a ranking by importance of invaded interest, *lex talionis* is not a principle of the criminal law as we know it (or, at least, not an important one). What legal system we know of would, for example, treat assassinating a public official as substantially *less* serious than assaulting a police officer with a gun? Such examples also make clear that there is a significant difference between *lex talionis* and our judgment of which crimes deserve most punishment. Even someone who favors capital punishment for assassins is unlikely to favor it for merely assaulting a police officer (and perhaps not even for selling heroin).

But there is something else about this list that deserves notice, something that may help to explain the enduring appeal of *lex talionis*. We can, I think, often understand why those surveyed might have responded as they did, even though we would not want (legal) punishment apportioned according to those responses. Indeed, often we might have responded similarly. But if we did, it would, it seems, be because we were answering a question about something other than deserved punishment, for example, about what we consider morally more blameworthy or personally more threatening. While it seems reasonable that such considerations should have a place in determining deserved punishment if a legal system is to maintain the allegiance of its subjects, it also seems that, as a matter of fact, they need not have all that large a place. That is why our intuitions of what the law should be do not seem to fit *lex talionis*, at least as represented in this survey's results.

We must conclude then that *lex talionis* cannot be the principle by which we proportion punishment to crime or the principle according to which we make intuitive judgments of proportion between punishment and crime. Must we draw the same conclusion concerning the unfair-advantage principle? Are the survey results we have been examining as damaging to that principle?

The answer is no. There are at least two reasons: First, such survey results cannot damage the unfair-advantage principle the way they damage *lex talionis* because the surveys asked the wrong question for determining relative unfair advantage. To get results directly relevant to the unfair-advantage principle, a survey would, for example, have to ask people to rank licenses to commit various crimes according to how much they would be willing to pay for them (as in so-called "market research surveys"). Second, the resulting ranking would itself only be raw material. The ranking would have to be fed into some economic model to determine what the fair market price of each license would be. Such a model would have to take into account both demand for the crime (that is, how many potential criminals are willing to commit the crime at a certain price) and supply (that is, how many such crimes society is willing to license). It seems then that the ranking such a model would generate is not likely to have more than the roughest resemblance to a ranking derived directly from the survey.

While an economic model is only one way to represent the constraints the unfair-advantage principle puts on what can be deserved punishment, it does provide an especially graphic way to understand both the critical power of that principle and the relation of unfair advantage to *lex talionis*. The harm the criminal might do is, of course, relevant to how much of a certain crime society will want to tolerate (and so to how many licenses it might put up for sale). Societies fear harm and will want to keep it to that minimum consistent with its other objectives, for example, a reasonable liberty or reasonable police budget. That is why *lex talionis* can make some sense of the criminal law as it is. The reason it cannot make more sense of it is that considerations of fairness do not allow society to apportion punishment simply to prevent harm. There is more to criminal desert than that. *Mens rea* is also relevant, as most forms of *lex talionis* recognize. But so is the "price" a criminal pays to undertake a certain crime (apart from the possibility of punishment). If committing a crime itself involves considerable risk to the criminal, then (all else equal) he deserves less punishment than would someone else committing an equally harmful crime with the same *mens rea* but with less risk to himself. *Lex talionis* cannot recognize such considerations except in the catchall category of "excuse." That is why it has such difficulty explaining the penalty for crimes like vehicular homicide. *Lex talionis* makes harm more central to punishment than it should be.

My frequent appeal to economics may suggest another objection to the unfair-advantage principle. That principle cannot (it might be said) be the principle implicit in the criminal law as we know it because the economic models appealed to seem to require more information than legislators usually have and more mathematical sophistication than they have had at their command until quite recently. The objection is correct insofar as it rejects the possibility that legislators (and judges) could explicitly engage in the sort of reasoning our auction involves. But I do not claim otherwise. All I claim is that such models provide a way of picturing their (and our) conception of criminal desert in much the way that economic models help us to understand why prices are what they are. The next chapter sets out the procedure I think legislators (and judges) actually follow. It corresponds to the rough-and-ready way most of us decide what price to pay for this or that. It does not require the sort of information the auction requires. But it also does not contribute to our understanding of what we do in the way that a model can, even if the model requires assuming that in practice we have information (or other resources) we can at best only approximate. Interestingly, *lex talionis* seems never to have suggested any model, only regulative metaphors like "an eye for an eye."

I conclude that retributivists should give up *lex talionis* for the unfair-advantage principle.

Notes

I should like to express my appreciation to the National Endowment for the Humanities for the year of support without which this article could not have been written; and to the University of Chicago for according me the privilege of a visiting scholar which made writing the paper much easier than it might otherwise have been.

1. H. A. Bedau. "Classification-Based Sentencing: Some Conceptual and Ethical Problems," NOMOS XXVII: Criminal Justice (1985): 102.

2. F. H. Bradley, *Ethical Studies*, 2nd ed. (London: Oxford University Press, 1962), pp. 26-27. Whether Bradley meant to make such a compromise

is another question. My impression is that he has been misread. Cf. B. Bosanquet, *The Philosophical Theory of the State*, 4th ed. (London: Macmillan, 1965), p. 212; and Bedau, p. 103.

3. See, for example, Michael H. Mitias, "Is Retribution Inconsistent Without *Lex Talionis*?" *Rivista internazionale di filosofia del diritto* 56 (Winter 1983): 211-230.

4. For a recent, extensive, and highly sophisticated discussion of this principle of morality, see Robert Nozick, *Philosophical Explanations* (Cambridge, MA: Harvard University Press, Belknap Press, 1981), pp. 363-393.

5. And not only to retributive theories. John Rawls makes the point that utilitarian theories such as Bentham's also include (something like) the formal version of *lex talionis*. "Two Concepts of Rules," in (among other places) *The Philosophy of Punishment*, ed. H. B. Acton (London: Macmillan, 1969), p. 114n.

6. Immanuel Kant, *The Metaphysical Elements of Justice*, trans. John Ladd (Indianapolis: Liberal Arts Library, 1965), pp. 101-102 (VI. 332-333) and pp. 132-133 (VI. 363-367).

7. Ibid.

8. Cf. Chapter Nine.

9. Cf. Chapter Four, pp. 94-96; and Chapter Eight.

10. For examples of the critical power of retributivism, see my two papers: "Setting Penalties: What Does Rape Deserve?," *Law and Philosophy* (April 1984): 62-111; "Guilty But Insane?," *Social Theory and Practice* 10 (Spring 1984): 1-23; and Chapter Six.

11. See W. D. Ross, *The Right and The Good* (London: Oxford University Press, 1930), pp. 62-63, for an example of someone who expressly limits justified punishment to the vindication of rights.

12. George Fletcher, "The Recidivist Premium," *Criminal Justice Ethics* 1 (Winter/Spring 1982): 54-59; and Hyman Gross, *A Theory of Criminal Justice* (New York: Oxford University Press, 1979), p. 40.

13. For those who see no advantage in separating those questions, I would suggest considering the advantages of separation as illustrated in Chapters Five and Seven.

14. *Ill. Rev. Stat.* (1983) Ch. 38, sec. 29-3.

15. This result seems to accord with practice. Courts do not respond to silly statutes by reducing the maximum penalty for violation. Instead, either they reinterpret the statute so that it is no longer silly, as in *City of St. Louis v. Fritz*, 53 Mo. 582 (1873) or *People v. Johnson*, 6 N.Y. 2nd 549, 161 N.E. 2d 9 (1959), or they invalidate the statute, as in *Park v. State*, 42 Nev. 386, 178 P. 389 (1919) or *Meyer v. Nebraska*, 262 U.S. 390 (1923). Courts seem to be concerned about the penalty only when the statute is neither silly nor "fallen into desuetude." See, for example, *Weems v. United States*, 217 U.S. 349 (1910) or *Solem v. Helm*, 463 U.S. 277, 103 S. Ct. 3001, 77 L Ed. 2d 637 (1983).

16. *Ill. Rev. Stat.* (1983) Ch. 38, secs. 9-3 and 12-4.1 (and sec. 1005-8-1).

17. Kant, p. 133.

18. See, for example, Gross. On p. 438, he proposes to proportion punishment to "culpability" (which, for him, includes harm done or risked as well as *mens rea*), while on the next, he proposes to proportion punishment so that the criminal does not get away with his crime. But he can say nothing about how to do either except to argue that it is a "rational" decision. Perhaps he could have said more if he had seen that he had failed to distinguish *lex talionis* ("culpability") from the unfair-advantage principle (taking back the unfair advantage so the criminal does not get away with his crime).

19. *Ill. Rev. Stat.* (1983) Ch. 38 sec. 9-3 (and sec. 1005-8-1).

20. *Ill. Rev. Stat.* (1983) Ch. 38, sec 9-2 (and sec. 1005-8-1).

21. See, especially, Chapters Ten.

22. For example, this seems to be what Gross has in mind, pp. 439-440.

23. V. Lee Hamilton and Steve Rytina, "Social Consensus on Norms of Justice: Should the Punishment Fit the Crime?" *American Journal of Sociology* 85 (March 1980): 1117-1144.

24. Peter H. Rossi et al, "The Seriousness of Crimes: Normative Structure and Individual Differences," *American Sociological Review* 39 (April 1974): 224-237, esp. pp. 228-229. These results are so bizarre that many philosophers are tempted to dismiss them out of hand (when it is necessary instead to understand both their appeal and ultimate irrelevance). So, perhaps it is worth pointing out that not only foggy-minded sociologists have taken this study seriously. Among those citing it respectfully is the U.S. Supreme Court in *Solem v. Helm*, p. 292.

4

How to Make the
Punishment Fit the Crime

Though the retributive theory of punishment has recently enjoyed a startling revival,[1] one seemingly decisive objection remains. It has been stated:

> The retributivist's difficulty is that he wants the crime itself to indicate the amount of punishment, which it cannot do unless we first assume a scale of crimes and penalties. But on what principles is the scale to be constructed, and how are new offenses to be fitted into it? These difficulties admit of no solution unless we agree to examine the consequences to be expected from penalties of different degrees of severity: i.e., unless we adopt a utilitarian approach.[2]

The objection is to retributivism both as a theory of what a judge should do (act-retributivism) and as a theory of what the legislature should do (rule-retributivism). But the objection strikes hardest at retributivism as a theory of legislation. The judge at least has the statutory maximum (and perhaps minimum) to limit his discretion, the legislative intent to guide him. The legislature has only the principles of punishment (and perhaps certain constitutional constraints). The objection does not deny that there are non-utilitarian principles by which to scale crimes: shock, injury to victim, similarity to crimes already on the books, and so on. The objection is that each of these principles is incomplete, counter-intuitive in important applications, and anyway always less satisfactory than a utilitarian principle. The objection is that, without a utilitarian scale of crimes and penalties, retributivism is at best vacuous.

By "retributivism" I mean any theory of punishment claiming at least (1) that the only acceptable reason for punishing a person is that he has committed a crime, (2) that the only acceptable reason for punishing him with such-and-such severity is that the punishment fits the crime, and (3) that the fit between punishment and crime is independent of the actual or probable consequences of the particular punishment or the particular statutory penalty.[3]   When contrasting retributivism with utilitarianism, I mean by "utilitarianism" not the general ethical theory but merely any theory of punishment making the fit between punishment and crime depend upon the actual or probable consequences of the particular punishment or statutory penalty. I do not intend anything I say here to affect the debate between (ethical) utilitarianism and competing ethical theories. Indeed, I hope to convince even the devoutest act-utilitarian that there is good reason not to make direct appeal to utility when imposing a punishment or enacting a penalty.

I shall argue that there is a retributive principle for setting statutory penalties, that the principle should sometimes yield statutory penalties different from those a utilitarian principle would yield, that the retributivist penalty appears morally preferable where it differs from the utilitarian, and that the retributivist penalty is the one more likely to be chosen in practice.

Because the setting of statutory penalties is supposed to be the major difficulty for retributivism, I shall say little about what judges do until Chapter Eight. I do not intend my silence to suggest that judges should behave in a way much different from the way I argue legislatures should. I just do not think the distinction between act-retributivism and rule-retributivism important.[4]

Because "justification" and certain other crucial terms have been used with importantly different meanings of late, I shall begin my discussion by going over what should be familiar ground.

Punishment and the Criminal Law

Punishment is an evil imposed by an institution having the six features listed in Chapter Two.[5] The criminal law provides the central cases of punishment. A theory of punishment must come to terms with the criminal law or fail. What goes on in clubs, corporations, universities, and other associations of persons is relevant only insofar as close to what goes on in the criminal law. What parents do with their children, owners with their pets, or the wind with the countryside, is at best peripheral.

The criminal law is but one means of social control. Others include terror, incapacitation, and conditioning. The criminal law differs from these in presupposing people who (1) can follow rules or not as they choose and (2) can be persuaded to follow rules by the distant prospect of set penalty. The criminal law would have no use where people were not more or less rational, where, that is, people did not adjust their acts to take into account possible consequences far off, uncertain, and limited. The insane, the feebleminded, the immature properly do not come under the criminal law. They are brought into court only to be sent elsewhere.[6] The criminal law does not, however, require a society of crafty deliberators or practical Newtons. The criminal law requires only that, somehow or other, people generally adjust their acts to take the penalties into account (or, for other reasons, stay clear of wrongdoing).[7]

Punishment (so understood) cannot be conceived apart from the criminal law (or some close analogue). To ask the justification of punishment as an institution is then to ask the justification of the criminal law as a whole. To ask that is, however, to ask for one of two justifications. "The criminal law" may refer either to the criminal law in general (*the* criminal law) or to this or that system of criminal law (the criminal law we live under). To ask the justification of the first is to ask why a rational person should prefer a system of criminal law, given a choice between a fair representative of the criminal law and a fair representative of any alternative method of social control. To ask the justification of a particular system of criminal law is, in contrast, only to ask why a rational person should prefer that system over any alternative system of criminal law. (For the purpose of justification, a method of social control or system of criminal law is an alternative to another only insofar as the two are possible but incompatible methods of ordering the same affairs of the same persons.) What I shall now argue is that neither the justification of the criminal law in general nor the justification of a particular system of criminal law entails a utilitarian principle for setting penalties (a principle, that is, which would make the choice of penalty depend upon the actual or probable consequences of having a particular penalty on the books).

Justifying the Criminal Law in General

There is surprisingly little disagreement about what justifies the criminal law in general. A rational person would (it is agreed) prefer the criminal law to any alternative method of social control because the criminal law serves the interests of rational persons better than does any alternative. Only the criminal law can order certain important social relations so as to allow rational persons to plan and act, without ordering society so completely that there is little at once worth planning and free from the defeating interference of authority.[8]

Though it may seem obvious that, for most domains of conduct, the criminal law thus strikes the best balance between protecting persons and respecting them, we must consider why that is so to see that the general justification of the criminal law entails no utilitarian principle for setting penalties. We may treat what follows as if it were an ethical utilitarian argument. But it would be wise to notice that the argument is not necessarily utilitarian. We shall not have to say whether the benefits justifying the criminal law accrue to society as a whole or to everyone individually. Thus, we shall not have to decide between utilitarian and "contract" theorists. We shall also not have to say whether the benefits justifying the criminal law are merely contingent facts about this world or conceptual truths about rational persons (and all the possible worlds where they may be found). Thus, we shall also not have to decide between ordinary consequentialists and those who found ethics upon a priori truths.

The criminal law maintains order by laying down rules, threatening punishment if the rules are not obeyed, and carrying out the threat often enough to keep the threat alive. The criminal law need not establish social tranquility. It does enough if it holds the commotion of life below a roar. The primary rules need not forbid all conflict between persons or even all undesirable activity. The rules need only forbid the more substantial harms and regulate major conflict. The threatened punishments need not be so frightful that no rational person would risk them. The punishments need only be frightful enough to make crime relatively rare. It does not matter whether the punishments accomplish this by assuring those who wish to obey the rules that others will not take advantage of that obedience, or by frightening off most of those who might otherwise commit crimes, or by satisfying the resentment of those who might otherwise take revenge, or by instilling a horror of the forbidden acts, or by keeping most criminals where they cannot commit crimes, or by some combination of these or other means. What does matter is that the criminal law maintains at least a modicum of order.

Every law takes with one hand while it gives with the other. The criminal law can nevertheless preserve for persons a sphere of action free from the interference of authority (as well as from the interference of other persons) in at least four distinct ways. First, so long as the primary rules are not too many or too broad, the criminal law justifies interference with persons only in a limited and predictable way, that is, only for disobeying a rule the person could have obeyed. Second, so long as the procedure of the criminal law is reasonably designed for its purpose, the criminal law will rarely interfere with a person except when he has in fact disobeyed a rule. Third, when someone has disobeyed a rule, the criminal law justifies only that interference to which the *act* corresponds, the statutory penalty. The criminal cannot be punished for what he is, only for what he has done. The penalty cannot be freely tailored after the act so that, had the criminal known in advance what the penalty would be, he would never have committed the crime.[9] And last, because penalties are foreordained (and so long as they are not too frightful), the potential criminal can treat each penalty as the price of the corresponding forbidden act. The criminal law might not long survive if everyone treated penalties that way all the time. But there is much to be gained if people do treat them that way sometimes. All human rules fail of sense now and then. A law made to be disobeyed (occasionally) serves our interests better than one which, threatening penalties too frightful to risk, pretends to be the work of a god.[10]

This is the criminal law we are to compare with other methods of social control. Its superiority is considerable, so considerable that it remains preferable though penalties are set in any number of radically different ways. Even drawing statutory penalties from a hat would not undo that superiority as we just described it (provided, of course, penalties in the hat were neither trivial nor too severe). But, if the justification of *the* criminal law does not exclude (on the basis of actual or probable consequences) such a silly method of setting penalties as drawing from a hat, it cannot require a principle linking particular penalties to particular consequences. The justification is too strong to rely upon the consequences of choosing penalties according to any particular principle (though not so strong as to survive choosing penalties by any principle whatever). Hence, there is nothing in the justification of criminal law in general to entail a utilitarian principle for setting penalties.

Justifying Particular Systems of Criminal Law

The justification of a particular system of criminal law may seem to lead directly to a utilitarian principle for setting penalties, even if the justification of the criminal law in general does not. To justify a particular system of criminal law should in part mean justifying it against systems very much like it and so (it may seem) against those differing from it only by a single penalty. We may, for example, throw open the statute book, notice that the penalty for kidnapping is one to five years imprisonment, and ask why the maximum penalty is not death. To ask that question is, it seems, to compare two systems differing only in the penalty for kidnapping, to suppose there is good reason to prefer one penalty over the other (as indeed there is), and to ask what that reason might be. What might it be? Surely (it will be said) the only reason one could offer would be the overall advantage (actual or probable) of living under one system rather than the other. It seems then that the justification of a particular system of criminal law entails appeal to a principle of setting penalties and that the principle appealed to will be utilitarian.

Legislatures do choose between penalties; we do argue about whether this or that choice is justified. There is no doubt about that. The question is whether justification must be in terms of the actual or probable consequences of slightly different systems of criminal law. The answer is that it cannot be. Consider how strange a justification in such terms is. We would compare two complete systems differing only in a single penalty. We may perhaps imagine them on a counter, side by side, ticking like clocks. But where are we to get two such systems? Systems of criminal law are not (like clocks and beakers) available through laboratory services. We cannot even come close to laying two such systems side by side. If we compare two contemporary systems, we must compare systems differing at least in personnel, history, and surrounding society, even if we can find two systems with the same procedures and statutes. And we are not likely to get two systems with procedures or statutes with more than a family resemblance. If instead we compare two successive states of one system of criminal law, we have the same problem. The successive states will differ in personnel (death caring little for our inquiry), history (the change of penalty being potentially as important as what the penalty is changed from or to), and surrounding society (fashion, business cycles, war, and so on caring as little for our inquiry as death does). Even the other statutes and procedures cannot be counted on to remain fixed during the comparison. The life of the law is no more to be pent up than life in general. Above that picture of legal systems ticking away side by side towers a vanity of intellect so enormous it deserves a name. I would suggest "the fallacy of omnipotent science" (the fallacy being to suppose that whatever experiment we can imagine — however indistinctly — is within the power of science).

It might seem that I am unfair. After all (it will be said) we do not have to lay systems side by side. We can compare them less fancifully. We can use statistical procedures to isolate the crucial variables, follow the effects of those variables in different systems, and so compare penalties. Or we could construct a mathematical model of the particular system of criminal law, hypothesize various penalties, and in each case deduce the consequences just as a physicist would do if he wanted to know the effect on pressure that heating a fixed volume of gas to such-and-such temperature would have. Or, at least, we can perform "thought experiments."

Same fallacy. Some day we may be able to do such wonders (though the next section casts doubt even on that). Certainly we cannot do them today. Who knows what the consequences would be if, say, Illinois adopted death as the maximum penalty for kidnapping? Would there be fewer kidnappings, more, or the same number as now? Would there be any sentences of death? Would Illinois be better off, worse off, or much the same as now overall? We can guess, of course. But we cannot do more. There is no mathematical model of society from which to make deductions about the actual or probable consequences of such a penalty. There will be none tomorrow, or the next day. And without some model, we cannot even perform thought experiments. Nor can we hope the statisticians will help. They do not have the data they would need. They do not know what procedures to use. And perhaps, given the data and procedures, they would face a problem of such magnitude they would still not be able to get significant results. Their computers, time, and other resources are finite. Much that is possible is far from practical.

If we cannot now find out what would be the actual or probable consequences of making such a dramatic change in the penalties of a single state, what are we to make of the claim that we are to decide *every* penalty by considering the consequences? What are we to do when the choice is between two and three years imprisonment? The trouble with the utilitarian principle of setting penalties is not so much that it leads us astray as that it leads not at all.

Still (someone might respond), the utilitarian theory provides an ideal toward which we can strive guided by other means until science can come to our aid. We must reject that response too. Under the circumstances in which penalties are in fact chosen, we would not know whether we moved toward or away from the ideal. We simply cannot do what utilitarianism tells us to do.

Nor will it help to respond that we *must* be able to make such comparisons because we make them all the time. The question is what we do when we justify one penalty against another. What I have argued so far is that we cannot justify one penalty against another by comparing two systems of criminal law differing only in one penalty or (what is supposed to come to the same thing) by comparing directly the actual or probable consequences of adopting each penalty. I admit we do talk about the "consequences" of this or that penalty (especially about whether the penalty will "deter"). I only deny that such talk has anything to do with the actual or probable consequences of the penalty. How can that be?

Inside the Criminal Law

Before I answer that question, I should like to draw an analogy between scientific theories and systems of criminal law. The analogy will, I hope, make what I say about deciding penalties less disturbing and so more convincing.

It is commonly held that a scientific theory consists both of claims that can be tested (more or less) directly ("experimental laws") and of claims that can be tested only by testing the theory as a whole ("theoretical laws"). Both kinds of law are, of course, "empirical" and "contingent," but the proof of one is quite different from the proof of the other. Experimental laws, though deducible from the theory as a whole and important in its defense, can survive the theory's overthrow. They ultimately rest upon experiment, not deduction. While claims *for* the theory, they are (more or less directly) claims *about* the world. Theoretical laws cannot likewise survive a theory's overthrow. They draw their content from the theory as a whole. Every change in the theory changes them, too. A name may move from theory to theory but the connection between entities referred to is familial, not personal. While theoretical laws are claims *within* a theory, they are not quite claims about anything. They are vehicles for reaching the world, not points of interest in it, abstractions, not tangible objects. Consider, for example, that part of Bohr's theory of the atom stating that electrons have an electrical charge of 0 (4.77 X 10^{-10} electrostatic units). It contains both an experimental and a theoretical claim. The experimental claim is that 0 is the minimal electric charge. That claim can be confirmed by any number of experiments without any commitment to Bohr's theory as a whole. That claim is about the world. The theoretical claim is that there are electrons. That claim has one meaning within Bohr's theory (a particle with such-and-such properties) and other meanings in succeeding theories (a particle or wave packet with somewhat different properties). Bohr's claim that there are electrons cannot be confirmed apart from his theory of the atom because the claim draws its meaning from that theory. The claim is only a claim within the theory, standing or falling with the theory as a whole.[11]

A system of criminal law is like a scientific theory in this way: certain claims about a system are, like experimental laws, capable of proof independent of the system as a whole. Others are not. For example: the claim that, if at least one kidnapper in ten is put to death, the rate of kidnapping will not exceed one per 10,000 persons in the jurisdiction, is an "experimental law." The claim can be understood without supposing any particular system of criminal law, can be confirmed in any number of jurisdictions (if it can be confirmed in any), and may be true even of a system which is hardly a system at all (so long as it makes kidnapping a crime). In contrast, the claim that the death penalty is the most effective deterrent of kidnapping is, though superficially like the other claim, a "theoretical law." The claim does not itself say anything about the rate of crime if death is put into the kidnapping statute. "Deterrent" does not have any relation to actual or probable crime without assumptions about the rationality of criminals, the efficiency of police, the likelihood that the penalty will not itself make the crime glamorous, and so on. Similarly, "death penalty" does not itself mean that anyone will fear for his life, be put to death, or anything else. Reaching a claim about the actual or probable consequences of making a certain crime capital requires consideration of the full machinery of a particular system of criminal law. So, the claim that death is the most effective deterrent of kidnapping is a claim *within* a particular system, a deduction from its presuppositions, a vehicle by which the system reaches the world. That claim, unlike the first, stands or falls with the particular system of criminal law. By itself, it can neither stand nor fall.

This analogy makes the inquiry discussed in the previous section seem more dubious. Even an omnipotent social scientist could not freely change penalties in a system of criminal law while holding all else constant. The presuppositions of the criminal law generate certain principles of punishment. Those principles guide the operation of the system as a whole and decisively settle all sorts of particular questions. One can easily change the words of a statute (well, relatively easily, since even such a change would require much political power, acumen, or luck). But one cannot control what happens thereafter. A certain statutory penalty may be declared unconstitutional while one much like it would not be; it may be nullified by a jury or prosecutor where one much like it would not be; and so on. For some penalties, there is only a grave of paper unless the whole system is remade to suit. An omnipotent social scientist cannot study penalties apart from particular systems of criminal law, cannot directly compare the actual or probable consequences of penal provisions of different systems, and cannot freely change penalties within a particular system without making one system into another. So, even an omnipotent social scientist is not likely to learn much from the study of statutory penalties. For those interested in the actual or probable consequences of living under a particular system of criminal law, what is important is the system as a whole. The penalties themselves are nothing.[12]

Now, back to the question at the end of the previous section: I can admit that we talk about the "consequences" of this or that penalty while denying that such talk has anything directly to do with the actual or probable consequences of the penalty because I believe such talk goes on *within* the criminal law. The claims involved are "theoretical" and therefore to be defended by appeal to the presuppositions of the particular system of criminal law, not by direct appeal to the world (which is to say, not by direct appeal to the actual or probable consequences of particular penalties). The dispute which is now our concern would have been impossible if both utilitarians and retributivists did not suppose the claims of deterrence (and other "consequences") were "experimental laws." The utilitarians are right to claim that the "consequences" of a penalty should be considered in deciding what penalty to adopt. They are wrong only in supposing that "consequences" has here the same meaning as it has in (ethical) utilitarianism generally. Having justified the criminal law as a system, they are no longer free to argue as if it were not a system. Similarly, the retributivists are right to claim that the actual or probable consequences have nothing to do with deciding particular statutory penalties. They are wrong only in supposing that their claim rules out considerations of deterrence and other theoretical "consequences." They too have not understood how much justifying the criminal law as a system entails. The criminal law has the richness and power of a physicist's theory.

Seven Easy Steps to a Fitting Penalty

The time has come to offer an alternative to the utilitarian procedure for setting penalties. In this section, I shall state the alternative, explain its relationship to the presuppositions of the criminal law, and explain what makes it retributive rather than utilitarian. The alternative may be stated in seven steps:

1. Prepare a list of penalties consisting of those evils (a) which no rational person would risk except for some substantial benefit and (b) which may be inflicted through the procedures of the criminal law.
2. Strike from the list all inhumane penalties.
3. Type the remaining penalties, rank them within each type, and then combine rankings into a scale.
4. List all crimes.
5. Type the crimes, rank them within each type, and then combine rankings into a scale.
6. Connect the greatest penalty with the greatest crime, the least penalty with the least crime, and the rest accordingly.
7. Thereafter: type and grade new (humane) penalties as in step 3 and new crimes as in step 5, and then proceed as above.[13]

Step 1. The criminal law, as noted above, presupposes persons who can follow rules or not as they choose and can be persuaded to follow rules by the distant prospect of set penalties. The list of penalties should therefore consist of just what no rational person subject to the system of criminal law in question would risk except for some substantial benefit. Nothing less would be persuasive. The list may vary somewhat from society to society. For example, in a society of honor a single slap across the face publicly administered by the common hangman may be a penalty only death could exceed in severity; while, to us, such a penalty seems lighter than a five-dollar fine (and so, amounts to no penalty at all).

The list of penalties should not contain any evil commonly believed beyond the power of the criminal law to inflict. Eternity in hell, for example, though once the greatest penalty in Christendom, would not be appropriate in the criminal code of Illinois. Who would believe Illinois to have such power? The list of penalties should also not contain anything the procedures of the criminal law are commonly believed unwilling to inflict. Exile to the moon, for example, though today a penalty within the power of some governments, is still one no government would be willing to pay for. Hence, it too would make an empty threat.

The list will, I think, usually include death, loss of liberty (e.g., by imprisonment or supervision), pain (e.g., by flogging or hard labor), loss of property (e.g., by fine or forfeiture), and mutilation (e.g., by branding or amputation).

Step 2. An inhumane ("cruel and unusual") penalty is one the criminal law would sometimes inflict if available. The penalty is, nevertheless, to be struck from the list because most members of the society object to it on principle (and independent of its utility within the criminal law). ("Most" is defined by the political constitution of the society.) We may be willing to use inhumane penalties on some people. We may believe inhumane penalties to be effective deterrents. What we object to is their general use. We find such use morally shocking. We prefer to take the risk of operating our legal system without such penalties.[14] (Flogging and mutilation would, e.g., be struck from the list in this society as inhumane.)

Step 3. Penalties need to be put in an order the potential criminal can appreciate. That is the point of step 3.

Dividing penalties by type is grouping them so that each group contains all those penalties, and only those penalties, differing from one another only by degree. For example: fines (that is, taking money or its equivalent in property) constitute a single type of penalty. Fines differ from one another only in the amount taken. A "fine" of a day in prison or of an arm is, however, a penalty of a different type. Such a "fine" is not simply a greater taking. It is a different taking. No rational person would prefer to risk a greater fine rather than a lesser (all else equal); so, fines differ only in degree. But some rational persons (though surely not all) may prefer to risk a day in prison rather than a fine of this or that amount while others may prefer a fine of this or that amount rather than a day in prison; so, fines differ from imprisonment in type. Where a penalty is of mixed type — thirty lashes of the whip and $500 fine, one year in prison and two years supervision thereafter, or the like — it should be treated as a type different from those of which it is mixed.

Once divided by type, the penalties of a type should be ranked from least to greatest. The least penalty is the one any rational person would risk if (all else equal) he had to choose between risking it and risking any other penalty of that type; the next least is the one any rational person would risk if he had to choose between risking it and risking any other type except the least; and so on up to the greatest. Where a type of penalty has a huge number of degrees, these should be reduced to a manageable few. That may be done either by selecting certain round number (e.g., ten dollars, fifty dollars, and so on) or by grouping the penalties into ranges (e.g., one to ten dollars, eleven to fifty dollars, and so on), or by some combination of these.

Once penalties are typed and ranked in this way, they can be combined into an ordinal scale. The scale may branch like a tree (each branch being a type of penalty), be an interweave of vines (each vine being a type of penalty), or be otherwise messily multiplex. Such complexities, though often inconvenient (and best avoided), are not important here. (So long as we are concerned with more than one type of penalty, there is no interesting unilinear system of preference all rational persons must share.) What is important is that there be a single direction to the ordering (least penalty of one type nearest least penalty of other types) and general (if rough) agreement about where to start and end a type (e.g., fines to begin before prison time and end at one year in prison). Of course, no penalty should ever be preferable to one *below*.

Step 4. The list of crimes should contain any act the legislature forbids on pain of penalty. A crime may be an act itself morally objectionable, or objectionable for some other reason, or even an act the legislature just madly chose to object to. The procedure for setting penalties works independently of the wisdom of the legislature in establishing crimes (except that the unwisdom of the legislature may reappear in step 5 as a lack of "seriousness").

Step 5. The crimes, like the penalties, must be in some order. Dividing crimes by *type* is grouping them by "intent" (that is, by what a rational person would ordinarily aim at if he did the act, whatever else he might aim at). The minimal aim of both theft and blackmail is getting another's property. These crimes are, then, both of one type. The aim of murder, mayhem, or vandalism is not ordinarily gain. So, none of these crimes is of the same type as theft or blackmail. We group crimes by intent because we set penalties so that the potential criminal will have reason to choose the lesser crime rather than the greater when he chooses his crime. Intent tells us what the criminal will be choosing between. Whether a criminal's aim is revenge or gain, he will *not* ordinarily choose between a type of theft and a type of murder. There are, of course, exceptions (the gunman who chooses between robbing a bank and contracting to kill, the revenge seeker who wonders whether his intended victim loves money more than life, and so on). The criminal law is not concerned with such exceptions ("mere motive"). But, when an exception becomes common, there is reason to define a new crime, the peculiar aim of individuals being grouped as a new intent (e.g., "use of a weapon for unlawful gain" or "taking vengeance").

Once divided by type, the crimes of each type should be ranked from least to greatest. The least crime is the one a rational person would prefer to risk (all else equal) given a choice between risking it and risking any other of that type; the next least is the one a rational person would prefer to risk given a choice between it and any other of that type except the least; and so on.[15] The ranking of crimes need be no finer than the ranking of penalties, and the more diverse the society, the less fine it is likely to be. We may distinguish between, say, grand and petty theft, simple and aggravated theft, and so on, because such distinctions do mark significant differences in what we (as rational persons) fear. But, because we (as rational persons) need not agree on every detail (e.g., on whether a theft of fifty dollars is to be feared significantly more than a theft of five dollars), the distinctions of rank (e.g., between kinds of theft) cannot be very fine. And, in fact, they are likely to be quite crude. Illinois, for example, recognizes only five "classes" of felony (plus capital crimes) and three "classes" of misdemeanor.

The existence of a particular ranking for a particular society is, of course, a contingent fact. But the existence of some ranking or other shared by all rational persons in a society is virtually guaranteed by the need of every society to agree on a few things just to exist and the possibility of making the ranking of crimes crude enough to mirror that minimum agreement. If one doubts the existence of such agreement for *this* society, he has only to go to a statute book and ask himself whether the rankings generally mirror his fears (and whether — all else equal — a person who ranked crimes much differently would be rational). For example: does he not (all else equal) fear grand theft more than petty theft? Would it (all else equal) be rational to fear them equally, much less to fear petty theft more than grand theft?

This method may put several seemingly different crimes — for example, burglary and blackmail — in the same rank. That does not mean there is no difference between them, only that there is no general reason (given the society in question and the abstractness necessary for legislation) for rational persons to prefer to risk one rather than the other. Which is preferable: to lose one's property by burglary or blackmail? Well, it depends, doesn't it?

Once crimes are typed and ranked, they can be combined into an ordinal scale. What I said of the scale of penalties applies equally to the scale of crimes. The scale may well resemble a New York subway map. What is important is that, for each crime but the most serious, we prefer to have it occur rather than any ranked immediately above. Thus, if we have the two lines (a) first-degree murder, second-degree murder, manslaughter (where there is intent to kill but suitable provocation) and (b) aggravated kidnapping, simple kidnapping, unlawful restraint, first-degree murder should be closer to aggravated kidnapping than to unlawful restraint and unlawful restraint nearer to manslaughter than to murder. The two lines need cross only where the kidnapping is so aggravated that it amounts to second-degree murder (e.g., where the victim dies because of the bad treatment he receives from the kidnappers even though they did not intend his death).

Step 6. Connecting the two scales is more or less mechanical. The least penalty should, of course, be assigned to the least crime; the greatest penalty, to the greatest crime. The lines connecting scales should never cross. Crossing lines would mean giving the potential criminal a reason to choose the crime we would rather he not choose should he be choosing between that one and some we ranked lower. The number of lines meeting at any single crime or penalty should be kept as few as possible. To have many lines meet at one crime is to make unclear what penalty the criminal may expect if he chooses to do the crime and so to tell him less about how we rank that crime relative to others than we could tell him. To have too many lines meet at one penalty is to tell the criminal we do not care which of those crimes he chooses when we do care.

Where several penalties are ranked together (say, ten lashes, thirty days in jail, and fine of $300), there may be local reasons for assigning only one to a particular crime (e.g., lashes to assault, jail to false imprisonment, or fine to petty theft). There may also be local reasons for putting all three into each statute, leaving the judge to decide who gets what. There may even be local reasons for not using certain penalties for certain crimes. "Local reasons" may include the likely educational effect of suffering what one has made another suffer, the satisfaction of resentment likely from such exact mirroring of the wrong (that is, the penalty's "expressiveness"), the unpopularity of certain penalties with certain social classes, and so on. While such reasons *are* utilitarian, they do not concern the scale of penalties or the proportion between penalty and crime, only the choice among penalties ranked equally severe.[16]

Step 7. Neither appearance of new penalties nor the commoner appearance of new crimes should present any new problem for the procedure outlined here. A new (humane) penalty will either belong to an old type or constitute a new type. If of an old type, ranking the penalty will be a matter for clerks. If of a new type, fitting it into the scale will require only the same crude agreement required to make up the scale in the first place: "Most rational persons would prefer to risk this rather than that." A new crime will also either belong to an old type or constitute a new one. If of an old type ("Larceny by computer is just larceny by trick"), ranking the crime will be easy enough. If, however, the crime is of a new type ("No, larceny by computer is the only crime where the minimal aim is both fun and profit"), then we must compare it with various crimes more or less analogous and already on the books, asking which we would prefer to risk, just as we did to establish the scale initially.

The procedure outlined here may appear clumsy compared to Bentham's mathematics or the equally nice proposals of twentieth-century utilitarians. I make no apology, believing the clumsiness to recognize a certain indeterminacy in what is rational. The procedure may, however, also appear to differ from the utilitarian in no other way. It will be worth a paragraph to make clear how much it does differ.

To scale crimes, the procedure outlined here takes into account the preferences of rational persons in the society to which the system of criminal law applies. No doubt those preferences promiscuously reflect the actual consequences of particular crimes and may themselves affect the probability of such consequences. But a utilitarian principle would take such consequences into account directly and systematically. The procedure outlined here does not. If the two procedures yielded identical scales, it would be fortuitous. Similarly, to scale penalties, the procedure outlined here takes into account the preferences of the "potential criminal." The potential criminal (like his brother abstraction economic man) is not someone you will meet in an alley or discover prying open your window. He is there, of course. But he is there in each of us, more or less. A utilitarian procedure would take into account the preferences not of *the* potential criminal but of all those potential criminals we hope never to meet in an alley or at our window. The procedure outlined here needs no sociology, only such knowledge as everyone has, no statistics or experiments, only the procedures of a political constitution. A utilitarian procedure would need a mature sociology to be at all reliable. The procedure outlined here works without information about the actual or probable consequences of particular penalties. A utilitarian procedure would not (however much trouble it would have obtaining such information). Since the procedure outlined here sets penalties without directly taking into account the actual or probable consequences of particular penalties, it is the retributive principle promised at the beginning of this chapter.

Moral Desert

The procedure outlined here is also retributive in the most orthodox sense of apportioning punishment according to the criminal's (act-related) "illicit pleasure," "wickedness," and "moral desert."[17] The procedure assigns the most severe penalties (that is, the penalties the potential criminal most prefers not to risk) to the most serious crimes (that is, the crimes rational persons most prefer not to risk); the lighter penalties to the less serious crimes. Such an assignment makes the punishment a function of the special wrong a criminal does simply by committing the crime. What wrong is that? The criminal's act may be morally wrong, law or no law. But, even if his act would be morally indifferent were there no law, the obedience of others makes his disobedience a taking of unfair advantage (all else equal). Others, though they too might like to take such liberties as he has, did not.[18] He has something they do not. The unfair advantage is the "illicit pleasure" in every crime, whether jaywalking or murder, prostitution or stealing. What the criminal deserves from the law (for this act) is a punishment proportioned to that advantage (and to that advantage alone). But how (it may be asked) are we to measure that advantage?

We are not accustomed to think of crimes as objects of commerce. The idea of window-shopping for a crime seems wildly unrealistic when it does not seem just back-slappingly funny. We would rather people concentrate on obeying the law. Still, we can gain a better appreciation of the special wickedness of a particular crime by thinking of crimes as things to be bought and sold. Imagine a market in which the government sells licenses permitting the holder to break a specified law once (a sort of absolute pardon in advance).[19] The number of such licenses would have to be limited just as we now limit hunting and fishing licenses. The principle of limitation would be the same. Licensed acts (together with unavoidable poaching) should not deplete social order below the desired minimum.

How would prices be set? Let us suppose the licenses to be sold at public auction. Since the criminal law forbids only those acts some people would otherwise do, there should be no crime so great or so small that someone would not commit it if he could do so cheaply enough. Here would be the chance. Different licenses would, of course, fetch different prices. But there would be a pattern. Public auction (or any other relatively free market) would tend to make the price of a license rise with the seriousness of the crime (and so approximate the procedure outlined in the previous section). There are at least two reasons for that: First, the quantity of licenses would have to decrease as the seriousness of the crime licensed increased. (The more serious the crime, the fewer the social order can tolerate, all else equal.) Second, the demand for licenses is likely to increase with the seriousness of the crime. (If that seems unlikely given moral constraints on potential buyers, ask yourself whether you would prefer to have a license to steal or a license to jaywalk.)

We are now ready to measure unfair advantage: the criminal's (act-related) legal "wickedness" varies with the value of the unfair advantage he takes of those who obey the law (even though they are tempted to do otherwise). They are the society he wrongs by his crime. What he "owes" them is the price of his advantage. The price cannot be the cost of the property taken, bones broken, or lives lost. Such costs measure the private injury he has done, the damages he should pay or the restitution he should make his victims, not the value of the license he has taken simply by doing the crime.[20] What then does he "owe?" The obvious answer is the penalty provided by law. The price of the crime is the penalty the criminal law has set for the crime, the criminal law operating as a system of administered prices. Even that price may, however, not be what he should "owe" (what he "owes" the law morally speaking, his "moral desert" as a criminal). The administered price is not necessarily a fair price. A penalty is a fair price only if it corresponds to what a license to do that crime would fetch in a free market (the outcome of a fair procedure). The correspondence is not equality but homology, a relative correspondence. There is, after all, no decisive reason that the society should choose this or that minimum of social order; nor is there any privileged rule for converting dollars into years in prison, lashes of the whip, or the like.

So, a criminal has cause to complain if he is subject to a penalty not corresponding to the *fair* price of the license he has taken. The cause of complaint is the same whether the noncorrespondence is the work of judge or statute. The cause is unfairness, that is, his not being treated like (his not being charged the same "price" as) those who have acted with equal license. What he deserves for his act is a penalty corresponding to the license he took. What he got was something worse. To say that a criminal "owes" a certain penalty for his act is a metaphor, but to say that the penalty is what he deserves from the law (for his act) is only the literal truth.

Now, it might seem that, whether the penalty does correspond to the fair price of a license or not, "the criminal brought the punishment upon himself." He committed the crime knowing the penalty (or, at least, the criminal law must suppose such knowledge). Surely, he has no cause for complaint whatever the statutory penalty.

This objection would, I think, hold if criminal penalties were in fact set by a free market. Proving knowledge of the penalty in such a market would prove the punishment fair (fair because the procedure is fair). But the criminal law is like a system of administered prices, not like a free market. Other safeguards must replace the safeguards of the free market if we are not to risk treating the criminal worse than he deserves (for his act). We do not punish for bad business judgment, foolishness, or whatever else might have led him to "buy" an overpriced license. Proving that the criminal "contracted" a certain penalty cannot, therefore, prove the penalty fair. To prove the penalty fair is, on the contrary, to prove the penalty to correspond to the free-market price (to be fair because it corresponds to the outcome of a fair procedure). To prove that is to prove the penalty to correspond to the seriousness of the crime (as the auction analogy shows). And to prove that is to prove the penalty to correspond to the outcome of the procedure outlined in the previous section. Therefore, what in all fairness the criminal deserves (for his act) is a punishment corresponding to the outcome of the procedure outlined in the previous section. Anything else would be out of proportion to the crime. The procedure outlined in the previous section thus fulfills the traditional retributivist function of apportioning punishment to (crime-related) moral desert.

This argument provides a second justification for the procedure of the previous section. The first justification was that the procedure was derived from the presuppositions of the criminal law. Whatever justified the criminal law justified the procedure too. The second justification connects the procedure directly with moral desert. The procedure is justified because the penalties it generates are fair and because a procedure generating penalties different from those generated by it would be unfair. Like the first justification, this second depends on justification of the criminal law. Where we cannot justify application of the criminal law (e.g., to the insane), there will be no justifiable punishment and so both no proper punishment under the procedure of the previous section and no one morally deserving of (legal) punishment.

The Retributive Procedure in Practice: *Weems v. U.S.*

The discussion has necessarily been quite abstract so far. I dare not leave it that way. The most abstract theory must stand up in practice or fall. A theory of punishment that cannot guide action is only a scarecrow of theory. The retributive theory described above does, I believe, give a helpful guide to action even where utilitarianism does not.

This section offers an example of punishment disproportionate to the crime, demonstrates that the retributive procedure easily picks out the disproportion, and then considers what a utilitarian theory would have to say. The example comes from the law courts. I have chosen it for three reasons. First, a law case reminds us of the relation a theory of punishment has to the practice of punishment (the decisions actually to be guided, the information actually to be had at the moment of decision, and the consequences differing theories would actually have). The use of such a case forbids floating philosophically from this world to that ideal world where everything is more convenient. Second, judicial decisions are careful judgments persons of learning and experience actually made when faced with living detail and forced to decide what justice requires. They give valuable insight concerning what our own considered judgment might be. Third, the case chosen is itself a classic, a clear example of punishment not itself inhumane but still so out of proportion that it shocks. Had I made up such a case, it might have been dismissed as too contrived for it to matter what a theory had to say about it. But, coming straight from practice (and, indeed, having an important position to return to), it cannot be dismissed. The theory that cannot say something sensible about it plainly has not stood up where it most ought to. Such a case, though by itself not a refutation of utilitarianism, does at least pose a problem any utilitarian theory of punishment should resolve. But, combined with a satisfactory retributive theory (as I believe it here is), such a case constitutes something approaching a crucial experiment. If a utilitarian theory is no good here, what good is it?

The case, *Weems v. United States*, was decided by the U.S. Supreme Court in 1909 and remains a leading American case on the question of proportion between punishment and crime. Weems, a disbursing officer employed by the U.S. government in the Philippines, had falsified a cash book of the Captain of the Board of Manila by entering as paid out the small sums of 208 and 408 pesos, as wages to certain employees of the Light House Service. He was convicted of falsifying ("perverting") that public document "corruptly and with intent. . . ."[21] The statute under which he was charged, though dating from Spanish times, had been reenacted under authority of Congress. The statute set a maximum and a minimum penalty. Weems received a sentence falling midway between. He was "[to serve] . . . fifteen years of *Cadena*, together with the accessories of section 56 of the Penal Code, and to pay a fine of four thousand pesetas. . . ."[22] The terms *"Cadena"* and "accessories" require explanation: "[Those sentenced to *Cadena*] shall labor for the benefit of the state. They shall always carry a chain at the ankle, hanging from the wrists; they shall be employed at hard and painful labor, and shall receive no assistance whatsoever from without the institution."[23] The "accessories" are (1) civil interdiction, (2) subjection to surveillance during life, and (3) perpetual absolute disqualification. These penalties are defined as follows:

> Art. 42. Civil interdiction shall deprive the person punished as long as he suffers it, of the rights of parental authority, guardianship of person or property, participation in the family council, marital authority, the administration of property, and the right to dispose of his own property by acts *inter vivos*. Those cases are excepted in which the law explicitly limits its effects.
>
> Art. 43. Subjection to the surveillance of the authorities imposes the following obligations on the person punished.
>
> 1.That of fixing his domicile and giving notice thereof to the authority immediately in charge of his surveillance, not being allowed to change it without the knowledge and permission of said authority in writing.
>
> 2.To observe the rules of inspection prescribed.
>
> 3.To adopt some trade, art, industry, or profession, should he not have known means of subsistence of his own.[24]

The penalty of perpetual absolute disqualification is "the deprivation of office, even though it be held by popular election, the deprivation of the right to vote or to be elected to public office, the disqualification to acquire honors, etc., and the loss of retirement pay, etc."[25]

The punishment is shocking, isn't it? But why? The sentence is not "cruel and unusual" in the sense of inhumane. Taking the penalties one by one, there was nothing remarkable about them in 1909; and, except for the chain (and the permanence of the surveillance), there is still nothing remarkable about them today. If the sentence is "cruel and unusual," it is only because fifteen years in prison (and 4,000 pesetas fine) is too much. But the punishment is certainly not too much for any crime. We would have no qualms about imposing such a penalty for, say, murder. It would, after all, be less severe than life imprisonment or death. So, if the sentence is "cruel and unusual" at all, it is so only because it is too much for trying to embezzle

616 pesos by falsifying a public record. But why should the penalty be too much for that?

The retributive procedure outlined above would have us answer that question by comparing the falsification of public records with crimes of the same type to see whether the severity of the penalty corresponds to the seriousness of the crime. That, in fact, is the procedure the majority of the Court adopted.[26] Here is part of what they uncovered:

> There are degrees of homicide that are not punished so severely, nor are the following crimes: . . . forgery of bonds and other instruments for the purpose of defrauding the United States, robbery, larceny and other crimes . . . If we turn to the legislation of the Philippine Commission we find . . . that forgery of or counterfeiting the obligations or securities of the United States or of the Philippine Islands shall be punished by a fine of not more than ten thousand pesos and by imprisonment of not more than fifteen years. In other words, the highest punishment possible for a crime which may cause the loss of thousands of dollars, and to prevent which the duty of the State should be as eager as to prevent the perversion of truth in a public document, is not greater than that which may be imposed for falsifying a single item of a public account.[27]

The court had no trouble drawing the obvious conclusion: " . . . [This] contrast shows more than different exercises of legislative judgment. It is greater than that. It condemns the sentences in this case as cruel and unusual. It exhibits a difference between unrestrained power and that which is exercised under the spirit of constitutional limitations formed to establish justice."[28] Because even the minimum penalty for falsifying official documents was twelve years of *Cadena*, the Court declared the statutory penalty unconstitutional and set Weems free.[29] "It is," the Court held, "a precept of justice that punishment for crime should be graduated and proportioned to offense."[30]

Of the six justices participating in the case, two dissented. Their dissent (written by Justice White, Justice Holmes merely joining) is instructive. The dissent sounds utilitarian, yet its concern is not proportion in punishment as such but the propriety of letting courts decide such matters.

> [If] it be that the lawmaker in defining and punishing crime is imperatively restrained by constitutional provisions to apportion punishment by a consideration alone of the abstract heinousness of the offenses punished, it must result that the power is so circumscribed as to be impossible of execution, or at all events is so restricted as to exclude the possibility of taking into account in defining and punishing crime all those considerations concerning the condition of society, the tendency to commit the particular crime, the difficulty of detecting the same, the necessity for resorting to stern measures of

repression, and various other subjects which have at all times been deemed
essential to be weighed in defining and punishing crime.[31]

There is an ambiguity in this passage. What *might* be thought wrong with
"abstract heinousness" (seriousness) as a standard of proportion is that it
fails to take into account the rational concerns of a particular society.
Stealing a horse is abstractly no worse than stealing money. Yet, in an
unpopulated country where horses are the only means of transport, stealing
a horse may be much the same as firing a gun at someone well within range.
The dissent would certainly be right to counsel against abstracting crime
from the conditions of the society where the crime is committed. But
seriousness is not abstract in that sense. (See step 5 above.) If all that
worried the dissent were such abstraction from the rational concerns of
society, the conclusion to draw is that the case should be sent back to the
Philippine courts for rehearing on the question of special conditions justifying the special penalty. The dissent does not draw that conclusion. What it
concludes is that no court should delve into questions of proportion. Why?

An unstated premise must be hidden in the shadows. Ordinarily, there is
nothing in judicial supervision of abuse to make the exercise of a legislative
power "impossible." For the dissent, what is wrong with "heinousness" as a
standard of proportion is not its abstractness but its indefiniteness. The
standard would (they fear) give the courts a free hand to invade the legislative power. Why? A good utilitarian should not believe that. Utilitarians
have traditionally been the ones to argue that "heinousness" is not an
arbitrary term but a shorthand for just those "considerations concerning the
condition of society" that the dissent wishes to have the legislature take into
account.[32] If "heinousness" is no harder to prove than any other fact, why
not let courts delve into such facts? The law knows how to grant presump-
tions in favor of a decision-maker, distribute burdens of proof, and otherwise
protect the legislative or executive power from meddlers — without closing
off review where discretion has clearly been abused. The majority were not
willing to act until convinced that they had before them more than mere
"different exercises of legislative judgment." Why are the minority not
willing to do the same?

Apparently, the minority does not believe "heinousness" to be just another
fact. They should as utilitarians, but they do not. Behind the concern about
who should decide questions of proportion is, it seems, the fear that there is
no standard by which to decide; the fear that, if judges can enter into such
decisions at all, there is no rational limit to what they can review; the fear
that the question before the Court is really whose arbitrary judgment should
define crimes and punishments. While the majority had no difficulty deciding what seems a clear case to us as well, the minority cannot understand
why it is clear and so tremble at the cases to come. Their utilitarianism blinds

them to the difference between obvious injustice and ordinary legislative discretion. Why should that be?

Both White and Holmes are practical men who know what judges and legislators can do. They must realize that neither judge nor legislator can in practice find out what necessarily must be found out to defend any conclusion about "heinousness" as *they* understand it. And so, they conclude that to give the power to decide "heinousness" (as they understand it) is to give power by its nature arbitrary. The power to find abuse of such power is simply the power to usurp power.

Here is confirmation of the conclusions drawn above. What seems to be wrong with utilitarianism is not so much that it leads us astray as that it leads us not at all. If it seems to utilitarians that I have been unfair, let them explain how this case (or one like it) should have been decided given the information actually available to the courts and legislatures in 1909 (or the information available today). They must, I believe, either adopt the method outlined above or take up the position Holmes and White retreated to. They will not, I believe, be able to provide a utilitarian decision of this case.

Judges, Retribution, and Clemency

By now it is evident why I consider the distinction between act-retributivism and rule-retributivism unimportant. Act-retributivism is the fallback position for theorists who would like to claim more. If what I have argued here is sound, there is no need to fall back. What may not be so evident yet is that, if there is any weakness in the defenses of retributivism, it is in the old stronghold, sentencing. The legislature works deep inside the great machine of criminal law; the judge, out where that machine cuts into the world. The legislature has only to follow my seven easy steps to do all it can or should; but the judge must and does do more. She looks to the person as well as to the act, to reformation as well as to punishment, to mercy as well as to justice. It is her business to know when to sentence with the fullest severity and when to suspend a sentence entirely, when to put a criminal on probation instead of sending him to prison, when to let the new sentence be served concurrently with others instead of afterward. The judge often seems to do less than justice. I do not, however, consider such judicial gentleness either evidence against my claims for retributivism or mere "rummaging about in the serpent-windings of utilitarianism." I do consider that gentleness something deserving explanation. I shall sketch that explanation here (reserving the full explanation till Chapter Eight).

We must conceive of sentencing as proceeding in two quite different stages. The first stage is retributive. Once a person is found guilty of a crime, the judge types and ranks the crime according to the procedures described above, exercising discretion the legislature has left him to continue the work of refinement it did not dare to complete in advance. Typing should be trivial. A single statute ordinarily deals with only a single type of crime. Ranking is not much harder. The judge imagines (or, more likely, remembers) the least someone could do to violate the statute, what someone might do in addition to make the violation more serious, and how serious the violation must be before being the worst possible under the statute. (The extremes should, of course, be representative rather than bizarre.) The judge then places the actual crime in the appropriate rank (perhaps one of a half-dozen or so). Here is the place for him to consider all mitigating circumstances (duress, provocation, necessity, and so on) and aggravating circumstances (exploitation of a position of trust, extreme brutality, helplessness of victim, and so on). The judge next takes the difference (to give an exact name to a rough process) between the maximum and minimum sentences permissible under the statute, divides the difference into as many ranks as he has ranks of crime, and chooses the sentence corresponding to the rank of the particular crime. The judge has now done all that justice requires. He has found the penalty to fit the crime. He cannot justify a sentence more severe than that by any other consideration. For example, for him to sentence in the following way would be unjust: "The statutory maximum is ten years. I have decided that the crime deserves five years. But, because so many people are committing this crime these days [or because the criminal is such a bad person], I am going to sentence him to the maximum — five years for what he did and five more years for what others might do [or for what he is]."

The second stage in sentencing is not retributive. It cannot be because all retributive considerations are taken into account in the first stage. The crime has told us all it can. The second stage stands to retribution as promise-breaking stands to promising. The second stage concerns exceptions, not the general case. Here is the place for considerations of personal character, family situation, hope of reform, overcrowding of prisons, and so on. The theory of this stage is properly a part of the same theory of clemency covering decisions not to arrest or not to prosecute; commutations, pardons, and amnesties; and paroles, furloughs, good-time remissions, and similar reductions in severity of deserved punishment. While the theory of clemency is well beyond the scope of this chapter. I must make three observations to avoid misunderstanding of what I have already said.

First, the principles of judicial clemency (like those of clemency in general) cannot allow clemency to be too common, predictable, or generous. The criminal law is possible without clemency but not without deterrence. Where clemency becomes the rule, there is no deterrence; the method of social control is no longer criminal law; and so, that principle of clemency would not be the principle of exceptions familiar to the criminal law.

Second, the principle of judicial clemency should not be direct appeal to utility. Judges, though in no position to gauge accurately the general disutility of this or that act of clemency, are only too well placed to recognize its utility to the prisoner. A judge who always aimed directly at the greatest good of the greatest number would probably do more harm than good. A judge may, of course, consider the consequences of various sentences, but such consideration will be quite selective (and, being selective, they are *not* utilitarian).[33]

Third, judicial clemency is not necessarily unjust (though like acts do not lead to like sentences). The criminal who receives clemency has nothing to complain of (except what anyone has to complain of when given better than he earned). The criminal who has committed the same crime as another but not received clemency may also have nothing to complain of. The principles of clemency should be principles all rational persons in the society would prefer if they had to choose between those principles and none at all. A grant of clemency according to such principles is nothing one can rationally complain of on principle (however much one may think another principle of clemency better or wish he too had received clemency under this one). Punishment is what a rational person deserves for his act; clemency, what he deserves for other reasons (perhaps only because of some official's arbitrary grace). There is no injustice so long as each criminal receives what he deserves.[34]

Notes

I read part of an earlier version of this paper before the Philosophy Colloquium of Illinois State University, January 26, 1979, and before the Philosophy Club of the University of Chicago, April 13, 1979. I should like to thank those present for their comments. I should also like to thank Richard Epstein for his helpful editorial advice on two later drafts, and my old criminal law professor, Yale Kamisar, for asking all the right questions.

1. See Chapter One.

2. S. I. Benn and R. S. Peters, *The Principles of Political Thought* (New York: Free Press, 1965), p. 219 (originally published in 1959 under the title of *Social Principles and the Democratic State*). The same objection is more fully made in Stanley I. Benn, "An Approach to the Problem of Punishment," *Philosophy* 33 (October 1958): 334-337. Hugo Adam Bedau repeated the objection in "Retribution and the Theory of Punishment," *Journal of Philosophy* 75 (November 1978): 601-622.

3. Compare Edmund L. Pincoffs. *The Rationale of Legal Punishment* (New York: Humanities Press, 1966), pp. 2-16. I have much changed the wording of Pincoffs' "claim iii" to bring out the inconsistency between what

Benn argues in the above quotation and what I argue. I nonetheless believe that the principle I defend below is one of "desert" in something like the traditional retributivist's sense. I explain why below.

4. I do not, I might add, think the distinction entirely pointless. As I shall explain below, judges do act in ways importantly different from the way legislatures do. The difference is not, however, so much a function of the act-rule distinction (though it is in part a function of that) as it is a function of which of two stages of sentencing the judge is in. The first stage follows (I shall argue) the same principles of punishment the legislature follows; while the second follows principles of clemency, something the legislature cannot possibly do. The act-rule distinction invites us (though it does not require us) to conflate those two stages.

5. Pp. 26-27. Compare Benn and Peters, p. 202; Herbert Morris, *Monist* 52 (October 1968): 475-501. All differences between this definition and the one Benn borrows from Flew are, I believe, simply explications of what the argument makes clear is there all along. The definition ignores the specific problems posed by vicarious criminal liability, collective criminal liability, "crimes of status," retroactive laws, secret laws, and other troublesome rarities.

6. See Michael Davis, "Guilty But Insane?," *Social Theory and Practice* 10 (Spring 1984): 1-23.

7. Compare E. Van den Haag, "On Deterrence and the Death Penalty," *Ethics* 78 (July 1968): 280-89; and Steven Goldberg, "On Capital Punishment," *Ethics* 85 (October 1974): 75-79. To say that the criminal law presupposes knowledge of penalties is not to say either that knowledge of the penalty is an element of any crime or that many people actually know the penalties when they contemplate crimes. Quite the contrary. To say that the criminal law *pre*supposes knowledge of penalties is to say that the criminal law proceeds as if particular criminals have such knowledge *whatever the facts may be*. The "criminal" who proves himself *incapable* of such knowledge will, of course, be judged incompetent and excused from criminal justice. The criminal who proves the penalty could not have been known to *anyone* (e.g., because the statute was never published) should be excused on a technicality. But the criminal who proves only his own ignorance of the penalty will be convicted even more easily than one who proves himself similarly ignorant of the primary rule he violated. Indeed, he will be convicted as easily as the criminal who proves himself an expert in the law. "Ignorance of the law is no excuse" may not be true of law in general, but it is certainly true of particular penalties. The discovery that most criminals were in fact ignorant of the penalty when they broke the law would be interesting as a piece of sociology but strictly irrelevant as a point of law. How can that be? Must not the criminal law heed the facts? Not always. Outside a theory, particular facts do not have much to say. Just as a scientific

theory may ignore anomalies, so the criminal law may ignore some dis-
coveries inconsistent with its presuppositions. And, just as a theory will
stand so long as it handles the phenomena with which it deals better than
does any alternative, so the presuppositions of the criminal law need not be
rejected so long as the criminal law seems (all things considered) preferable
to any alternative method of social control. Even the criminal himself may
(as Morris has reminded us) prefer to be treated as a rational agent rather
than as the unfortunate fool he may in fact be.

8. See, e.g., Morris, "Persons and Punishment," pp. 477-478; H.L.A. Hart,
Punishment and Responsibility: Essays in the Philosophy of Law (New York:
Oxford University Press, 1968), esp. pp. 28-53; and Rolf E. Sartorius, *In-
dividual Conduct and Social Norms* (Encino, Calif.: Dickenson Publishing
Co., 1975), esp. pp. 106-109.

9. Thus, this analysis of criminal law identifies the use of indeterminate
sentences as foreign to the criminal law, a practice tending to reduce the
benefits the criminal law provides rational persons by letting them know the
consequences of their acts. (By "indeterminate sentence" I mean a sentence
where the maximum is either undefined or so uniformly high as to leave the
parole board virtually full discretion. For more, see Chapter Eight.) Reform
theory—with its preference for indeterminate sentences—is, on this
analysis, not so much a theory *of* punishment as a theory of *alternatives to*
punishment.

10. I am not here talking about excusing conditions. What I have in mind
are cases where we would say, "Yes, I would have done just what you did had
I been in your place; but the law cannot recognize such cases as an exception." Civil disobedience is perhaps the sort of case that comes most readily
to mind, but such oddities as *Regina v. Dudley and Stephens* (Q.B.D. 1884)
are closer to the paradigm. Such cases are fit subjects for clemency as
explained later.

11. I have relied on Ernest Nagel, *The Structure of Science* (New York:
Harcourt, Brace, & World, 1961), esp. pp. 82-85, for what I say of scientific
theory.

12. Compare John Rawls, "Two Concepts of Rules," *Philosophical Review*
64 (January 1955): 3-32. Rawls's distinction between the concept of rule as
"summary" and rule as "practice" is different from the distinction between
claims within the system and claims for the system. His distinction is
important for his celebrated contrast between justifying a practice and
justifying actions falling under a practice. My distinction concerns *two* ways
a claim (but not the same claim) may be proved. Such a claim may be used
either in justifying a practice (e.g., having this statute) or in justifying an act
under a practice (e.g., imposing this sentence under the statute or enacting
this statute under a particular system of criminal law). Yet, whatever the
differences, the two distinctions seem to lead to the same conclusion:

"[Where] there is a practice, it is the practice itself that must be the subject of the utilitarian principle" (Rawls, p. 30). The utilitarian principle cannot reach particular sentences (or, though Rawls concludes the opposite, particular statutory penalties).

13. This procedure was suggested by J. D. Mabbott, "Punishment," *Mind* 48 (April 1939): 152-167, p. 162. Benn's attack upon the possibility of a retributive scale is his answer to Mabbott's suggestion. See Benn and Peters, p. 218. This chapter may be thought of as the response Mabbott should have made to that attack.

14. For a somewhat fuller discussion of what makes a penalty inhumane, see my "Death, Deterrence, and the Method of Common Sense," *Social Theory and Practice* 7 (Summer 1981): 145-77, esp. pp. 167-171.

15. What is feared is not a state of affairs as such (e.g., death or loss of property) but an act (e.g., being intentionally killed or being intentionally deprived of one's property for gain). Murder is not the same type of crime as, say, involuntary manslaughter (since the murderer intends death while the perpetrator of involuntary manslaughter does not). Now, certain acts (such as blinding) are crimes not everyone can suffer. Others (such as treason or cruelty to animals) are crimes no one can suffer. Such crimes should, of course, still be ranked with those everyone can suffer. So, we must suppose each person ranking crimes to consider how much he fears each crime being committed against himself *or* someone (or something) for whom he cares. If someone cared little or nothing for anyone or anything but himself, he would rank many crimes lower than the rest of us would. For the same reason, changes in our concern for others (e.g., infants, dogs, the insane, trees) may have an important effect upon what we punish and how much we punish it.

16. Compare the discussion of "characteristicalness" in Jeremy Bentham, *The Principles of Morals and Legislation* (New York: Hafner Publishing, 1948), pp. 192-193.

17. I do not omit "moral blameworthiness" by accident. Blameworthiness is not, like the terms of my litany, associated with the "moral accounting" of retribution (except at the stage of clemency). Compare William Kneale, *The Responsibility of Criminals* (Oxford: Oxford University Press, 1967), pp. 25-30. This pamphlet is reprinted in full (except for the dedicatory opening paragraph) in James Rachels, *Moral Problems* (New York: Harper & Row, 1971), pp. 161-187. See also Chapter Nine.

18. Notice that the claim here is not that everyone — except the criminal in question — has restrained himself from committing the crime in question. There are crimes few of us find tempting enough to require restraint lest we commit them; and perhaps no crime tempts everyone. Few men — and even fewer women — are tempted to commit rape. The rich seldom have any interest in armed robbery. The poor are likely to be equally uninterested in

committing stock fraud. And so on. The claim here is only that some of those who did not break the law in question would have done the forbidden act but for the law (or penalty) and that it is these over whom the criminal would gain unfair advantage if he were not punished for breaking the law in question. There will ordinarily be such people because a law failing to restrain anyone (either because everyone with the urge to break the law does or because no one — except this one criminal — has any urge to break it) is either ineffective or pointless (and so not likely to be a law at all). But what if there were a law one, but only one, person had any urge to break? How would he take unfair advantage of anyone by breaking *that* law? I have already answered that question in Chapter Two: The criminal still benefits from the restraint of others who might break other laws from which he benefits (just as *they* benefit from his keeping laws he would rather not keep). The woman who has no urge to rape may yet have an urge to castrate. The unfairness here would depend upon a more complicated practice than before (upon a system of laws rather than a single law); but there is no other difference. Still (it might now be asked), what if the criminal in question is the only one with any urge to break any law whatever? What if he is a man among angels? While I am not sure this last question deserves an answer, it certainly has one: Yes, according to the retributive theory, this criminal would *not* deserve legal punishment; and, it seems to me, the theory is right:

> *"It was wrong to do this," said the angel.*
> *"You should live like a flower,*
> *Holding malice like a puppy,*
> *Waging war like a lambkin."*
>
> *"Not so," quoth the man*
> *Who had no fear of spirits;*
> *"It is only wrong for angels*
> *Who can live like the flowers,*
> *Holding malice like the puppies.*
> *Waging war like the lambkins."*
>
> — Stephen Crane

19. Strictly, this analogy applies only to completed crimes. Attempts would have to be licensed with only partial or conditional pardons and so a license to attempt would always be worth less than a license to do the full act. You would be pardoned only if you did not succeed. The market analogy seems to explain what retributivists and utilitarians alike have found perplexing, i.e., why we should punish failures less severely than successes. Compare Lawrence Becker, "Criminal Attempt and the Theory of the Law

of Crimes," *Philosophy and Public Affairs* 3 (Spring 1974): 262-294, with Chapter Five.

20. For the opposite (and, I think, mistaken), view, see J. P. Day, "Retributive Punishment," *Mind* 87 (1978): 498-516.

21. *Weems v. United States*, 217 U.S. 349 (1909), pp. 357-358.

22. Ibid., p. 358.

23. Ibid., p. 364.

24. Ibid.

25. Ibid., pp. 364-65.

26. For a different interpretation of *Weems*, see Herbert Packer, "Making the Punishment Fit the Crime," *Harvard Law Review* 77 (April 1964): 1071-1082, esp. 1075.

27. *Weems v. U.S.*, pp. 380-81.

28. Ibid., p. 381.

29. Ibid., p. 382.

30. Ibid., p. 367.

31. Ibid., pp. 387-88.

32. Compare Bentham on "mischievous acts," pp. 152-77.

33. For a fuller discussion of why principles of clemency should not be direct appeals to utility, see Alan Wertheimer, "Deterrence and Retribution," *Ethics* 86 (January 1976): 181-99. This point about clemency is evidently not obvious. Benn expressly claims that judges *should* sentence according to their judgment of the utility of each sentence (Benn and Peters, pp. 222-26). My remarks should not be interpreted as denying the special sort of act-utilitarianism Sartorius argues for. All I want to deny is the possibility of any act-utilitarianism not building in complex factual assumption equivalent to a ban on direct appeal to utility for clemency.

34. For a different view, see Michael Clark, "The Moral Graduation of Punishment," *Philosophical Quarterly* 21 (April 1971): 132-40. Clark has, I think, confused the two stages I distinguish.

PART TWO

Applications

5

Why Attempts Deserve
Less Punishment
Than Complete Crimes

Rifle ready, an assassin lies in wait. He aims carefully as the intended victim comes in view but holds fire until only a few yards separate them. Then he pulls the trigger. The "victim" walks on, unaware that only a faulty cartridge has saved him from death.

A would-be robber enters a bank, goes to a teller window, hands in a threatening note, and displays a toy pistol. An alert guard, seeing the "weapon," immediately intervenes. The robbery has aborted.

These are both attempts to commit a serious crime.[1] Should they be punished as severely as the corresponding complete crime? The answer of most legal theorists today is: Yes. That is surprising for two reasons.

One reason for surprise is that the answer clearly goes against common practice. Most legal systems statutorily provide for penalties for attempts substantially less severe than for the corresponding complete crimes. And some jurisdictions (for example, Illinois) which for a time yielded to the theorists (especially the American Law Institute's highly influential *Model Penal Code*) have gone back to providing lesser penalties for most attempts. Legal theory is seldom so out of step with practice.

The other reason the theorists' answer is surprising is that it is (virtually) *the* theorists' answer. That a few theorists should set themselves against practice is hardly worth notice. We expect theory to be (to some degree) a criticism of practice. But that so many theorists, retributivists and deterrentists, rehabilitationists and incapacitationists, could agree in the face of opposed practice certainly is worth notice. When, as here, the agreement arises not from each appealing to some common principle external to their several theories, but from distinct principles, each internal to the theory in question, we have a state of things inviting one to conclude, "Well, there must be something to it."

Perhaps there is. And perhaps too it would be worthwhile to find out what "it" is. Nevertheless, I shall not do that here. Instead, I shall try something more risky and so more interesting. I shall try to show that the theorists, though nearly unanimous, are mistaken. I shall argue that, if we accept the version of retributivism outlined above, we must recognize the injustice of punishing attempts as severely as we punish complete crimes because attempts *deserve* less punishment. Most retributivists will, I hope, find the argument decisive. Deterrentists, rehabilitationists, and incapacitationists will, I suppose, not find it even relevant except insofar as they recognize justice as an external constraint on what may be derived from their respective theories. But, because most non-retributivists today recognize justice as at least a factor to be considered along with deterrence, rehabilitation, or incapacitation, the conclusion drawn here should be of interest even to them.

There is also a more practical reason for interest in the conclusion drawn here — at least for Americans. The United States Supreme Court recently revived the doctrine that punishment must be proportioned to the seriousness of the offense. At first, the doctrine was applied only in capital cases. But it has now been extended to cover cases involving a life sentence for repeated conviction of minor felonies.[2] There is no principled reason not to extend it further (though there may well be reasons of policy preventing such an extension soon). The conclusion drawn here suggests one way in which it might be extended. If punishing a criminal more than he deserves for his crime is unjust, and if attempts deserve less punishment than the corresponding complete crime, it seems to follow that any state which in fact punished an attempt as severely as the corresponding complete crime would risk having the sentence overturned as unconstitutional because the punishment for the attempt was out of proportion to the crime.

Two Problems of Attempt

Legal theorists have until recently attended so little to attempts that it would not be much of an exaggeration to say that "the problem of attempts" is a discovery (or invention) of this century.[3] There are really two problems. One is what we might call a "problem of demarcation"; the other, a "problem of proportion."

The problem of demarcation is to set limits to what can justifiably be punished as attempt. The problem has one aspect for virtually all deterrentists, rehabilitationists, incapacitationists, and even traditional retributivists, but another aspect for certain contemporary retributivists. For deterrentists, rehabilitationists, and incapacitationists, there is no difficulty about explaining why attempts should be punished. If the purpose of the criminal law is to prevent certain acts and if punishing criminals is (in one way or another) the means by which the criminal law achieves that purpose, then the only question is how early is too early to begin preventing. For traditional retributivists, there is also no difficulty about justifying the punishment of attempts. If the purpose of punishment is, say, to "annul" the evil intention embodied in an act, then whether the act failed or was completed is irrelevant to whether the act should be punished. The problem for such retributivists, as for non-retributivists, is not so much to *justify* punishing attempts as to justify *not* punishing "mere preparation."

The problem of demarcation has a different aspect only for those retributivists who conceive punishment as proportioned to a certain sort of (nonlegal) *harm*. Each complete crime has (they say) its characteristic harm (which, indeed, is what justifies making it a crime). But attempts, because they are incomplete or failed crimes, cannot involve the same harm that the complete crime does. Attempts must (it seems to these retributivists) either do some other harm or be an exception to the principle that punishment should be proportioned to wrongdoing (since there would be nothing of a retributive sort to proportion punishment to). Because proportion between punishment and crime is the foundation of retributivism, such theorists have had to look for some harm characteristic of attempts. The results remain controversial at best.[4]

I shall say little more about this first problem here. I have identified it only to distinguish it from the one that now concerns me. If we think of this first problem as one of *demarking* the punishable from the non-punishable, then we may think of the second problem as one of *apportioning* punishment among punishable acts. We need not suppose that the principles that settle demarcation will settle proportion as well. Indeed, one lemma of the argument I shall make here is that the problems of demarcation and proportion are largely independent of one another.

Legal theorists have had less to say about the problem of proportion than about the problem of demarcation. They have generally supposed that the reason for making some act a crime should determine as well how much the crime should be punished. That supposition has generally led them to conclude that the lenient treatment of attempts is either utterly wrongheaded or at best justified by rather speculative considerations (for example, that failure to complete a crime shows lack of resolve or that the lesser penalty for attempts is an implicit recognition of the difficulties of proving intent in the absence of the complete crime). Let me briefly review those theories before examining the alternative.

Rehabilitationists have argued against leniency for attempts in this way: The purpose of punishment is to prevent socially dangerous acts by changing the dangerous person so that he is no longer a danger (and by holding him in a safe place until he is changed). One who attempts a crime is in general as dangerous as one who succeeds (unless the crime is broken off because of a change of heart). So, in general, punishment for attempt should be the same as punishment for complete crime. Since incapacitationists differ from rehabilitationists only in having given up hope of reform, their argument against leniency for attempts would differ only in that way.[5]

Deterrent theorists have reasoned only somewhat differently. We might put their argument this way: The purpose of punishment is to prevent socially dangerous acts by making them uninviting in prospect. A crime is just any act recognized as sufficiently dangerous to be worth discouraging by the threat of punishment. Hardly anyone plans a mere attempt. In prospect virtually all crimes are conceived as complete (and highly successful!). But insofar as criminals do consider the possibility that their crime might fail or abort, they should consider the lower penalty for mere attempt as making the attempt less uninviting than it would be were the penalty for attempt the same as that for the complete crime. "If we fail," they might say, "all we risk is 4-15 years. Only if we succeed need we worry about 6-30 years." The distinction between attempt and complete crime is therefore not only pointless but positively inconsistent with the purpose of punishment. So (the deterrentist would conclude), punishment for attempt should be the same as for the complete crime.[6]

Retributivists want to proportion punishment to wrongdoing rather than to some social good such as prevention of dangerous acts. Their reasoning about attempts should then be quite different from the three forward-looking theories already described. It has not been. Traditionally, the wrong in question was understood as moral wrong (law or no law), an evil intention realized in an act. What seemed important was the intention's having been realized in some act or other, not the particular way in which it was in fact realized. I am (it would be said) morally just as blameworthy for attempting to rob a bank and failing as I would be if I succeeded. I meant to succeed, and only, say, the bank guard's alertness prevented me from "making a haul." If punishment should be proportioned to moral blameworthiness, what I deserve for my attempts is just what I would deserve had I succeeded. So, attempts should (such retributivists held) generally be punished as severely as complete crimes.

More recently, retributivists have shifted their concern somewhat from the intention (or other state of mind) to the act itself. Wrongdoing, it is now often said, is a matter of what is done as well as of what is intended. For example, reckless driving is bad, but (it is said) killing someone as a result is morally worse. There are, I think, at least two forms of this "loss-based" approach. One kind would emphasize the harm done to individuals; the other, the loss of social discipline or security.[7] Both approaches would allow for treating some attempts as deserving less punishment than some complete crimes. But neither is altogether satisfactory. There appears, for example, little reason to conclude that I would do significantly more individual or social harm by completing a bank robbery (and being arrested as I left the bank) than I would if arrested *before* the teller gave me anything or *once* he gave me a bag of almost worthless paper. Yet, the loss-based approach seems to require us either to equate the attempt with the complete crime or to produce some reason to believe the complete crime would do significantly more harm than the attempt.

Hyman Gross provides an especially interesting example of (something like) this sort of retributivism. Gross does *not* argue that every attempt should be punished as severely as the corresponding complete crime. Instead, he proposes "a middle way," distinguishing between various kinds of attempt based on their "dangerousness." Some crimes become mere attempts because of (what Gross calls) "manifest impossibility" (for example, the use of what one knows to be a toy gun in an—"irrational"—attempt to kill a public official). Other crimes fail because of (what Gross calls) "overt impossibility" (for example, the use of a rifle everyone but the actor knows to be inadequate for the crime attempted). But most crimes that fail do so because of "covert impossibility" (for example, use of ammunition that, though ordinarily reliable, happens to be from a bad batch). According to Gross, a crime that fails because of covert impossibility should be punished as severely as the complete crime because the act was "as dangerous as it could be" and so, "harmful conduct" (even though "by chance" no harm occurred). Crimes that fail because of *overt* impossibility are, however, less culpable because they are less dangerous. And crimes that fail because of manifest impossibility are even less culpable because they are not dangerous at all.

There is something appealing in this, especially in Gross' handling of "manifest impossibility" (which seems to invite a straightjacket rather than a prison term). But there is trouble too. Gross' guiding principle is that the same conduct should receive the same punishment. To those who might object that attempts and complete crimes cannot be the same conduct because one is merely dangerous while the other is actually harmful, Gross responds that the harmfulness of conduct is a matter not of the harm done but of the harm risked. (He expressly rules out of the equation feelings to be assuaged, injuries to be compensated, and any other "differences that the occurrence of harm might make.") He defends that response by claiming that an attempt defeated by covert impossibility is as *blameworthy* as the complete crime would be. The assassin of our initial example is, it seems, "morally speaking" a murderer whether he succeeds in his attempt or not. Gross thus falls back on something like the traditional retributivist view that the criminal law punishes morally blameworthy acts (in proportion to their moral blameworthiness) because they deserve punishment law or no law. But he cannot fairly do that until he shows blameworthiness to be independent of actual outcome. And it is hard to see how he can do that since, for example, we ordinarily blame the reckless driver who kills someone much more severely than the reckless driver who happens to do no harm. Even Gross' subtlety seems unable to make the loss-based approach work.[8]

There is, however, a third form of retributivism, the one I have been arguing for. It proposes to measure wrongdoing by the *unfair advantage* the criminal takes by breaking the law rather than by the harm done or risked. This form of retributivism has not been systematically applied to the second problem of attempts. I shall attempt such an application here.

Unfair Advantage and the Problem of Proportion

Most retributivists today would, I think, accept the following propositions:

(a) that the criminal law of a relatively just legal system tends to main-tain a fair balance between the benefits and burdens of those subject to it;

(b) that providing for punishment if someone disobeys the law (in such a legal system) is justified, in part at least, because provision for such punishment helps to assure that the law will be obeyed; and

(c) that punishing someone for a particular act of disobedience (in such a legal system) is justified only insofar as the punishment is no more than what the act deserves.

Retribution is a theory of *just* punishment. The theory presupposes some-thing approximating a just legal system because it is hard to make sense of the idea of "just punishment" outside of such a system. Keeping in mind this connection between just punishment and just legal system, we can, I think, easily see why the three propositions retributivists accept together set surprisingly strict limits to the penalties that may be provided for attempts.

Doing what the law forbids while others abide by the law will take unfair advantage (provided the law is part of a relatively just legal system). That will be true even if what the law forbids is a mere attempt. The unfair advantage may, as explained earlier, be thought of as a "license" others do not have because they did not "take" it. We can gauge the unfair advantage of a particular crime by determining the value of the cor-responding "license." While any fair procedure for setting prices should serve to gauge the value, let us continue to use the auction in which everyone subject to the criminal law of a particular society may bid on a small number of "licenses" to do the act in question.[9] The problem of lesser penalties for attempts then becomes a) distinguishing the special unfair advantage one takes by committing a complete crime from that one takes by committing a mere attempt and b) gauging the relative value of these advantages as reflected in the price the appropriate licenses would fetch in an auction of the sort just described.

What to License?

If an attempt deserves less punishment than the corresponding complete crime, the license for the attempt must be worth less than a license to do the complete crime. But, what is it we would license if we licensed a mere attempt? How should we formulate a license to attempt? And how would that license differ from a license to commit the complete crime?

A complete crime ordinarily consists of: (a) a state of affairs the law is supposed to prevent, the *"actus reus"* (for example, the unlawful taking of another's property or an involuntary death at the hands of another); (b) some state of mind, the so-called *"mens rea"* (for example, the intent to do great bodily harm or a failure to exercise reasonable care); and (c) a certain connection between *mens rea* and *actus reus* (for example, a theft being the result of acting with the intent to deprive another of his property or a death that is a natural and probable outcome of what the actor knew himself to be doing). What constitutes the *actus reus* or *mens rea* of a "complete crime" (or the appropriate connection between them) will, of course, be determined by the statute creating that crime (or by the common law when the statutes are silent). A license for the complete crime would mirror the statute, pardoning in advance commission of the *actus reus* done with a certain *mens rea*. Would a license for attempt have the same structure? Let us begin with *actus reus*.

What makes an act a mere attempt is that the *actus reus* of the complete crime never occurs. The actor fails in his attempt. For example, the would-be bank robber is arrested before the teller hands him the money. Nothing of value is taken. The harm characteristic of robbery, forced deprivation of one's valued property, does not occur, even for an instant. The presence or absence of such characteristic harm seems to be crucial to the distinction between attempt and complete crime. The actor's plans can miscarry in all sorts of ways without reducing his crime to a mere attempt, provided he does the characteristic harm (or something like it). For example, if by mistake a bank robber robs the bank next door to the one he intended to rob, he is still guilty of robbery, not merely of *attempting* to rob the bank he intended. He did not do all he intended, but he did do the harm characteristic of robbery, intending to do just that, and that is all that he needs to do to commit robbery.

Since what makes an act an attempt is that the harm characteristic of the complete crime is not done, either an attempt will have a characteristic harm of its own or it will not be possible to identify the special *actus reus* of attempt without deriving it from the *mens rea*. I think it plain that we cannot in general specify a harm characteristic of attempt. For example, suppose that two men enter a bank, each waving a gun, and that one intends to kill a certain teller while the other only intends to rob the bank. And suppose too that each is arrested just before he can complete what he set out to do. The one who intends to kill the teller will be guilty of attempted murder while the other will only be guilty of attempted robbery. They will be guilty of different attempts even though each has performed exactly the same ("outward") act in making his attempt.

There are, of course, some crimes even the attempt of which ordinarily includes harm characteristic of *lesser* offenses. For example, attempted bank robbery ordinarily includes one or more assaults. The robber must put the teller in "reasonable apprehension of battery" to get him to hand over the money. That harm characteristic of assault will, however, hardly explain the penalty for attempted robbery. We punish attempted robbery much more severely than assault, however aggravated. For example, in Illinois, aggravated assault is a class-A misdemeanor (maximum of one year imprisonment) while attempted armed robbery is a class-1 felony (4-15 years imprisonment).[10] The second problem of attempts becomes interesting only if we assume that talking about attempts is more than a roundabout way of talking about lesser complete crimes (and their characteristic harms).

There are also certain "attempts" that do have their own characteristic harm. For example, assault is often thought of as an attempt to commit battery. The "assaulter" intends "an unlawful touching" but fails and that is why he is guilty of assault rather than battery. Thought of in that way, assault is a true attempt. But assault can also be thought of in a way giving it a characteristic harm of its own. An "assault" ordinarily puts someone in fear of battery. Many statutes define "assault" in terms of that *fear*. Thus, Illinois defines "assault" as placing another "in reasonable apprehension of receiving a battery."[11] Under such statutes, there would be assault even if the "assaulter" intended no more than to place his victim in reasonable apprehension of receiving a beating (*rather than* to beat his victim or otherwise "touch" him). "Assault" so defined would not be a crime of attempted battery but itself a complete crime (though one making express reference to another). The person who intended battery but only achieved assault would be very much like the person who intended to kill his victim but achieved only bodily harm. The intended harm would be enough like the harm he did to count as within the intention (or within what he risked by what he did). We must, then, be careful to exclude from the class of attempts all those "attempts" that have a characteristic harm. For our purposes, attempts are, as such, harmless.

Because (as we shall assume hereafter) attempts do not characteristically do harm in the way complete crimes do, attempt must be a crime primarily of *mens rea*. But not any *mens rea* will do. Attempts seem to require a certain *mens rea*. For example, a reckless driver does not "attempt" negligent homicide just because his driving is grossly negligent but "fails" to result in death. Certain crimes like reckless driving cannot be attempted even though they can easily be committed. An attempt requires an intent, an intent to bring about the *actus reus* of a complete crime (or something like it). Attempts are distinguished according to the complete crime intended. Entering a bank waving a gun is attempted bank robbery if the actor intends to rob the bank but attempted murder if he intends to kill a teller.[12]

A license to attempt would, then, have to identify a certain act, the *actus reus* of the *complete* crime (for example, robbery), and pardon the license holder for intending to do such an act and beginning to do it, but *not* pardon him for doing the harm characteristic of the complete crime. A license to attempt is, by definition, silent concerning the actuality of the *actus reus* of the corresponding complete crime.

Perhaps the notion of "beginning a crime" deserves a word or two. Some may want to define "beginning" so that the interference with liberty from cutting off "mere preparation" is less than the interference with liberty from crimes allowed to get beyond that stage. Others may insist that the line between mere preparation and actual attempt be drawn so that the attempt itself seems too close for comfort (for example, because it inspires insecurity once reported). And others may want to think of "beginning" in other more or less restrictive ways. We need not concern ourselves with that here. That is a matter of demarcation. Whatever the demarcation, our problem would be the same, that is, to determine whether licenses to attempt would be worth less than "licenses to succeed."

Each license for attempt will have to be written as if the corresponding complete crime were possible. (The license must be written to cover an act a would-be criminal can do and no one can even begin to attempt what he believes impossible.) That does not rule out punishing those who attempt the "legally impossible," that is, those trying to do what, if successful, would in fact be no crime at all. Possibility as represented in a license to attempt is possibility as the actor sees it, not as it is in fact. So, there could be a law making punishable as an attempt doing something in the belief that what was done was a crime. For example, we could punish as attempted theft taking one's own umbrella believing it to be another's or as attempted smuggling the covert importation of nondutiable lace in the belief that it was dutiable. We could even have a law to punish as "generic attempt" those acts the actor intends to be unlawful even though there is no traditional category of crime into which to put what the success would be, for example, marrying someone in the belief that all marriage is illegal, and intending in that way to begin a life of crime. Whether prohibition of such attempts would be wise is, of course, a matter of demarcation that need not concern us here. I am simply pointing out that, while what constitutes an attempt will depend on what the complete crime would be, it will not necessarily depend on whether the intended crime is possible in fact or in law.[13]

What Price Attempts?

Now that we have distinguished mere licenses to attempt from licenses to commit the complete crime, we are ready to gauge the relative value of these two kinds of license. I should like to do that by considering three potentially serious objections to the conclusion I want to draw. Each rests on an incomplete understanding of our auction. That, anyway, is what I shall try to show. In the course of showing that, I will, I believe, show as well that (in general) a license to attempt a certain crime will be worth substantially less than a license to commit the complete crime but still substantially more than no license at all.

The first objection we must consider purports to show that mere licenses to attempt would not be bought at the auction we are using to model considerations of fairness. Given the function of the auction, this would amount to showing that, according to the retributive approach taken here, attempts deserve no punishment whatever. If this objection could be made out, it certainly would discredit our approach. It would reveal the retributivism assumed here to be more at odds with common practice than the other theories of punishment seem to be.

We might put the first objection this way: It seems that a mere license to attempt would be worth nothing at all. Hardly anyone undertaking a crime plans to fail. But, a mere license to attempt is no more than a "license to fail." So (it seems), no one would want such a license. What no one wants, no one would bid for and what no one would bid for will be worth nothing at our auction. So (the objection concludes), licenses merely to attempt would be worth nothing because no one wants them.

This objection seems to rest on the assumption that, for every person intent upon some crime, there will be a license to commit that (complete) crime at a price he can afford. Only on that assumption is it possible to show that there would be no demand for mere licenses to attempt. Otherwise, it seems that such a license would certainly be worth something. Most would-be criminals would, we may suppose, recognize the possibility of failure even if failing is not in their plan. If there were too few "licenses to succeed" to go around, might not would-be criminals reason that a "license to fail" is better than no license at all? "Well," we might imagine them to explain, "with a license to attempt this crime, at least we're covered if we fail."

So, the objection assumes that the number of licenses to commit complete crimes will always be large enough to satisfy the demand. The objection fails because that assumption is quite unreasonable. For almost any crime, society cannot afford (or, at least, will not tolerate) as many instances of it as people would commit were there no law prohibiting it. That is the most common reason for making an act illegal. So, licenses to succeed would, for most crimes, be (far) too few to meet the demand. Some people who intend to succeed will not be able to get a license to succeed and will either have to make do with a "license to fail" or go without a license — which, for our purposes, means either not committing any crime or instead engaging in "poaching."

The objection cannot be saved by pointing out that it is possible to "poach" rather than buy a license. "Poaching" must itself be a crime. (Were it not, there could be little reason to buy any license.) And, for our purposes, "poaching" must be a crime of a special sort, that is, one which carries penalties of a different order or kind from those we are equating with the penalties an ordinary legal system imposes. "Poaching," as we understand it here, is a crime against the market we are imagining, a crime against the way we are modeling the problem, a "meta-crime" having no counterpart in the domain we are using the model to understand. So, for example, life imprisonment, death, or some inhumane penalty might be reserved for poachers.

"Poaching" has, then, a small but special role in our model. We need not suppose our criminals to be completely "law abiding" within the model (that is, to commit crimes only when they have a pardon in advance). We need only suppose that they would like to keep their (punishable) lawbreaking to a minimum (because they do not want to be punished) and that buying licenses permits them to avoid punishment (without making the crime itself too expensive to be worth committing). The society will, of course, do its best to discourage "poaching" by making the punishment for that crime severe. But, we may suppose, it is either unwilling or unable to punish "poaching" severely enough to assure that no one would dare to "poach." No large society has been able to rid itself of crime, however horrible the punishments imposed.

How then shall we imagine these licenses to work? Licensing can keep punishable lawbreaking to a minimum whether we imagine a license to attempt to work by pardoning the entire crime provided it fails (or aborts) or instead by forgiving part of the punishment the criminal would otherwise receive. But because our concern here is whether a lower penalty for attempt is what justice requires, though what justice requires of us who have no auction to set penalties, not what justice requires of the society in our model where penalties are set by the fair procedure of an auction, our conclusion will be less open to suspicion if we imagine the license as pardoning the entire crime *provided it fails* (or aborts) rather than as forgiving part of the penalty for the complete crime.

This way of imagining a license to attempt also fits nicely with our analysis of the distinction between licenses to attempt and licenses to commit a complete crime. We are supposing that licenses merely to attempt license only *mens rea* with the resulting act (provided it is not the *actus reus* of the complete crime). So, a license merely to attempt cannot pardon a complete crime (or pardon such a crime completely) because a mere license to attempt cannot pardon the *actus reus* of the complete crime. A license to commit the complete crime must, on the other hand, pardon failure too because every success includes the *mens rea* of failure (with the resulting act) as well as the harm characteristic of success.

This suggests another reason for potential criminals to buy a license to attempt, but one operating even if they already have the corresponding license to succeed (provided a license to attempt is less expensive). *If* a mere license to attempt were less expensive than a license to succeed at the same crime, potential criminals might buy the appropriate license to attempt as a backup. "Why waste a license to succeed," they might reason, "to pardon a failure if we can get pardoned by turning in a cheaper license to attempt?"

So, there should be some demand for mere licenses to attempt, especially if they cost less than licenses to succeed. But, would licenses to attempt *cost less*? That brings us to the second objection. This objection purports to show just the opposite of the first, that is, that a license to attempt would be worth just as much at our auction as a license to commit the complete crime. Showing that would, of course, amount to showing that, according to the approach taken here, attempts deserve the same punishment as the corresponding complete crimes. The objection would, if proved, be less serious than the first. The "different" retributivism championed here would have led to roughly the same conclusion as its competitors did. We would not have shown it to be better (or worse) than its competitors in the handling of attempts. This second objection is, then, while not quite as serious as the first, still serious enough.

The objection assumes a role for "protective associations," that is, groups of law-abiding citizens who buy license to keep them out of the hands of criminals. We might put the objection this way: Whatever the criminals may think about the relative value of licenses to attempt and licenses to succeed, the protective associations would fear attempted crimes just as much as complete crimes. They would not want people "out there" seeing whether they would succeed or fail at this or that crime. They would want potential criminals to be faced with the choice of "poaching" or obeying the law. They would (the objection runs) bid up the price of licenses to attempt just as they would the price of licenses to succeed. So, licenses to fail should cost about the same as licenses to succeed.

This objection rests in part on the assumption that protective associations can determine the price of any particular license to attempt. That assumption is correct. The society we are imagining — like our own — must choose to tolerate a certain level of disorder because it is unwilling or unable to do what is necessary to reduce that disorder further. The protective associations exist to reduce that disorder further by buying up (and not using) licenses what would otherwise be bought up (and used) by potential criminals. The protective associations would, we may suppose, have substantial assets, far more than most criminals would have. So, for any particular license offered at auction, some protective association should be able to outbid any individual criminal (and so, be able as well legitimately to bid up the license to the highest price criminals are willing to pay). But, like the assets of any criminal, the assets of the protective associations must be finite. While there may be no practical limit to the price they can pay for any particular license, there will be a limit to the total number they can buy. And because of that, they cannot control the price of licenses in general.

The objection seems to need the further assumption that our auction is a one-time affair in which all the licenses are auctioned from a fixed supply the protective associations do not affect by what they do. That is not what should be assumed. Such an assumption would make our model less realistic (and so, less useful) than need be. What should be assumed is that those running the auction will calculate from time to time the amount of social disorder (or whatever) the previous selling of licenses produced. If the social disorder produced last time was too great, they would want to lower the number of licenses offered for sale this time. If the social disorder produced last time was tolerable, the auctioneers would be able to offer the same number of licenses this time. And if the social disorder produced last time was lower than expected, they would be able to offer even more licenses without exceeding the limit of disorder the society is willing to tolerate. We must, of course, suppose our auctioneers to want to offer as many licenses as possible consistent with tolerable social disorder so as to produce the maximum revenue permitted – the equivalent in our society of keeping the costs of law enforcement as low as possible consistent with maintaining a certain level of "law and order."

The continuing nature of the auction together with the limited resources of the protective associations makes the associations far less important than required for the objection. The protective associations buy licenses to prevent their use. Any license a protective association buys will, then, *not* be a claim on the fund of public order. Such licenses will instead produce almost pure profit (much as the sale of postage stamps to collectors does for the post office). So, of course, the auctioneers will want to offer substantially more licenses than the protective associations can buy. The *use* of those "surplus" licenses (even when combined with unavoidable "poaching") will not produce disorder beyond the limit society has set. So, it is certain that, in the long run, the criminals will get a good share of the licenses. Because the protective associations must budget their resources and because the number of licenses offered at auction will depend upon the effect on social order of the last offering, the number of licenses offered for auction must in general exceed by a substantial amount the number the protective associations can buy.

It may seem, then, that protective associations are engaged in a foolish undertaking, that they would be able to accomplish just as much did they do nothing at all. That is not quite so. They guarantee that the price of this or that license will not fall too low (that is, so low that it no longer reflects how much people in general fear that crime being committed). If the would-be criminals stop bidding too soon, a protective association could buy the bargain and at least assure that that crime will not be committed then (or, at least, not at such a low price). Of course, part of the price of that purchase may be more licenses put on the market next time. But that is a problem for next time. The protective associations might reasonably be formed with the short-range goal of preventing certain licenses from being used. Once formed, they might continue operating because, should they leave the auction, there would be a sudden glut of licenses. Their exit would trigger a "crime wave." Such a crime wave might, of course, be prevented if the associations notified the auctioneers of the planned withdrawal far enough in advance. Let us suppose they could. They would still have good reason not to withdraw. Withdrawing would leave the criminals free to pick up bargains or even to form conspiracies to keep prices low.[14]

So, it seems, whether there are protective associations or not, there will be some licenses would-be criminals will be able to buy. It also seems that licenses merely to attempt will be useful to would-be criminals, though not as useful as licenses to commit the corresponding complete crimes (since a license to attempt would pardon only a failure, while a license to commit the complete crime would pardon the attempt even if it succeeds). So, any rational would-be criminal should be willing to bid significantly more for a license to succeed than for a mere license to attempt. Since the actual price of licenses will in general be determined by what the would-be criminals bid, not by what the protective associations bid, licenses merely to attempt should in general be worth less than the corresponding licenses to succeed.

That brings us to the third objection. This one, while tacitly rejecting the second, still threatens to discredit our approach. The objection is that all mere licenses to attempt should be of equal worth, since all license approximately the same thing, failure. This objection purports to show that, according to our version of retributivism, attempted murder deserves no more punishment than, say, attempted theft.

We might state the objection in this way: It seems that the number of licenses to commit various complete crimes will in general be proportioned to the seriousness of the characteristic harm that sort of crime does. For example, we would expect a society to issue fewer licenses to murder than licenses to steal because societies find it easier to tolerate theft than murder. But (the objection continues), attempts do no harm (though they may risk it). Attempts differ from one another (primarily) in *mens rea*. Depending on the intention of the actor, the same (harmless) act could be attempted murder or only attempted robbery. So, society has no more reason to limit licenses for one sort of attempt than licenses for another. And so (the objection concludes), it seems that (insofar as quantity is the determinant of price), all licenses to attempt should sell for the same price.

This third objection makes an important point. Society might justifiably be said to have no reason to limit the number of licenses to attempt (that is, no reason to punish attempts) except insofar as there is some connection between attempts and the harm society seeks to prevent by prohibiting the corresponding complete crimes. Where there is no such connection, a license for one sort of attempt is likely to sell for no more than a license for another — because the selling price of both should be *nothing*. Consider, for example, two licenses to attempt what Gross called the "manifestly impossible." One license would, let us suppose, pardon an attempt to kill using means everyone including the actor knows to be insufficient (for example, killing someone by "shooting" him with what is obviously a toy pistol). The other license, let us also suppose, would pardon stealing from those even the thief knows to have nothing to steal (for example, picking pockets even the thief knows to be empty). A society might issue an infinite number of such licenses without fear of suffering any significant loss of order. If the society we are imagining issued all licenses of that kind it could issue, the price such licenses would fetch at the auction would be nominal (supposing anyone to be moved to bid on them at all). So, whether or not it is wise to outlaw attempting the manifestly impossible, it is certainly unjust to punish those who commit such attempts.

The fallacy of the third objection is that it generalizes this insight to cover all attempts. While Gross may have made too much of risk, this objection makes too little of it. Most attempts do risk the harm of the corresponding complete crime. Their failure cannot be known in advance by the would-be criminal (as in the case of manifest impossibility) or even by the society generally (as in the case of what Gross called "overt impossibility"). Society therefore has good reason to limit the number of licenses to attempt (even though, as we are supposing, attempts as such never do harm). Each license to attempt held by someone without the corresponding license to succeed is an invitation to poach. "If I fail, I'm safe," the would-be criminal might reason, "and I'm willing to take my chances if I succeed." It seems that generally the greater the number of "real" attempts (that is, attempts that fail, if they fail, only because of "covert impossibility"), the larger the number of crimes that will succeed. Whatever reason there is to fear the complete crime is, then, also a reason to fear the corresponding attempt (though it is not as strong a reason). Whatever reason there is to limit the number of licenses to commit a certain crime will also be a reason to limit proportionately the number of licenses to attempt it. So, insofar as quantity of licenses determines price, there should be some proportion between the price of a license for the complete crime and the price of a license for the corresponding attempt.[15]

Concluding Remarks

The auction is, of course, only a way to help us see better the unfair advantage criminals take in *our* society when they attempt or succeed at this or that crime. So, it is now time to summarize the foregoing argument in the language of unfair advantage with which we began: Someone who attempts a crime but fails to do the harm characteristic of success still (ordinarily) risks doing that harm. He deserves punishment for risking that harm because even risking such harm is an advantage the law abiding do not take. He deserves less punishment for the attempt than he would for the complete crime because being able to risk doing harm is not as great an advantage as being able to do it. To attempt murder, for example, is not worth as much as to succeed at it. The successful murderer has the advantage of having done what he set out to do. The would-be murderer whose attempt failed has only had the *chance* to do what he set out to do. The difference is substantial.

Because even the criminal guilty only of attempting a serious crime takes a substantial advantage the law abiding do not, he deserves substantial punishment for what he did. But because merely attempting a serious crime is substantially less of an advantage than actually succeeding at it, such a criminal deserves substantially less in punishment for the attempt than he would for the complete crime.

There is an important difference between this argument and that Gross made to show that attempting the "covertly impossible" deserves the same punishment as committing the complete crime while attempting the "overtly impossible" deserves less punishment. Because I think Gross has presented the best systematic treatment of attempts to date, it will, I think, be worth our time to contrast briefly his treatment with ours. Gross' argument turned on degree of "culpability"; the argument made here turns instead on degree of "unfair advantage." Though (as noted in Chapter Three) most retributivists seem to take these two notions to be equivalent, the punishment of attempts is one place where they prove to be strikingly different.

Let us begin with attempting the *covertly* impossible. Gross observes that a person whose attempt turns out to be covertly impossible is just as culpable (that is, blameable) as the person who actually succeeds. Such a criminal fails to do the characteristic harm not because he is incapable of doing it or because he failed to do everything in his power to do it. He fails only "by chance" and chance does not reduce culpability.

We may agree with most of this. All we must deny is that punishment should be proportioned to "culpability" as such. *Our* position is that punishment should be proportioned only to a certain sort of culpability, the culpability specifically connected with "cheating," that is, with the unfair advantage one takes by breaking the law in question. While our criminal may be just as bad a person, just as culpable generally, whether or not he succeeds or fails at this or that crime, he is not therefore equally well off. To cheat successfully is to take a greater advantage than one takes by cheating unsuccessfully. That is why a license to commit a complete crime is worth more (in our model) than a mere license to attempt the same crime (and it is that additional advantage which the additional punishment is supposed to "annul").

There is, of course, some connection between the advantage one takes by risking a certain harm and the advantage one takes by achieving it. The proportion may even vary from one category of crime to another with the proportion between attempts and successes. Attempts to commit crimes that are rarely successfully committed may deserve relatively little punishment while attempts to commit crimes that are almost always committed successfully may deserve a punishment much like that the complete crime deserves. But, an attempt, no matter how close to being a "sure thing," could never take the same advantage as the corresponding complete crime. There is always a significant difference between any probability of an outcome, even if the probability is one, and the occurrence of the outcome itself. For example, I can (all else equal) rationally exchange my dollar for yours. But I cannot (all else equal) rationally exchange my dollar for a ticket in a lottery even if I believe it to be a fair lottery in which only one ticket will be sold and the pot of which will consist of all money paid in for tickets. ("Lottery" implies risk and rational agents are in general "risk-averse.") So, if the punishment the criminal deserves for what he did should be proportional to the unfair advantage he took, the criminal guilty of an attempt always deserves less in punishment for what he did than the criminal who succeeded at the very same crime.

The distinction between "general culpability" and that "special culpability" corresponding to unfair advantage taken comes out no where more clearly than in attempting the *"overtly* impossible." According to Gross, the person attempting the overtly impossible deserves more punishment than the person guilty of attempting the manifestly impossible because what he did was more dangerous than attempting the manifestly impossible, but deserves less punishment than the person guilty of attempting the covertly impossible because what he did was less dangerous than that. Our conclusion must be the same. But our explanation is, I think, better.

Gross explains the lesser culpability of those who attempt the overtly impossible by appealing to the lesser danger such attempts pose. Certainly he is right to claim that overtly impossible attempts are less dangerous than covertly impossible attempts. But the trouble is that he must also claim that overtly impossible attempts are *more* dangerous than manifestly impossible attempts. The only difference between these two kinds of attempt is that, in a manifestly impossible attempt, even the criminal himself knows (in some sense) that what he is doing is harmless while in an overtly impossible attempt everyone but the criminal knows that. How does the criminal's knowledge in one case or ignorance in the other change the dangerousness of the act itself? I am at a loss to answer. Of course, the difference in knowledge may correspond to a difference in character. The person who would undertake an overtly impossible crime today seems likely to improve his technique in prison and succeed next time he tries, while the person guilty of a manifestly impossible attempt seems much more likely to go on failing harmlessly. But neither Gross nor I believe such facts about the person are relevant to determining what he deserves for his *crime* (though both of us are willing to allow such personal factors to count in mitigation of sentence). So, Gross' explanation of why it is just to impose some punishment for overtly impossible attempts seems to be no explanation at all.

What have we to put in its place? For us, the question must be whether the advantage one takes by attempting the overtly impossible is worth more than the advantage one takes by attempting the manifestly impossible. That question is not hard to answer. For a rational person, a license to attempt the manifestly impossible would be worth nothing. After all, why would a rational person attempt the manifestly impossible when he can do exactly the same physical acts legally (provided he does not intend to do what he knows he cannot do anyway)? He has it within his power to make sure at no cost that he will never need such a license. In contrast, a license to attempt the overtly impossible would have some use. Even a rational person now and then does something stupid. A license to attempt the overtly impossible is, in effect, insurance against one's own stupidity. The license pardons an attempt that fails because the would-be criminal did not think to "ask around," "case out," or otherwise exercise what even he would ordinarily recognize as reasonable criminal care. Such a license would, however, not be worth much. Because its use is more specialized than a general license to attempt (being useful only when a criminal fails to exercise ordinary criminal prudence), it would have to sell for less than a general license to attempt. So, the unfair advantage taken by attempting the overtly impossible must be less than that taken by any covertly impossible attempt but significantly more than that taken by any manifestly impossible attempt.

Notes

Work on this paper was begun under an Organized Research Grant from Illinois State University (June 1984) and completed under National Endowment for the Humanities Fellowship Grant FB-22388-84. I am grateful to both institutions for their support.

1. Though I shall ignore hereafter the distinction between failed and aborted attempts, it may be theoretically interesting. See, especially, Andrew Ashworth, "Criminal Attempts and the Role of Resulting Harm under the Code, and in the Common Law," *Rutgers Law Journal* 19 (Spring 1988): 725-772.

2. *Herman Solem, Warden, Petitioner v. Jerry Buckley Helm*, 103 S. Ct. 3001, 463 U.S. 277 (1983). For details, see Chapter Six.

3. There are at least two notable exceptions. See Plato, *Laws* IX: 877 (an interesting paragraph arguing for a lesser penalty for attempted murder than for successful murder); and Cesare Beccaria, *On Crimes and Punishments*, Ch. XIV (two sentences) and perhaps Ch. XXVII (one sentence). Bentham is notable for his absence.

4. See, for example, Charles R. Carr, "Punishing Attempts," *Pacific Philosophical Quarterly* 62 (January 1981): 61-68; and H. L. A. Hart, *Punishment and Responsibility* (New York: Oxford University Press, 1968), pp. 130-131. The retributive approach is now often represented by the formula $H \times R = P$ where H represents the harm the criminal did; R, the degree of his responsibility; and P, the deserved punishment). Given that representation, the problem attempts poses for retributivism is obvious. If H is zero (that is, if attempts do no harm), then deserved punishment must be zero too. Compare Chapter Three.

5. See, for example, Barbara Wootton, *Crime and the Criminal Law* (London: Stevens, 1963), especially pp. 32-57.

6. See, for example, *Lawrence C. Becker*, "Criminal Attempts and the Theory of the Law of Crimes," *Philosophy and Public Affairs* 3 (Spring 1974): 262-294; and Hart, 128-129.

7. For an extremely useful discussion of these (and other possibilities) see George Fletcher, *Rethinking Criminal Law* (Boston: Little, Brown, and Co., Inc. 1978), pp. 472. For an up-to-date version of the individual-harm approach, see R. A. Duff, "Auctions, Lotteries, and the Punishment of Attempts," *Law and Philosophy* 9 (February 1990): 1-37. Duff's paper is in part a criticism of the argument made here. I try to deal with his objections in Chapter Ten.

8. Hyman Gross, *A Theory of Criminal Justice* (New York: Oxford University Press, 1979), pp. 430-434. For similar criticism of Gross, see Michael Bayles, "Punishment for Attempts', *Social Theory and Practice* 8 (Spring 1982); 19-29.

9. Gross, it should be noted, accepts the idea of a "fair market value" for particular crimes but makes no attempt to work it out. p. 439.

10. *Illinois Annotated Statutes* (St. Paul, MN: West Publishing Company, 1983), ch. 38, secs. 8-4, 12-2, 18-2, 1005-8-1 (2), and 1005-8-3. Note too the

special provision for enhancement of the penalty for armed robbery, ch. 38 sec. 1005-8-2.

11. Ibid., sec. 12-1.

12. Compare Glanville Williams, "Problem of Reckless Attempts," *Criminal Law Review* (June 1983): 365-375. This is, however, not as clear to some people as it seems to Williams and me. See Note, *"State v. Grant*: Is Intent an Essential Element of Criminal Attempt in Maine," *Maine Law Review* 34 (1982): 479-494.

13. For a recent practical discussion of forbidding attempts to do the legally impossible, see Ian Dennis, "The Criminal Attempts Act 1981," *Criminal Law Review*. (January 1982): 5-16.

14. Protective associations in fact make sense only if we assume some market inefficiency. They can be eliminated if the market is large enough to prevent "cornering" and the licenses are liquid enough to make them good investments even for the honest. For more, see Chapter Ten. I am, please note, here defending protective associations only to be charitable to an objection. I am letting them into the model only to show the model can still get the result we want.

15. One reviewer for *Law and Philosophy* objected to the use of the auction as a model that "I would pay more to get a license for theft than for a license for manslaughter, because the latter is an unplanned crime. . . . [even though] I would pay more to prevent manslaughter than theft being committed against me." I do not have space here to provide a full response to this objection. But because it is one that may occur to many readers, let me at least suggest how I might answer it in full: The auction does not require that manslaughter be punished more, less, or the same as theft. These crimes do not belong to the same "type" (that is, they are not crimes a potential criminal would normally choose between). (See Chapter Four.) Because manslaughter and theft are not of the same type, their relative seriousness is not directly a matter of justice (if it is a matter of justice at all). The same would be true of the relative seriousness of theft and attempted theft, or of murder and (say) negligent homicide, *were there not other considerations making the one less serious than the other.* In this Chapter, I explain the relation between theft and attempted theft. I take up the relation between crimes differing only in *mens rea* in Chapters Seven and Ten.

6

Just Deserts for Recidivists

In 1973, a Texas jury convicted William Rummel of felony theft for obtaining $120.75 under false pretenses. The maximum sentence for the crime was then ten years' imprisonment. Rummel received a life sentence. There was no mistake. Under Article 65 of the Texas Penal Code, "Whoever shall have been three times convicted of a felony less than capital shall on such third conviction be imprisoned for life in the penitentiary." Rummel had been convicted of a felony twice before. In 1964, he had been convicted of presenting a credit card with intent to obtain by fraud approximately $80; and in 1969, he had been convicted of passing a forged check for $28.36. The 1973 conviction was his third. The life sentence was mandatory.[1]

Rummel appealed his sentence, arguing that life imprisonment was grossly out of proportion to his crime. On March 18, 1980, the United States Supreme Court, by a five-to-four majority, declared that Rummel's sentence was *not* demonstrably grossly out of proportion to his crime.[2] The decision received some scholarly criticism and no defense. Most criticism concerned the Court's apparent retreat from the standard for demonstrating gross disproportion that had been worked out in *Coker v. Georgia* three years before.[3] Some criticism concerned the rigidity and severity of the Texas recidivist statute itself (that is, its failure to distinguish between kinds of felony, to take account of time between crimes, or to leave room for a judge to consider such factors).[4] But only one critic of the Court's decision actually questioned the justice of recidivist statutes as such.[5] The question is nevertheless a serious one and one that a few legal theorists had already begun to discuss.[6]

The seriousness of the question can be estimated by considering a recidivist case the Supreme Court decided three years after *Rummel* — namely, *Solem v. Helm*. The facts do not differ much from those of *Rummel*. Most of the differences seem to make *Rummel* the more attractive candidate for announcing the doctrine that life imprisonment is too severe a punishment for recidivism when the underlying offense is relatively minor. Yet the Court "chose" *Helm* to announce that doctrine.

Jerry Helm had been convicted by a South Dakota court of trying to pass a "no account" check for $100. Ordinarily, the maximum penalty for the crime would have been five years' imprisonment (and a $5000 fine). Helm, however, had *six* prior felony convictions – three for third-degree burglary and one each for obtaining money under false pretenses, for grand larceny, and for third-offense driving while intoxicated. Under the South Dakota recidivist statute, any person having at least *three* prior convictions was supposed to be given a life sentence without possibility of parole (and a $25,000 fine). Helm was therefore sentenced to life imprisonment without possibility of parole. (How he avoided such a sentence three times before is not explained.)[7]

Helm appealed. On June 28, 1983, the Supreme Court declared his sentence "cruel and unusual" because the penalty was out of proportion to the crime. The decision was by five-to-four vote just as in *Rummel*. Justice Stewart, the only member of the Court to vote differently in *Helm*, did not write an opinion.

Legal scholars will probably not receive the Court's reasoning in *Helm* more kindly than they received it in *Rummel*. Certainly, the attempt to distinguish *Helm* and *Rummel* by making much of the mere technical possibility of parole for Rummel seems more daring than wise. The Court declined to declare the Texas statute unconstitutional "as applied in *Rummel*" (in large part at least) because the majority could not find a "bright line" separating constitutional from unconstitutional applications of the Texas statute. Justice Stewart's one-paragraph concurring opinion is simply the assertion that the Texas statute did not seem to fall below "the minimum level" the Constitution will "tolerate."[8] The Court (or, rather, Justice Stewart) found such a "bright line" in *Helm*. "This sentence," the Court asserted, "is far more severe than the life sentence we considered in *Rummel v. Estelle*."[9] That "bright line" requires distinguishing between the administrative discretion of parole boards and the executive discretion of clemency. The principles governing these cases remain shadowy at best.

My purpose here is to bring those principles to light. My concern is the justice of recidivist statutes, not their application to this or that particular case. I shall be concerned to determine what the law should be, not what it is. My conclusion is that, while some recidivist statutes can be consistent with principles of just punishment, a statute like that under which Rummel or Helm was sentenced cannot be (unless limited to persons convicted of the most serious crimes). The justification of recidivist statutes itself limits how much a recidivist can be punished for his recidivism. The analysis should provide the "bright line" the Court was looking for.

The analysis should do something else too. The argument I make here relies upon the principle of just deserts – that is, upon a version of retributivism. One traditional criticism of retributivism is that it has nothing significant to say about how much to punish. To say that punishment should be proportioned to wrongdoing is (this criticism asserts) to say no more than that a criminal deserves whatever the statute provides for the crime. I have already argued that the criticism is mistaken.[10] This chapter continues the argument. The application I make here of the principle of just deserts shows that that principle, properly understood, provides a standard against which to test the justice of statutory penalties. The application provides further evidence that the principle is far from trivial.

The question of justification is, of course, more than a question of just deserts, more even than a question of justice generally. There may be policies which, though just (in some reasonably obvious sense), would be unworkable, impose needless burdens on others, or otherwise prove unwise. All that hardly needs saying. Showing recidivist statutes to be consistent with the principle of just deserts is not all there is to justifying them. But showing them to be consistent with the principle must be a part of justifying such statutes for any person who recognizes justice as a constraint on what can be done with lawbreakers. And, if the principle is as nontrivial as I believe it to be, such a showing would have to have a major role in any such justification.

Recidivist Statutes

A recidivist is a "persistent," "habitual," or "repeat" offender — that is, a criminal who has been convicted of other crimes before he committed the crime of which he now stands convicted. He is not simply someone who is guilty of many crimes, but one whom previous conviction has not made a law-abiding citizen. I am not a recidivist if I pass two bad checks on two successive days and then am caught. I am a recidivist only if I pass one bad check, am caught and convicted, and then pass another bad check (and am again caught and convicted).

Recidivist "statutes" may be divided into three classes. Some recidivist statutes simply make previous conviction a factor weighing against otherwise deserved leniency. The recidivist receives a sentence more severe than he would have received had he not had a certain number of previous convictions. His sentence cannot be more severe than a first offender might receive for the same crime if there were other aggravating factors. Let us call such recidivist statutes "anti-leniency provisions." Because treating recidivism as a factor weighing against leniency seems to trouble very few, I shall say little more about such provisions. Our concern shall be the other two classes of recidivist statutes.

Most recidivist statutes seem to treat recidivism as if it made the underlying crime worse than any set of mere aggravating factors could. There are two ways in which this can be done. Some recidivist statutes provide for a higher maximum (and minimum) penalty for a second, third, or fourth offense while maintaining some proportion between penalty and most recent crime. For example, Illinois treats a second conviction of certain Class-2 felonies (three to seven years' imprisonment) as conviction of a Class-1 felony (four to fifteen years' imprisonment).[11] Such statutes seem to presuppose that repetition makes a crime *proportionately* worse than it would otherwise be, or shows the criminal to need *proportionately* more incentive to avoid the crime in question than the ordinary run of potential criminals of that sort (however aggravated their crimes).

Other recidivist statutes treat recidivism as a crime preempting the underlying offense. The punishment for which the criminal is liable under such a statute bears no necessary relation to his last crime or to the other one, two, or three crimes that make him a recidivist. Such statutes seem to presuppose that recidivism reveals the habitual criminal to be quite different from the ordinary criminal. The Texas and South Dakota recidivist statutes are extreme (but not unique) examples of this third class of recidivist statute. The penalty is both great and mandatory upon conviction of any felony (after two or three prior convictions). Other examples of this class leave some discretion to the judge or provide that only a certain term of years be added to the otherwise deserved sentence or restrict the class of felonies that can trigger the statute. Let us call all recidivist statutes of this third class "ungraded" and statutes of the second class "graded."

The distinction between graded and ungraded recidivist statutes is pretty rough. A significant number of statutes are not clearly one or the other. For example, is a recidivist statute triggered only by conviction of a violent felony very crudely graded or ungraded but of limited application? (I think it better to treat such statutes as ungraded.) Sometimes the problem is the context of the statute as much as the statute itself. For example, insofar as a statute allows the judge discretion in sentencing, we may not be able to tell from the statute itself whether the legislature intended the judge to take into account the seriousness of the particular crime in setting sentence. We may not be able to decide whether such a statute is in fact graded without examining other provisions of the criminal code or the case law of the jurisdiction. Sometimes the only way to find out is to interview legislators (or judges).

The distinction between graded and ungraded statutes is, however, not affected by what might (or does) happen *after* sentence is passed. Many states still invest parole boards with substantial power. A life sentence can, in practice, be only a few years if the parole board so decides; and the parole board may take into account the seriousness of a prisoner's crime when deciding whether he has served long enough. An ungraded statute may have much the same effect as a graded statute. Indeed, part of the reason the Supreme Court decided against Rummel was that he would be eligible for parole in twelve years, making his (minimum) sentence for recidivism little more than the maximum he could have received for his third crime alone. Though the court may have been right to consider the possibility of parole a factor mitigating the severity of the statute, I shall hereafter be concerned only with recidivist statutes as written (together with their statutory context). I shall assume that it is always better, all else equal, to have a statute that is itself just than to have an unjust statute combined with some mechanism of discretion that can sometimes do justice only by defeating the letter of the statute. Texas practice makes recidivism punishable by what is more or less an indeterminate sentence (with a twelve year minimum). Whatever objections there are to indeterminate sentencing (and there are many)[12] would apply to such a practice. But indeterminate sentencing is not the topic of this Chapter.

Recidivism and Theories of Punishment

Graded recidivist statutes seem to have one history and spirit; ungraded, another. Ungraded statutes seem to date only from the end of the nineteenth century. They typically apply very generally (that is, to anyone convicted of a certain number of felonies). They impose a severe penalty (for example, life imprisonment) but not for the sake of severity (or, at least, not for the sake of severity alone). Ungraded recidivist statutes have their roots in concepts of reform. The traditional defense of such statutes has been that, because earlier attempts at reform have failed, the only way remaining to prevent further crimes by this criminal is to imprison him indefinitely or, at least, until he is likely to have outgrown his criminal ways. Ungraded statutes have been the work of an articulate movement.[13]

Graded statutes, though having a much longer history, have not been the work of such a movement. The earliest American example of such a statute seems to be the New Plymouth colony's provision for burglary (and robbery). A first offense was punished by branding the letter *B* on the offender's right hand; the second offense, by branding with the same letter on the left hand and by a "severe whipping" as well; and the third offense, by death because the offender had proved "incorrigible."[14] The Massachusetts colony had a similar provision as early as 1642.[15] But recidivist statutes were not confined to New England. A Virginia statute of 1705 punished the first offense of hog-stealing by thirty lashes (or 10 fine); the second, by placing the thief in the pillory for two hours with his ears nailed, at the end of which time his ears were cut loose from the nails; and the third offense, by death.[16]

Such early statutes are a rarity. American law made no general provision for recidivism until the nineteenth century. Until then, each special provision for recidivism seems to have had a special story suggesting such statutes may have been thought of as mitigating the deserved punishment of first and second offenders rather than as enhancing the punishment of recidivists. The special stories also help to explain the relative rarity of such statutes. Under English common law until the nineteenth century (and its American counterpart until the Revolution), felonies were generally punishable by death, and such crimes as burglary, robbery, and grand theft would ordinarily be felonies. Thus, until 1647, hog-stealing in Virginia was so punished even upon a first conviction. The Virginia legislature then reduced the penalty to a year's penal servitude (or a fine of one thousand pounds of tobacco) because, though common, hog-stealing was seldom prosecuted.[17] The statute of 1705 seems to have been a compromise between the severity of the pre-1647 law and the leniency of 1647. Perhaps the legislature wished to be sure that "incorrigibles" got what they deserved.

Graded statutes seem to have their roots in concepts of deterrence and retribution. The traditional defense of such statutes is (a) that the higher penalty is necessary to deter those whom the lower penalty has not deterred or (b) that recidivism reveals a greater depravity deserving greater punishment (the "incorrigibility" of the New Plymouth statute).

The historical connection between kind of statute and kind of defense is, however, hardly more than a tendency. Various defenses may well appear where they should not. For example, as early as 1841, the Supreme Judicial Court of Massachusetts upheld a *graded* statute in part because the statute merely inflicted "a more severe punishment upon those who, having been once committed to the state prison, have failed of being reformed by the penitentiary discipline there administered."[18]   And in 1895, the U.S. Supreme Court gave these reasons (among others) for upholding an *anti-leniency provision* of Missouri's penal code: (a) that the statute "imposes a higher punishment for the same offense upon one who proves, by a second or third conviction, that the former punishment has been inefficacious in doing the work of reform," (b) that "the punishment for the second is increased, because by his persistence in the perpetration of crime, he has evinced a depravity ... which ... needs to be restrained by severer penalties," and (c) "that repetition of the offense aggravates guilt." The first reason concerns reform (or perhaps "special deterrence") – that is, the good effect of the particular punishment on the particular criminal's future conduct; the second, (general) deterrence ("the need to restrain by [threat of] severer penalties" all those whose depravity is too great to be restrained by lesser penalties); and the third, retribution ("aggravated guilt").[19]   In 1980, the Supreme Court quoted this same list when it upheld Texas' *ungraded* statute in *Rummel v. Estelle*.

Though the various defenses of recidivist statutes may sometimes appear side by side, they are not easily made compatible. Considerations of reform make *graded* recidivist statutes suspect. The prison that failed to reform a criminal one, two, or three times before is not likely to succeed this time just because it will have *proportionately* longer to work on him. The shock of imprisonment has not worked. Neither has the rehabilitation provided the criminal while in prison. So, it would seem, the only way left to prevent future crimes by this criminal is to hold him until he is no longer a criminal, however long that may be. There may or may not be any way to know in advance how long it will be before a certain criminal ceases to be a criminal. But what is almost certain is that, however long it will be, that time is not likely to be proportioned to the seriousness of the last crime. The logic of reform, as often noted, does not require any particular connection between past con- duct and future treatment. Failed reform suggests incapacitation, not a graded response.

Deterrence and retribution are more compatible with each other than either is with reform. Both require gradation of punishment. Considera- tions of retribution require gradation because crimes differ in seriousness and (according to retributive theory) what a criminal deserves for his crime varies with its seriousness. Considerations of deterrence lead to gradation in another way. The point of a system of penalties is (according to deter- rence theory) to discourage all wrongdoing insofar as possible and, where that is not possible, to discourage the greater wrong. A system of penalties punishing a minor felony in the same way as a major felony does not deter major felonies. The system is inconsistent with deterrence. For example, as far as one can tell from the Texas recidivist statutes, Rummel might as well have robbed a bank of a million dollars as obtained that $120.75 under false pretenses. Considerations of deterrence do not support such statutes.

Though deterrence and retribution are more compatible with each other than either is with reform, they are not all that compatible. While both recommend graded statutes, they do not necessarily recommend the same grading. Considerations of deterrence might, for example, suggest higher penalties for recidivists committing crimes hard to detect, the greater severity of punishment compensating for the greater temptation of "easy pickings." Considerations of retribution would, however, suggest more severe penalties only for recidivists committing more serious crimes, and a crime is not more serious just because it is hard to detect.

We must, then, make some decision about theories of punishment before we can consider whether recidivist statutes are just. Even if we agree that reform, incapacitation, deterrence, and retribution are all legitimate aims of punishment, we must still decide how they fit together in a theory of just punishment before we can proceed. The alternatives seem to be few.

Reform is not quite a theory of *just punishment* at all. The "medical model" upon which reform relies makes reform an alternative to punishment rather than punishment strictly so called. Punishment is an evil. Treatment, even forced treatment, is not an evil (or, at least, is not clearly so). The medical model also tends to make talk of justice more or less irrelevant. We understand what "incompetent medical treatment" is, what "excessive," "poor," or "unnecessary" treatment is. But we have no standard use for "unjust medical treatment." Whatever the merits of reforming criminals, it is, I think, now widely recognized that reforming them cannot be the primary determinant of what makes the punishment just.

Incapacitation fails as well as a theory of just punishment, but for quite different reasons. Incapacitation is certainly an evil for the one incapacitated. Incapacitation is, however, not an aim general enough to be the primary aim of punishment, just or not. Many punishments (for example, fine, suspended sentence, or restitution) simply do not incapacitate. Incapacitation is, at best, the reason for incarcerating rather than punishing in some other way. And, it is probably better thought of as only *a* reason for that. Given the fallibility of predictions of future conduct, it seems unjust to incarcerate simply because we suppose ourselves to be incapacitating a criminal. Incapacitation seems to be a legitimate reason to choose a certain mode or degree of punishment only when such a punishment would be just for other reasons and we are wondering whether we should show clemency.

Deterrence is an aim general enough to be the primary aim of punishment. Deterrence is, however, not itself an aim likely to lead to a theory of *just* punishment. Deterrence (as often noted) seems to justify public rather than private execution, abolishing the insanity defense to discourage those who might suppose they could escape punishment by feigning insanity, and perhaps exemplary punishment of some who do not deserve such punishment for what they themselves did.

Acknowledging such weaknesses, recent deterrent theorists have incorporated fairness into their theories to limit what can be done to deter.[20] The distinction between deterrent theorists and retributivists has become ever more subtle. Yet, insofar as deterrence remains distinct from retribution, there remains one serious objection not likely to be overcome. Deterrence requires one to choose penalties (in part at least) to discourage crime. The practical test of any penalty is supposed to be its effect on crime rate. Deterrent theory thus presupposes knowledge of the causal relation between penalties and crime rate (or, at least, some relatively reliable way to measure that connection) — that is to say, it presupposes a relatively sophisticated sociology of crime. That is exactly what we do not have. The variables connecting statutory penalty and crime rate are so many, so incompletely known, and so hard to keep track of that a sociologist's prediction of effect on crime rate of this or that change in statutory penalty is likely to be little closer to the mark than anyone else's. As a theory of how much we should punish, deterrence seems to be a practical dead end.[21]

That leaves retributivism. Retributivism is, of course, primarily a theory of *just* punishment. Punishment is, according to retributivism, justified because (and only insofar as) it is deserved — that is, because it is a fair return for the crime. Traditional criticism of retributivism has concerned not its justice so much as (a) the sense of punishing criminals as much as they deserve (is that not sometimes pointless cruelty?) or (b) the practical problem of proportioning punishment to desert (how do we measure criminal desert?). These criticisms have, I think, lately received answers sufficient to make retribution seem the most fruitful approach for both theory and practice.

The answer to the first criticism is that the advantages to everyone of a system of punishment proportioning punishment to wrongdoing are sufficient to make everyone prefer the principle of just deserts to any alternative principle. The advantages include some deterrence (because in general the greater wrongs are also the more tempting), personal security (because what one suffers in punishment will ordinarily be connected with what one knowingly does), and recognition of certain important rights of a person (for example, the right to have one's acts taken seriously). Proportioning punishment to wrongdoing does not, however, require that every criminal suffer as he deserves. Retribution is consistent with occasional clemency. Retribution merely forbids punishing a criminal *more* than he deserves, whatever the social advantage in deterrence, incapacitation, or reform.[22] That answers the first criticism.

The second criticism has been answered by working out in detail what retributivism requires. Under the banner of "just deserts," retributivists have recently proposed a number of model rules for sentencing.[23] I myself have tried to provide rules any legislature could follow to determine statutory penalties in accordance with desert.[24]

So, it seems, the question whether recidivist statutes can be justified must be understood to ask at least whether such statutes are consistent with retributivism. The question now is, What does a recidivist deserve?

Retributivist Approaches to Justifying Recidivist Statutes

There are two approaches retributivists might take to justifying recidivist statutes. One is to treat recidivist statutes as foreign to the criminal law, an exception to the general rule that punishment should be proportioned to wrongdoing. We might call this "the external approach." The other approach is to try to show that persistence in crime somehow makes the last crime worse or constitutes a distinct crime. The recidivist somehow *deserves* extra punishment. We might call this "the internal approach."

Retributive theorists have in fact had very little to say in defense of recidivist statutes. Hyman Gross may well provide the only example of the external approach. He dismisses recidivist statutes as "crude counterparts of civil commitment."[25] While he gives no argument for so treating them, it is not hard (given what he does say) to figure out what his argument would be: The recidivist is (Gross's argument suggests) not the sort of person the criminal law presupposes. The recidivist's persistence in crime after repeated detection and conviction makes it likely that he is someone lacking the personal resources necessary to be a law-abiding citizen. There is even some empirical evidence for this characterization of the recidivist (though Gross does not mention it). Sentences for serious offenses are ordinarily so long that few persistent bank robbers, rapists, or arsonists live long enough to qualify as recidivists. The typical recidivist is not too different from Rummel or Helm, a petty criminal, usually "shiftless, work-shy . . . , [one] for whom petty stealing represents the line of least resistance."[26]

There is much to be said against the external approach. Historically, retributivism has been a theory of punishment that made a point of *not* inquiring too deeply into what people in fact are. Part of treating people with respect (it was thought) is not to look behind the *persona*. Much of the appeal of retributivism comes from its insistence on treating the criminal with the same respect we would treat anyone else. Even the recidivist may prefer retributive punishment to the kindness that would hold him indefinitely for his own good or the good of others. The external approach amounts to an admission that retributivism has nothing useful to say about recidivist statutes. Retributivists may in fact have to make such an admission once all other alternatives have been exhausted. But there is no reason to make such an admission before then. I shall therefore ignore the external approach.

Representatives of the internal approach are even scarcer than representatives of the external. Andrew von Hirsch is the best example I have been able to find among reputable theorists. He is, as it turns out, not a good example. In *Doing Justice*, he asserted that "repetition alters the degree of culpability that may be ascribed to the offender."[27] Repetition following conviction is more culpable because (according to von Hirsch) the offender has persisted in behavior after having been forcefully censured for it through his prior punishment. The offender is now (von Hirsch *seems* to by saying) more culpable because he is defying the law as well as breaking it. Such defiance deserves additional punishment and that is what recidivist statutes provide.

Several retributivists have criticized *Doing Justice* for defending recidivist statutes in this way. Defiance (they argued) is a state of mind, not an act, and so does not deserve independent punishment though it might serve as a reason for not mitigating otherwise deserved punishment. Von Hirsch's response to that criticism was surprising. He agreed with it, denying only that he held the position criticized. He pointed out (correctly) that the discussion of repetition in *Doing Justice* occurs during a defense of proposed *sentencing* standards, not of standards for setting *statutory* penalties. His concern there was only whether previous convictions may properly be taken into account as a factor weighing against otherwise deserved leniency. While the argument may sound as if it could be used to defend graded or ungraded recidivist statutes, it was not so intended.

Having thus cleared up the misunderstanding of *Doing Justice*, von Hirsch argued that both graded and ungraded recidivist statutes are inconsistent with the principle of just deserts. His argument puts nicely the problem of providing an internal retributivist defense of graded or ungraded statutes. It is an argument from desert. The two-time offender does not, he says,

> deserve cumulated blame for both his misdeeds because he has been censured for the first act already. What the actor does deserve is the full measure of blame for the current act: he is no longer in a position to claim a scaled down response.[28]

To commit a crime is (for most retributivists including von Hirsch at that time) to gain an unfair advantage over those who do not commit it. Punishment (or clemency) reestablishes the balance between benefits and burdens by taking back (or at least doing away with) the unfair advantage. Once a criminal has served his sentence, he has "paid his debt to society." He is again no more deserving of punishment than he was before he committed the crime. His next crime gives him (so von Hirsch seems to suggest) another unfair advantage and it is that new unfair advantage that makes him deserve a new punishment. The new punishment is (the argument continues) necessarily proportioned to the new crime. The new crime sets the upper limit (even if it does not set a lower limit). That upper limit is the same whatever the criminal did before he did the act in question. Repetition does not itself make any particular act worse. But being a repeat offender does show one to be less deserving of clemency (at least less deserving than being a first offender would, all else equal). That is the only connection between repetition and desert. So even *graded* recidivist statutes necessarily punish a criminal more than he deserves for his act because they treat past crimes as factors *positively* aggravating the present act (rather than as factors merely weighing against the criminal's deserving clemency). "If the offender has a very large number of convictions," von Hirsch notes, then

> there may be an understandable desire to begin to respond more severely. But that would have to rest, in my view, on utilitarian notions (e.g., the notion that harsher measures need to be tried when lesser ones have failed so often before . . .), rather than on the idea of the offender deserving more punishment . . . [29]

In short, retributivism does not (accordingly to von Hirsch) have the resources to justify any recidivist statute (beyond anti-leniency provisions). The principle of just deserts justifies the use of anti-leniency provisions by invoking considerations *barring* the use of graded or ungraded recidivist statutes (supposing it is unjust to punish a criminal more than he deserves for his act).

For retributivists, then, the problem is to explain how a single *act* of wrongdoing can deserve more punishment than another if the two differ only in that the doer of one is a recidivist while the doer of the other is not. I shall present my solution in this way. First, I shall explain how the version of retributivism I have been defending requires us to set up the problem. Second, I shall show the problem can be solved once properly set up. And last, I shall consider certain likely objections. Answering those objections will bring us back to Rummel (and Helm).

The Special Advantage of Doing It Again

We may, I think, assume that recidivist statutes (other than anti-leniency provisions) punish a criminal *more* than he deserves for his most recent act or, at least, more than he would deserve for it were it not the last of a series. To assume otherwise would be to assimilate graded and ungraded statutes to anti-leniency provisions. The assimilation is implausible. Many recidivist statutes permit (and some require) a life sentence upon conviction of the triggering offense. To assimilate graded or ungraded statutes to anti-leniency provisions would be to declare that even the most minor felony may *deserve* life imprisonment, that all gradation in punishment of felonies is a matter of clemency (or, at least, of desert independent of the crime itself), and thus that the principle of just desert is largely irrelevant to questions of how much to punish. While some graded or ungraded statutes may be disguised anti-leniency provisions (for example, the Virginia hog-stealing law discussed above), most recidivist statutes do not seem to be. Most seem designed to punish a criminal more than he would deserve for what he did were he not a recidivist. I know of no reason to suppose such statutes are not what they seem.

The principle of just deserts does not allow a criminal to be punished more severely than he deserves for what he did. Punishment is justified (according to the principle) only insofar as proportioned to the unfair advantage the criminal took by his crime (unless part is forgiven for reasons of personal desert, public policy, or the like considerations independent of the crime itself). Punishment undoes the unfair advantage a criminal takes by committing the crime. Punishment "pays a debt to society" that the crime creates, a debt that is owed until paid or forgiven. The principle of just deserts looks at the crime to set the maximum penalty, looking at the criminal only for reasons to show clemency. If the principle allows for graded or ungraded recidivist statutes, the recidivist must deserve punishment for what he did more severe than a first offender would deserve for what he did. The recidivist must take an unfair advantage that a first offender does not take by an otherwise identical act. The crime triggering the recidivist statute must either itself be worse than the crime a first offender commits (all appearances to the contrary notwithstanding) or the recidivist must take an unfair advantage in addition to that taken by committing the triggering crime.

Let us first consider the possibility that the crime triggering the recidivist statute could be worse (that is, deserve more punishment) merely because a recidivist did it. The harm done would (by hypothesis) be the same whether a recidivist or a first offender did it. There would, therefore, be no reason to fear the act more simply because a recidivist was doing it. And, if there is no reason to fear the act more simply because a recidivist was doing it, how could a recidivist take a greater unfair advantage by doing the act than would a first offender doing an act otherwise identical? In other words, given the auction we have imagined, what reason could there be for the "price" of a "license" to be higher because a recidivist won the bidding?

Well, there are some reasons. That the person bidding for a particular license is a recidivist may affect what he or others are willing to bid for the license. For example, a professional criminal is likely to know how to put the license to better use and so would be willing to bid more. Others, seeing what the professional bids, may also bid more, supposing her to have an eye for undervalued licenses. Such reasons may also have a place in the justification of recidivist statutes. They are, however, not relevant now. Our concern is what the recidivist deserves for his act, whatever else he may be or do (apart from the bare fact of his previous convictions).

A recidivist is not necessarily a professional criminal or someone likely to commit many crimes before he is caught. While some recidivist statutes do require proof of criminal life beyond the fact of previous convictions, most do not. The typical recidivist may (for all the language of the typical recidivist statutes indicates) be an amateur who got caught each time he tried to break the law. The typical recidivist either deserves his punishment simply for being a recidivist (rather than for being a professional criminal, "poacher," or the like) or he does not deserve punishment for being a recidivist (but for being something else). To assume (without proof) that recidivists are professional criminals, criminals who have gotten away with many crimes before being caught for this one, or anything of the sort, would make recidivists liable for punishment when we cannot prove they deserve it (or, at least, when we have not proved they deserve it).

Since presuming guilt in that way seems unjust, we must hereafter imagine the auction so that the identity of this or that bidder will have no effect upon the ultimate price. Let us imagine that the bidders do not know who is buying. Many of those at the auction may, for example, be professional agents hired by anonymous principals. The bidders may know the agents, but they cannot know the principals. The agents may, however, have to reveal certain information (for example, identity or credit rating of principals) to be permitted to act for them. Such information would be revealed in confidence to the "management" of the auction, not to the other participants. Such arrangements are not all that uncommon at auctions where the fact that a certain person was bidding would lead others to bid more than they would otherwise (for example, because the person is known for spotting good values).

That brings us to considerations apart from the crime triggering the recidivist statute. We might, I think, suppose that recidivist statutes could be justified by analogy with provisions for parole revocation. What recidivist statutes really do (we might suppose) is to take account of what the criminal deserved for his previous crimes. He did not receive full punishment for them before because he was shown leniency. We suspended part of his debt to society on condition he contract no more. He has now contracted more and so brought down on himself the old debts he would otherwise have been free of.

The appeal of such an analysis is undeniable. Under it, recidivist statutes would be no harder to justify than is reimposing a suspended sentence when the terms of suspension have been violated. But the problems of such an analysis are undeniable too. Let me point out three. *First*, ungraded statutes do not seem well suited for analogy with statutes providing for parole revocation unless conviction of even two or three minor felonies is enough to make someone deserve long imprisonment. Because at least part of what shocks us about Rummel's life sentence is that he does not seem to deserve it even for all three offenses together, the analogy with parole revocation would at most provide a justification for graded statutes (and ungraded statutes with low minimum sentences). *Second*, even graded recidivist statutes do not much resemble statutes governing revocation of parole. The previous convictions are the primary determinant of what a parole violator suffers if he is found to have violated parole. His present conviction is the primary determinant of what a recidivist suffers if he is found to be a recidivist. And *third*, recidivist statutes *never* give credit for time served for previous convictions (or otherwise take into account what the recidivist has suffered for his previous wrongdoing). A recidivist may have served the maximum sentence each time and still receive the maximum enhancement allowable under the recidivist statute. No one, as far as I know, has argued that such an enhancement would be unjust.

These problems together make it seem reasonable not to try to analyze recidivist statutes on analogy with parole revocation. We must instead suppose the recidivist to be someone who "paid his debt to society" for each of his past crimes before he committed the crime triggering the recidivist statute. While not having a "clean slate," he nevertheless has a slate clear of outstanding "debts" apart from those incurred by his most recent crime.

What he deserves now is, of course, a function of his criminal record. His criminal record is what makes him a recidivist. But what he deserves is not a function of what he deserved in punishment for the previous crimes and has yet to suffer. If recidivist statutes are justified, they are justified because a recidivist deserves more punishment for what he did this time even if he got what he deserved for each of his previous crimes.

So, to say that a recidivist deserves more punishment for what he did than would a first offender for the same act must be to say simply that the recidivist (by an act seemingly identical to that of a first offender) takes an unfair advantage which the first offender does not take. But what might that advantage be? That advantage must, I think, be a "second-order" advantage — that is to say, *the unfair advantage of taking more than one's fair share of unfair advantage*. Even the bare statement of the advantage suggests why theorists have overlooked it. How can there be a "fair share" of "unfair advantage"? A good question. Having thus identified the special advantage a recidivist must take (if he takes any special advantage at all), we must now try to make sense of it. I shall use the auction described above to do that. Of course, that auction is a heuristic device, not a device of proof. Once we understand the advantage a recidivist takes that other criminals do not, we may forget the auction. We need only apply what the auction has revealed to the criminal law as we know it. So, back to the auction.

The Relative Seriousness of Recidivism

Being able to commit a crime with impunity is, we agreed, an advantage if others cannot do the same. That is the advantage corresponding to the punishment a criminal deserves for his crime. *Being able to buy a license* giving one such impunity should be an advantage too if not everyone else can do the same. This second-order advantage is the advantage that must correspond to the punishment a recidivist deserves for his recidivism. We can easily imagine a procedure for gauging what such a second-order advantage would be worth.

Imagine that our "crime auction" is permanent and holds daily sessions (like a stock exchange). Anyone may enter a bid as often as he likes without charge provided he did not buy a license on another day, or provided he did not buy certain licenses on other days (or a certain number of them), or provided he did not do so within a certain period. The details are not important now. Each variation simply corresponds to a different recidivist statute. The recidivist is to be thought of as someone who, having bought one or more licenses on one or more previous days, returns to buy again. The recidivist may be distinguished from the (ordinary) multiple offender. The multiple offender is to be thought of as someone who buys more than one license on a single day.

Imagine too that, even if someone has made the disqualifying purchases, he can still gain entry if either he agrees to limit his bidding to certain crimes (that is, to those that would not trigger the recidivist statute) or he has a *special* license-to-enter. The procedure need not be complex. The "management" could check credentials at the door. Agents could be required to reveal their principals (and would do so truthfully). Every name could be checked against the record of previous purchases. Someone who had made the disqualifying purchases could either be tagged to limit his bidding or sent down the hall to get a license-to-enter.

Down the hall would be a second auction, one at which one could buy a license allowing its owner to enter the first auction, to bid on certain licenses, and to buy any for which he was the highest bidder, just as if he had never made the disqualifying purchases. The exact terms of such a second-order license would correspond to what a particular recidivist statute designated as the "triggering offense." Though it is customary at auctions for one to pay for what he buys before getting it, we must imagine our "second-order auction" to work otherwise. Recidivists do not "pay" for their recidivism until they "pay" for the triggering offense. So, to make the analogy between the criminal's unfair advantage and the price of auctioned licenses as close as possible, we must imagine that the purchaser of a license-to-enter would not have to pay for it until (and unless) he had bought the appropriate first-order license. The second-order license would be free unless used to make a first-order purchase.

The recidivist is, then, someone who (unlike a first offender) needs two licenses to commit a crime with impunity — a first-order license for the crime in question and a second-order license permitting him to buy the first. Thinking of the recidivist in this way suggests several questions relevant to the justification of recidivist statutes. Would a recidivist pay any more than a first offender to do the same act? How much more would he pay (assuming he would pay more)? How much would it be fair to make him pay for the second-order license (if it is fair to make him pay anything)? Why would it be fair? How are such considerations relevant to the justice of actual recidivist statutes? These questions are closely related, each but the first presupposing an answer to the one before. Let us take them in order.

Would a recidivist pay any more than a first offender to do the same act? Of course. The would-be recidivist has no choice if he is to be a (licensed) recidivist. He must (we are supposing) have a first-order license to commit his crime and a second-order license to get the first. The price of the first-order license will be set at an auction in which he will have to bid against would-be first offenders. Unlike the would-be recidivist, first offenders would not have to take account of the price of a second-order license when deciding how much to bid. The price of a second-order license would be a surcharge only recidivists have to pay. The would-be recidivist must operate under a competitive disadvantage.

Why then would anyone (or, at least, any rational agent) become a recidivist? The answer must be that a first-order license is sometimes worth enough to the would-be recidivist for him to be willing to buy it even with the surcharge (and even though no one else is willing to pay the price). We need not inquire whether the would-be recidivist is willing to pay what others are not because he is willing to accept a smaller "profit" than others are, or because he is a "more efficient producer of crime," or because he enjoys crime more than those bidding against him. Every auction has its highest bidder. All we need do for our purposes is assume that would-be recidivists are (for these or other reasons) not necessarily priced out of a fair auction of first-order licenses. Such an assumption is, I think, plausible.

Or, at least, it is so long as the price of a second-order license is not high. How much then would a would-be recidivist have to pay for his second-order license? Well, that depends. First-order licenses are limited in number (we have assumed) to preserve a certain degree of social order, but second-order licenses need not be limited for that reason. Recidivism as such does not add to the number of licensed crimes. Recidivism merely affects the distribution of first-order licenses among would-be criminals. As we have imagined the situation so far, the auction's "management" could, if it chose, even issue as many second-order licenses as there were would-be recidivists.

But that is not the most interesting possibility. Our auction is (we may assume) a business competing with other businesses (for example, the stock market or land speculation). Would-be recidivists must (let us assume) have a second-order license only because a government regulation requires it (for reasons we shall consider when we come to the question of fairness). The government does not, however, set the number or price of such licenses. Management is free to adopt any fair procedure it chooses for distributing licenses. Management might set a price and let price limit demand, or limit the supply and let supply determine price, or combine one or both these strategies with some merchandising gimmick. Whatever management does, it will do (we may assume) to make the largest profit possible from sale of second-order licenses. If (as we have already imagined) management decides to sell licenses by auction, they would have to limit supply. If there were enough licenses to go around, who would bid more than a penny?

Does keeping the supply of second-order licenses below demand mean that the price of such licenses will be high? I think not. A would-be recidivist pays for a second-order license only if he buys a first-order one too. He will buy a first-order license only if the price of the second-order license does not eat up whatever makes a particular first-order license seem attractive to him at the price (while all other bidders are at least indifferent). The difference between the maximum some nonrecidivist is willing to pay and what a would-be recidivist is willing to pay is not likely to be large. Indeed, the difference is likely to be so small that the management might well wish to sell a relatively large number of licenses (at low prices) or to offer a range of licenses (each pardoning a certain kind of crime). A would-be petty thief may, for example, not be able to pay the price a would-be bank robber would be willing to pay for a second-order license. The management would miss out on a whole market if it auctioned only a relatively few general second-order licenses on which both the would-be thief and the would-be bank robber had to bid.

How much would it be fair to make a would-be recidivist pay for a second-order license? If the outcome of a fair procedure is itself fair, then it would be fair to make a would-be recidivist pay whatever he bid to win the second-order auction. But the auction we have imagined is fair (given our previous assumptions) if, and only if, it is fair to require a second-order license of a would-be recidivist. Is that fair? Arguably, yes. The auction we have imagined assures that (in general at least) crime pays. That is, one would not ordinarily buy a first-order license if one did not expect to benefit. The price of a particular first-order license is not only a fair price (because the auction itself is a fair procedure) but also a price allowing one to benefit from committing the crime (or, at least, to achieve a net gain in expected utility by the purchase). Because society can tolerate only so much crime, the benefits of crime must be a scarce good. Considerations of distributive justice would require (or at least would permit) distributing even such a peculiar good as evenly as possible (all else equal). Requiring recidivists to pay what amounts to a surcharge to commit additional crimes gives non-recidivists a better chance of getting a first-order license than they would otherwise have. Reducing the recidivist's "profit margin" helps to distribute the "profits of crime" more evenly than they would otherwise be distributed. Given that we must have a certain amount of crime and that crime is profitable, it seems only fair to regulate crime to assure that more people (rather than fewer) get to share in the profits.

Why not then simply forbid recidivism outright (since that would make the distribution of criminal profits even more even)? That is a question our imagined auction certainly does suggest. But it is not a question we need take much time with. We might as well ask, Why not forbid all crime rather than auction off licenses? We could, of course, have imagined our auction differently. We could, for example, have imagined it with a flat prohibition on buying more than one first-order license in a lifetime. But, had we imagined it that way, we could not have used it to gauge the unfair advantage a recidivist takes that a first offender does not take by the same (first-order) crime. We formed our model to help us gauge unfair advantage. Unfortunately, the form suggests a question having no counterpart in any actual system of criminal law. The criminal law (in effect) forbids recidivism by forbidding the triggering offense. To forbid recidivism as well by special statute is redundant unless violating that statute carries with it an added penalty. The criminal law need not make special provision for recidivism. But, if it does, the provision will be the analogue of a second-order license, not of a flat prohibition.

Objections and Replies

Earlier I said that recidivist statutes (whether graded or ungraded) may be thought of as providing punishment for the unfair advantage of taking more than one's fair share of unfair advantage. At the time, that statement probably had all the clarity of a communication from Delphi. By now, though, it should seem clear enough. The auction has helped us to see what that special unfair advantage might be and, indeed, helped us to make a rough estimate of its size. If we think of the value of that special advantage as the price the appropriate second-order license would bring in a (relatively) free market (for example, our second-order auction), it seems that the special advantage a recidivist takes simply by being a recidivist must be a *small fraction* of the advantage corresponding to the advantage of committing the triggering first-order crime. If punishment should be proportioned to the unfair advantage a criminal takes by his crime, the recidivist cannot deserve much punishment for his recidivism. The maximum punishment should be no more than a small fraction of the punishment for the triggering offense (assuming that punishment itself to correspond to what is deserved for that offense). So, the argument of the last section seems to show that many recidivist statutes, especially ungraded statutes with high minimum sentences, must punish some recidivists (for example, all persons guilty of only lesser felonies) far more than they deserve. Such statutes are (according to the principle of just deserts) unjust.

Many will, I think, find this analysis implausible. Some may find it so because the notion of "fair share of crime" itself seems so bizarre that it must call into question any conclusion dependent on it. How can there be a "fair share" of such a thing? Others may be willing to allow that even criminals can divide loot fairly but refuse to accept the auction as a measure of desert. The auction has (it might be said) nothing to do with the realities of the criminal law. Crime is not licensed, even retroactively. Crime is suppressed as much as it can be and condemned when it cannot be suppressed. Still others would accept the analysis, auction and all, did it not lead to a conclusion seemingly so against practice. The analysis shows that penalties for recidivism are far too high. The analysis thus impugns the practice of a century. How could so many legislatures (and courts) have been so wrong for so long? Forced to choose between the wisdom of an age and the new analysis given here, many may choose against the analysis. Others, while not finding any one of these (or other) objections telling, may yet find the sheer number decisive. Where bees gather, there must be honey.

Such objections do raise substantial questions. But, upon examination, they will be found not to raise questions that cannot be answered satisfactorily. They certainly do not, I believe, provide sufficient reason to reject the analysis. Some merely misunderstand the limited problem addressed. Some call for clarification of what has already been said. Some make important points but not ones weakening the analysis. And some simply disappear in the course of answering others. While I can not deal here with all the objections that might be raised, I can, I think, say enough about the most obvious to give potential critics reason to believe that I might be able to dispose of their objections too and to suggest how I might do it. I hope this strategy will not appear too evasive.

One sort of objection might be put this way: The very notion of a "fair share of crime" imports into the theory of punishment what belongs nowhere or, if it belongs somewhere, belongs in a theory of distributive justice. My analysis (it is objected) treats punishment as a means of distributing goods, not just as a means of correcting wrongs. That simply confuses corrective justice with distributive justice. Let us call this "an objection from justice."

There are two replies to be made to this objection. The first is that it misunderstands what I set out to do. My purpose is *not* to provide a full defense of recidivist statutes but merely to *explain* what punishments for recidivism can be justified under the principle of just deserts (given the existence of recidivist statues). To explain that, I had to explain as well what would be required to justify recidivist statutes (as a part of the *criminal* law). And I have defended recidivist statutes against one criticism — that is, the criticism that they are *all* inconsistent with the principle of just deserts. I have argued that *some* are not. But I have made no positive defense of such statutes (and, indeed, my own opinion is that, apart from anti-leniency provisions, the law is probably better off without them). My chief conclusion is that justifying recidivist statutes presupposes the second-order notion of a "fair share of crime." *If* that notion is incoherent, confused, or otherwise fatally flawed, so too (given my analysis) is any *just-deserts* defense of recidivist statutes. Recidivist statutes must then be defended on other grounds or not at all. If, however, as I believe, the notion of a "fair share of crime" is not incoherent, confused, or otherwise fatally flawed, recidivist statutes (graded and ungraded) can be justified under the principle of just deserts — but only if the penalty is limited to a small fraction of the penalty for the triggering offense. Objections to the notion of a "fair share of crime" are, then, not exactly objections to the argument presented here.

That is my first reply to this objection from justice. My second is that the case for some fatal flaw in the notion of "fair share of crime" has yet to be made and there is reason to believe it cannot be made. "Fairness" is a principle more general than "justice." One cannot be just without being fair, but one can be fair without being just. That greater generality is what makes possible a coherent notion of "fair share of crime" (if such a notion can be coherent in a way that the notion of a "*just* share of crime" cannot be). The principle of just deserts is what makes that generality useful. The principle requires punishment to be proportioned to unfair advantage of a certain kind — that is, the unfair advantage one takes by lawbreaking. The principle is a just principle because the proportion it requires is permitted by justice (or perhaps because it serves the ends of justice in some positive way — for example, by reestablishing at least in part the balance of benefits and burdens of a reasonably just legal system which the crime disturbed). The principle of just deserts is, however, silent about what the laws should prohibit. The principle simply requires that if certain acts are prohibited on pain of punishment, the punishment be limited in a certain way. The question of just deserts arises only if recidivism is prohibited — that is, only if the law has been structured as if the recidivist had taken some advantage the first offender had not.

So, the analysis given here cannot confuse corrective justice with distributive justice. The criminal law prevents wrongs by prohibiting certain acts. One cannot *correct* an injustice by prohibiting it. The criminal law corrects injustice only by punishing (or forgiving). Insofar as recidivist statutes punish prohibited acts (within a relatively just legal system), they are concerned with corrective justice in a way consistent with serving distributive justice (that is, in the way the criminal law in general does that). Punishment under recidivist statutes helps to reestablish the preexisting fair balance between benefits and burdens.

This point may perhaps best be brought home by considering another (more particular) objection from justice. It might be objected that the argument for the permissibility of recidivist statutes given here would require the same treatment of (ordinary) multiple offenders as of recidivists. Multiple offenders seem to get much the same advantage as do recidivists — that is, all get an unfair share of crime. If distributive justice *requires* recidivist statutes, why (the objection goes) does it not require similar statutes governing multiple offenders? Why should multiple offenders receive no "enhancement" of penalty for committing a series of crimes before being convicted when recidivists receive an "enhancement" for the same crimes because punctuated by convictions? How can that be fair?

The answer is simple. Our analysis is in fact silent about whether (distributive) justice requires multiple offenders to be punished much like recidivists. Our auction does not allow for the possibility *only* because we did not bother to provide for it. The procedures of the auction could be changed to allow just one unlicensed "purchase" in a lifetime. Nothing we have said *requires* the exact arrangement we have imagined. Certainly, the similarity between recidivists and other multiple offenders is a reason to treat them alike (whether by enhancing the punishment of both or of neither). But it is only *a* reason. The dissimilarities may be reasons for distinguishing them. We generally go easy on first offenders, whether they have committed one crime or several. We like to give people "a second chance" (in recognition of how easy it is for us to go wrong). We tend to think of multiple offenses as a single "spree." We hope the lesser penalty will prove effective in discouraging future criminal activity. And so on. The principle of just deserts does not stand in the way of such leniency. Whether the principles of *distributive* justice do is a question beyond the scope of this paper. (I must admit, however, that I do not see why a just legal system could not maintain a fair balance between benefits and burdens even if it showed substantial leniency to multiple offenders while not showing such leniency to recidivists.)

Still another objection from justice would question the justice of *rationing* crime. Would it not (it might be asked) be fairer to let the market control altogether? The requirement of two licenses for recidivists amounts to unjustified interference with the normal operation of a free market. And, if that is so, then the auction as described cannot (it might be concluded) in fact provide any help in understanding how recidivist penalties are to be justified. Underlying this objection is (it seems to me) the assumption that a free market is always *the* fairest way to distribute any good. To assume that is to assume too much. We may admit that (under circumstances such as we have assumed) a perfectly free market is *a* fair way to distribute licenses. But we need not admit as well that it is fairer than a market that puts some restrictions on who gets what. Equality in distribution is itself commonly recognized as a good independent of the equality of opportunity a perfectly free market serves.

The objection nevertheless calls our attention to an important point. If recidivist statutes are to be justified (not just shown to be permitted by the principle of just deserts), their defenders will have to point to some good beyond the fairness of punishing more those who have taken a greater share of unfair advantage than the first-offender has. Fairness might well be consistent both with having recidivist statutes and with not having them (though one sort of fairness may pull in one way while another sort pulls in another).

That brings me to a second sort of objection, one emphasizing the disanalogy between the purpose of the criminal law (for example, preventing certain acts) and the purpose of our auction (that is, licensing certain acts). The disanalogy must, of course, be admitted. The question is how important the disanalogy is.

My view is that, given the principle of just deserts, the disanalogy is not important. The principle of just deserts (like the principle of deterrence) generates a "tariff theory" of punishment. Statutory penalties have the structure of a price system. The criminal must "pay" for what he does at the rate determined by what he does. The "prices" are, of course, not set to encourage crime, to make a "profit" for the state, or the like. Rather, under the principle of just deserts, the "price" is set to be a *fair* return for (a *re-attribution* of) the crime. The criminal law is like a system of administered prices, not like a system where price is set by a fair procedure that will (as in a free market) guarantee the fairness of any purchase. The statutory penalty is not necessarily what the criminal *justly* "owes" for his crime. Just as a price charged under a system of administered prices can be unfairly inflated (even if people are willing to pay it), so the statutory penalty can be too severe for a crime (even if people commit the crime knowing the penalty). And just as we can check the fairness of an administered price by comparing it to the price charged in a free market for equivalent goods, we can check the fairness of a statutory penalty by comparing it to what would result under a procedure we know to be fair. The auction model used here is simply one way of turning a hard question of substantive fairness into an easier question about what would result under a fair procedure. Any tariff theory of punishment makes analogy with pricing mechanisms natural. Describing punishment as "paying the price for one's crime" is certainly not a recent innovation. So, the burden of proof falls on those who wish to claim that my analysis should be rejected simply because of the disanalogy between the purpose of punishment and the purpose of the auction.

A third sort of objection takes the auction model seriously enough to raise questions about the connection between the economics of the model and the "economics" of crime. What analogue (it might be asked) is there in society to the "poaching" of the model? If there is no analogue, why should we treat the model's results as authority for setting penalties in society?

Such an objection is easily answered. Models *never* have all the properties of what they model. If they did, they would not be models but the very thing that was to be modeled. Models work by simplifying, mirroring some aspects of a process at the cost of distorting or ignoring others. Every model has its price. The hard question is whether the price is worth paying. My view is that the auction model is worth the price here. There is, I think, something intuitively right about it or at least something extremely convenient. It suggests questions worth asking (as well as some not worth asking). It has helped us to grasp an idea which at first seemed incomprehensible. And it has helped us to derive a conclusion about recidivist statutes which is at least not obviously wrong. Insofar as that is so, there can be no objection to it just because the mechanisms of the model do not all have exact counterparts in the criminal law.

Something similar can be said about the "extreme rationality" our auction seems to assume. It is not necessary for us to claim that criminals in fact think like the stockbroker-criminals of our auction. We need only claim that in fact criminals are rational enough so that thinking of them in this way is revealing. Such a claim is, of course, controversial, but not among retributivists. Retributivism has always had to begin with rational agents because retributivism supposes moral agents, and one cannot be a moral agent unless one is rational. The controversy has not even been between retributivists and deterrentists. Deterrence, like retribution, supposes rational agents, though for a somewhat different purpose. The only theorists who are likely to find little revealed by thinking of criminals as rational agents are reformists (and incapacitationists). That is no surprise since their central thesis is that criminals need reform (or incapacitation) because there is something wrong with them, and that "something" is usually a mental illness or incapacity rendering them to some degree not rational (in the sense the rest of us are). So, any objection to the degree of rationality we have assumed is not so much an objection to my analysis as to the general enterprise that retributivists and deterrentists share. It is, in other words, an objection so fundamental that it should not be answered in a chapter with the limited purpose this one has.[30]

The last sort of objection I want to consider now is an appeal to "common practice." The assumption is that any correct theory of punishment must be a theory of the criminal law more or less as we know it. Any theory calling into question much of practice must be flawed somewhere and it is the theorist's job to figure out where. In the meantime (it is said), practical people may properly ignore the theory.

I accept this assumption. But I do not think any objection to what I have argued follows from it. The practice my argument challenges is already breaking down. It is now commonly recognized that much of the practice of punishment during the last century or so was shaped by the theory of reform, about which we have come to have grave doubts, both because it has failed in practice and because it requires us to treat persons in ways we have come to see as morally suspect.[31] We can easily understand how people who accepted that theory would do what people in fact did. But we need not count what they did while attempting to follow *that* theory as evidence against the claim that certain conclusions follow from a different theory. An objection from common practice could threaten the argument presented here only if the practice in question belonged to a period (for example, the eighteenth century) when punishment was understood (more or less) retributively. If the conclusions drawn here were much at odds with such practice, there *would* be good reason to suppose the argument to be fallacious. Practitioners might then prudently fold their arms and wait for theorists to expose the fallacy. But the conclusions drawn here are, I believe, plainly *not* at odds with such retributive practice.

Indeed, it seems to me that even recent practice is a good deal less against our conclusion than may at first appear. The practice appealed to is pretty thin even if it is longstanding. Recidivist statutes seem to have been much less often used than one would expect from reading them. For example, Helm should have gotten a life sentence upon his fourth conviction, but did not get it until his seventh. Recent practice is also far from uniform. Many recidivist statutes are merely anti-leniency provisions. Many more leave the courts free to proportion punishment to crime.[32] Practice under such statutes may well be consistent with the conclusion drawn here. Recent practice is also far from static. When *Rummel* was decided, seven states still had recidivist statutes about as harsh as that of Texas. When *Helm* was decided, just three years later, the number had dropped to five. One of the seven (Washington) had substituted an anti-leniency provision for its ungraded statute. Another state (West Virginia) had its recidivist statute declared in violation of the state constitution's requirement that punishment be proportioned to wrongdoing.[33] *Helm* certainly appears to be part of a trend. So, insofar as the analysis given here raises questions about the justifiability of recidivist statutes, especially about ungraded statutes with high minimum sentences, the analysis may both explain why such statutes are doing so badly in the present just-deserts environment and claim that common practice supports its conclusions rather than calling them into doubt.

Conclusions: *Rummel* and *Helm* Revisited

The foregoing observations suggest a somewhat different reading of *Rummel* and *Helm*. The majority in *Rummel* may now be understood to have argued in effect that, taking the possibility of parole into account, Rummel's life sentence was (or, at least, could reasonably be expected to turn out to be) only a small fraction greater than the maximum sentence he could receive for his third offense alone. The penalty for the third offense (with no leniency) would have been ten years' imprisonment. A minimum "life sentence" was twelve years. The difference is only two years. So, *supposing* parole to be granted Rummel as soon as he became elibible, Rummel would in fact not be punished more severely under the Texas statute than would be permissible under our analysis. The *indeterminacy* of Rummel's "life sentence" made it hard to say the sentence was grossly out of proportion to the crime. On the other hand, the minority in *Rummel* may be understood to have argued that, because parole is discretionary under Texas law, the calculation of what Rummel deserves in punishment must ignore the possibility of parole. A life sentence is a life sentence. The difference between a maximum of ten years for the third offense itself and a maximum of life imprisonment for recidivism is enormous. So, the life sentence is out of proportion to the crime (even taking into account the recidivism).

Under our analysis, then, the dispute between majority and minority in *Rummel* has nothing to do with the "subjectivity" or "objectivity" of the various tests of proportionality. The dispute concerns only *what* one should test. Once there is agreement to take the possibility of parole into account or to ignore it, the principle of just deserts will quickly give an answer in all but a few borderline cases (of which *Rummel* is not one). Determining whether a recidivist is getting what he deserves is no harder than making many other determinations that the law looks upon as (more or less) routine. Indeed, under the analysis given here, determining what a recidivist deserves seems much easier than, say, deciding whether the right of privacy bars a state from requiring the doctor of a fourteen-year-old to notify her parents before performing an abortion on her or whether a swastika constitutes "fighting words" if its being displayed at a meeting is likely to cause a riot.

So, under our analysis, the decision in *Helm* should have been unanimous. That it was not may be attributed to a number of factors not likely to carry as much weight the next time the Court hears a similar case. The most important of these factors were, I think, an inability to distinguish *Helm* from *Rummel* on any defensible principle and an unwillingness to overrule *Rummel* only three years after handing down that decision. If that is why the minority did not join the majority, we may expect them to come over soon. Whether they do or not, I hope it is now plain that they *should*.

Notes

Work on this chapter was begun under an Organized Research Grant from Illinois State University (June 1983) and completed under National Endowment for the Humanities Grant FB-22388-84. I am grateful to both institutions for their support.

1. *Rummel v. Estelle*, 100 U.S. 113 (1980).

2. *Ibid.*

3. See, e.g., Note, "Constitutional Law — Texas Habitual Offender Statute Does Not Violate the Eighth Amendment," *American Journal of Criminal Law* 8 (July 1980): 209-216; Note, "Constitutional Law — Criminal Law — Cruel and Unusual Punishment," *Cincinnati Law Review* 49 (1980): 725-737; Note, "Constitutional Criminal Law — Eighth Amendment," *Tulane Law Review* 55 (February 1981): 560-576; and Note, "Rape, Recidivism, and Capital Punishment," *Ohio Northern University Law Review* 9 (January 1981): 99-119. For a more judicious and forgiving (but still quite critical) discussion, see Note, *"Rummel v. Estelle*: Sentencing without a Rational Basis," *Syracuse Law Review* 32 (Summer 1981): 803-840.

4. See, eg., Joshua Dressler, "Substantive Criminal Law through the Looking Glass of Rummel v. Estelle: Proportionality and Justice as En-

dangered Doctrines," *Southwest Law Journal* 34 (February 1981): 1063-1130, as well as the following written before the Supreme Court handed down its decisions: Note, *"Rummel v. Estelle*: Cruel and Unusual Punishment," *South Texas Law Journal* 19 (Fall 1978): 709-715 and Note, "Recidivism and the Eighth Amendment," *Notre Dame Law Journal* 55 (December 1979): 305-315.

5. Dressler.

6. See, e.g., Katkin, "Habitual Offender Laws: A Reconsideration," *Buffalo Law Review* 21 (Fall 1971): 99-120; G. Fletcher, *Rethinking Criminal Law* (Boston: Little, Brown & Company, 1978), pp. 463-466 (1978); and von Hirsch, "Desert and Previous Convictions in Sentencing," *Minnesota Law Review* 65 (April 1981): 591-634.

7. *Solem v. Helm* 103 S.Ct. 3001, 463 U.S. 277 (1983).

8. *Rummel*, at 1145.

9. *Helm*, pp. 297.

10. See Chapter Four and Five.

11. *Ill. Rev. Stat.* ch 38 33A-3 (1981).

12. For a summary of such criticisms (and a partial bibliography), see Chapter Eight.

13. See, e.g, MacDonald, "A Critique of Habitual Criminal Legislation in Canada and England," *University of British Columbia Law Review* 4 (May 1969): 87-108; and Katkin, *supra* note 6.

14. *New Plymouth Colony Laws, Statutes, Etc.* 1623-1671, at 249 (Boston 1836).

15. *The Colonial Laws of Massachusetts*, 1660, at 127 (Boston 1889).

16. Arthur P. Scott, *Criminal Law in Colonial Virginia* (Chicago: University of Chicago Press, 1930), pp. 226-227 (1930).

17. Scott, 226.

18. *Plumbly v. Commonwealth*, 43 Mass. (2 *Met.*) 413, 415 (1841).

19. *Moore v. Missouri*, 159 U.S. 673, 677 (1895), I have given this language the usual gloss, but I must admit to a sense that retributive considerations may underlie even the appeal to failed reform. The statute in question merely required recidivists to be sentenced to the maximum penalty allowable for a first offender whatever the other aggravating or mitigating factors, and so even the reference to reform may be read as noting the absence of a reason for giving the criminal less than he deserves for his crime.

20. See, e.g. John Rawls, "Two Concepts of Rules," *Philosophical Review* 64 (January 1955): 3-32; T. Honderich, *Punishment: The Supposed Justifications*, especially 148-189 (1971); H. L. A. Hart, *Punishment and Responsibility: Essays in Philosophy of Law*, especially 1-27 & 220-237 (1968); and Alan Goldman, "The Paradox of Punishment," *Philosophy and Public Affairs* 9 (Fall 1979): 42-58.

21. This point, though often made, seems to need repetition. For a defense of it, see Chapter Four.

22. See, e.g., Herbert Morris, "Persons and Punishment," *Monist* 52 (October 1968): 475-501.

23. H. Perlman and C. Stebbins, "Implementing an Equitable Sentencing System: The Uniform Commissioners' Model Sentencing and Corrections Act," *Virginia Law Review* 65 (November 1979): 1175-1183; A. von Hirsch, *Doing Justice: The Choice of Punishment* (1976); and *Twentieth Century Fund, Fair and Certain Punishment: Report of the Twentieth Century Fund Task Force on Criminal Sentencing* (1976). For more see Chapter Eight.

24. See Chapter Four.

25. Hyman Gross, *A Theory of Criminal Justice* (1979), p. 40.

26. The quotation is from an English report cited approvingly in Katkin, 107. The American experience seems to be the same — Katkin, 108.

27. Von Hirsch, *Doing Justice*, 85.

28. Von Hirsch, 597-598. Cf. Fletcher, "The Recidivist Premium," *Criminal Justice Ethics* 1 (Winter/Spring 1981): 54-59.

29. Von Hirsch, "Desert," 619 n.64.

30. I have, however, dealt with this question elsewhere. See my "Death, Deterrence, and the Method of Common Sense," *Social Theory and Practice* 7 (Summer 1981): 145-178 and "Guilty But Insane?," *Social Theory and Practice* 10 (Spring 1984): 1-24.

31. See Chapters One and Eight.

32. *Rummel*, 1151-1152.

33. Note, "Recidivist Statutes — Application of Proportionality and Overbreadth Doctrines to Repeat Offenders," *Washington Law Review* 57 (July 1981): 573-598.

7

Strict Liability: Deserved
Punishment for Faultless Conduct

> There can be no crime, large or small, without an evil mind. In other words, punishment is the sequence of wickedness. Neither in philosophical speculation, nor in religious or moral sentiment, would any people in any age allow that a man should be deemed guilty unless his mind was so.[1]

Keith Baker's cruise control stuck in the accelerate position without warning, causing his car to accelerate. Baker tried to deactivate the device, repeatedly hitting the off and coast buttons and tapping the brake. The cruise control was off within a few minutes, but not before the Kansas highway patrol clocked him at seventy-five miles per hour in a fifty-five mile per hour zone. Baker received a ticket for speeding, had the cruise control fixed, and appeared in court to explain why he was entirely without fault. No one disputed his evidence, not even his claim that the cruise control had seemed in perfect working order until the instant it stuck. Nevertheless, the judge disallowed the evidence, convicted him of speeding, and fined him ten dollars and costs.[2]

Baker appealed. The appellate court sustained the conviction.[3] If the car's brakes had failed (the court reasoned), Baker might have been excused. Brakes are necessary to operate a car. Cruise control is not. A driver who installs cruise control does so for his own convenience and must suffer the consequences should the device malfunction.[4] Those consequences include conviction for speeding under the relevant statute.[5] The appellate court did not say that Baker should not have installed the cruise control, that he should have known better than to use it on that day, or that he should have done something else to prevent the speeding. What it did say was that by activating the cruise control, Baker had "caused the act of speeding" and that sufficed for conviction.[6]

Probably no one thought the worse of Baker for speeding in the way he did or for the resulting conviction. No one claimed that Baker intended what happened, that he took an unreasonable risk, or that his speeding was the consequence of any improper, unreasonable, or negligent act. The court's only concern was that his voluntary choice led, however unwittingly, to the speeding prohibited under a statute that did not make absence of "criminal intent" relevant to guilt.[7] His conduct, though faultless, was still subject to punishment. Baker's case is typical of most strict liability in the criminal law. Even the maximum punishment possible upon conviction was relatively light.[8]

Here, it seems, is a relatively straightforward instance of that most troubling of notions — "punishing the innocent." Baker had, of course, done what the law prohibited. He operated his car in a way that caused it to exceed the speed limit. He was *not* innocent if innocent means only "not in violation of the law." But innocent often means something more than that. For example, a legal system that punishes the insane for doing what they could not know to be wrong might quite intelligibly, and damningly, be said to punish the innocent. Yet, such punishment would, under that legal system, still be punishing those who had in fact violated the law. There is, then, at least one sense of "innocent" beyond the legal sense — a sense relevant to what the law should be. In this sense, "innocent" means "without (moral) fault." This is the sense we usually have in mind when we worry about punishing the innocent.

The received view is that any legal system that punishes faultless conduct is, in that respect, unjust.[9] There may be sufficient reason to excuse such a system. But the question would be one of excuse, not of justification. According to this view, we may have to tolerate the system, but only until we can correct it. We would be treating people worse than they deserved, and only necessity could excuse that.

I want to challenge this view. But I do not want to do so in any of the usual ways. In particular, I do not want to make the challenge by direct appeal to actual or probable consequences. We do not have enough information for that; and, even if we did, the resulting argument would probably not be decisive. The force of the received view seems to originate in non-utilitarian considerations of justice that a utilitarian counterargument would leave untouched. I also do not want to make the challenge by merely rebutting the common arguments *against* strict liability. That has been done already.[10] Such parrying of arguments, even when successful, seems to produce intellectual stalemate rather than persuasion. The best way to challenge the received view is, I think, on its own ground, that is, by arguing affirmatively for the unlikely proposition that one can deserve punishment for faultless conduct not only according to the law as it is, but also according to the law as justice would allow it to be. That is what I propose to do in this chapter.

Defining the Problem

Strict liability should not, of course, be confused with absolute liability, though these terms are often used interchangeably. A statute holds someone strictly liable insofar as it rules out such excuses as "I didn't mean to," "I didn't know," and "I was careful."[11] In contrast, a statute holds someone absolutely liable insofar as it rules out, *in addition to these excuses*, such excuses as "I didn't do that, it just happened," "someone else physically moved my hand against my will," or "there was no way anyone could have prevented it."[12] If strict liability does away with the "guilty mind" requirement, absolute liability does away with the "guilty act" requirement as well, leaving something very close to a mere event, reflex, or external cause.[13] Like most legal distinctions, this one is a bit fuzzy. But, for our purposes, that should not matter.[14]

Cases of strict liability in the criminal law can be found as early as the middle of the last century.[15] Today, strict liability is common in statutes concerning: the sale of liquor, impure foods or drugs, and misbranded articles; acts affecting the safety, health, or general welfare of the community; serious crimes such as murder, bigamy, rape, and possession of narcotics; and traffic and other motor vehicle regulations. In general, liability is not strict with respect to every element to the offense. The less severe the punishment for an offense, however, the more likely that liability will be strict with respects to more elements. In crimes of strict liability, the judge will usually consider the actual degree of "evil mind" at sentencing, reserving the lightest penalties for those who, like Baker, were not even negligent.

Strict liability has never been popular. The *Model Penal Code* sought to eliminate it "whenever the offense carries a possibility of sentence of imprisonment,"[16] permitting strict liability only for minor offenses such as Baker's. And even that use seems to have been the Code's curtsy to necessity, not an endorsement. No offense provided for in the Code itself imposed strict liability.[17] Most of this century's legal theorists, including Jerome Hall, Glanville Williams, and H.L.A. Hart, have condemned it.[18] Indeed, until recently, no general theory of the criminal law had a place for it.

That has now changed. Hyman Gross, in *A Theory of Criminal Justice*,[19] has proposed an analysis giving strict liability a small but respectable place within his general theory. Gross distinguishes between two kinds of strict liability statutes: those concerning serious offenses with severe penalties, and those concerning minor offenses with light penalties.[20] Gross argues that statutes of the first kind are best understood as not imposing strict liability at all. Some of these, for example, those statutes prohibiting statutory rape or bigamy, are thought to impose strict liability because of misconceptions concerning the harm the law seeks to prevent.[21] Others, including felony murder, are thought to impose strict liability because the law mistakenly treats the act in question as riskier than it actually is.[22] Either way, once one identifies the harm that the statute actually seeks to prevent, it become obvious, Gross thinks, that absence of fault with respect to that harm is, or at least should be, a good excuse.[23] For example, an Illinois statute forbids sexual intercourse with a child under eighteen years of age, but disallows the defense that the accused "reasonably believed the child to be of the age of 18 or upwards."[24] According to Gross, disallowing this defense shows that the harm the statute actually seeks to prevent is sexual intercourse with any young person.[25] The age of eighteen is just an arbitrary cutoff, not a material element of the crime. A mistake about age, then, would not be a mistake about a material element of the crime and liability for that crime would not, in that respect, be strict.[26]

Since statutes of this first kind do not, according to Gross, really punish the innocent, we need not concern ourselves with them yet. Gross' discussion of statutes of the second kind, those establishing minor offenses, tries a different approach to the problem of punishing the innocent. Such crimes, according to Gross, punish conduct of minimum, but still significant, culpability.[27] Persons convicted of such crimes deserve some punishment for what they did, just not very much.[28] Such strict liability punishes small faults in conduct, not faultless conduct.

This conclusion approximates both the reasoning and language of the *Model Penal Code*.[29] It is nonetheless interesting. The impulse behind the Code seems to be utilitarian. That utilitarians should be able to accommodate strict liability is not surprising. Indeed, it is the Code's obvious hostility to strict liability that is surprising. Gross, however, is close to those theorists one would least expect to make provision for strict liability, that is to say, retributivists. To justify punishment for an offense of strict liability, a retributivist would have to argue *either* that culpability can exist without fault *or* that fault can exist without an evil mind—without intent to do the forbidden act, recklessness, or actual negligence. Retributivists traditionally have argued neither. Yet, as Gross clearly sees, he must make one of these arguments or admit that any punishment of someone guilty of a strict liability offense would amount to punishing the innocent when, as in Baker's case, the evidence of innocence is before us. Gross makes the second argument. He tries to show fault can exist without an evil mind. This is not surprising given his understanding of fault, wrong, and culpability.

For Gross, the difference between "faulty doing" and "wrongdoing" is important. Both fault and wrong imply that the actor's conduct fell below the standard of correct conduct. Fault implies no more than that, but wrong implies as well that the circumstances of the act do not excuse. So, to say that someone guilty of a strict liability offense deserves punishment is according to Gross, not to say that he did wrong, except in the technical legal sense. In cases of strict liability, Gross observes, "[n]ot only is there absence of wrongdoing . . . but the prohibited act might have been excused if only the law allowed the excuse."[30]

Thus, for Gross, fault, not wrongdoing, is essential to culpability. Fault requires the possibility of taking reasonable precautions to prevent what is prohibited. If such precautions are possible, then liability for doing what is prohibited is at most strict, and the actor is culpable. If such precautions are not possible, liability for doing what is prohibited is absolute and the actor is not culpable.[31]

Gross is not the only theorist to have recently advanced these ideas,[32] but he is the most perceptive and systematic. His analysis of strict liability rests on what he calls the "principle of culpability," the same principle he uses to elucidate much of the criminal law. Gross summarizes the principle in this way: *"Criminal liability is just only when it is for an intentional act that illegitimately poses a threat of harm with which the law has concerned itself."*[33] If we accept this principle, and if culpability must be proportioned to fault, fault must arise when intentional action meets a certain standard — the standard of posing an illegitimate threat. Strict liability could be justified only for an act posing an illegitimate threat.

This analysis is inadequate. To see why, assume that Gross would agree Baker deserves punishment and then try to understand how, according to Gross, punishing Baker could be just. Since any conduct that does not satisfy three conditions for faultiness would, according to Gross, not come under the principle of culpability, we should begin our evaluation of Gross' analysis of strict liability by ensuring that Baker's conduct satisfied those three conditions.[34]

The first condition is that the risk in question be of a kind the actor can appreciate.[35] Baker, it seems, could appreciate the risk a malfunctioning cruise control posed. That is why he had the cruise control fixed as soon as it started to give him trouble. Baker's conduct thus satisfies the first condition.

Gross' second condition is that the actor be able to prevent the harm.[36] That Baker could get the cruise control fixed once he learned something was wrong shows his ability to prevent the malfunction if only he had learned of it in advance. Could he have learned of the problem *in advance*? He certainly could have taken his car to a reputable mechanic to have the cruise control checked. Nothing suggests that the problem would not have been discovered during a checkup. So, he probably could have prevented the malfunction — if only he had tried hard enough.

Gross' third condition is that preventing the harm should not make the risk-threatening activity impractical.[37] This last condition also seems to be satisfied. Even if cruise control owners like Baker had to have the device checked once a month, the expense would probably not be so great that no one would use cruise control.

We are now ready to consider whether punishing Baker is consistent with Gross' principle of culpability. We may distinguish the three requirements the principle lays down (which should not be confused with the three conditions just discussed). First, the act in question must pose a "threat of harm with which the law has concerned itself."[38] Second, the act must be intentional.[39] Third, the threat of harm the intentional act poses must be illegitimate.[40] Does Baker's conviction satisfy all three of these requirements?

Baker's speeding did pose a threat of harm with which the law has concerned itself. The law has undertaken to prevent speeding because speeding risks serious accidents. So, the first requirement is satisfied.

The second requirement also seems satisfied. Baker's conviction was for an intentional act — causing his car to speed by entrusting its operation to the cruise control. The speeding was not intended or consciously risked. Indeed, it probably was not even the result of a failure to maintain the car as a reasonable person would. Nevertheless, entrusting the car's operation to the cruise control is as intentional an act as any for which society imposes criminal liability. If anything more were demanded for the act to be intentional, for example, actual foresight of the danger, the liability in question would be ordinary rather than strict.

That leaves only the third requirement of the principle of culpability. To hold Baker culpable for entrusting the operation of his car to the cruise control, his act must, according to Gross, also have posed an illegitimate threat of harm. For Gross, illegitimacy is a matter of "weighing-in-balance" the harm that is done or threatened by the conduct in question against the legitimate interests that the conduct serves.[41] Cruise control need not itself pose an unreasonable risk for using it to be illegitimate. Its use could be illegitimate because the risk posed, though reasonable in itself, is nonetheless not in the service of an interest sufficiently important to prevail against countervailing interests. Contrasting cruise control with brakes, as the court did,[42] will illustrate this.

Brakes are necessary for the operation of any car and, in that sense, their use is involuntary if we are to use cars at all. If driving cars serves important enough interests, then driving with brakes that could fail even if reasonably maintained would not be conduct sufficient to support a conviction for speeding when the failure of well-maintained brakes caused the speeding. Cruise control is, in contrast, not necessary for the operation of a car. So, according to Gross, the legitimacy of its use will depend on a different balance of considerations, for example, the balance between the safety of others and the convenience of the driver. Convenience is an "illegitimate interest" when balanced against another's safety.

This explanation of Baker's case, though obviously appealing, is still troubling. Unless we wish to say that the appellate court erred in its decision to let Baker's conviction stand, we seem forced to say that Baker was at fault because entrusting his car to the cruise control *illegitimately* risked harm to others — or instead that Baker was *not* at fault for so entrusting his car but still *deserved* punishment for what he did. Because Baker's case is so typical, saying the court erred would amount to giving up the enterprise of justifying strict liability in the criminal law. We are thus left with the other two alternatives.

Gross chooses the first. On this alternative "minimum culpability" implies "minor fault" (the lowest grade of "evil mind"). On the second alternative, it does not. The first alternative has the advantage of completely domesticating "strict liability." Strict liability in the criminal law would then rest on something like negligence.[43] The only difference between strict liability and negligence liability would be that the standard of care in strict liability would be higher — not just reasonable care but what we might call "super care." The difference is nevertheless significant. While the test of negligence is process-oriented,[44] the test of super care is outcome-oriented.[45] Super care, while not necessarily unreasonable, is still by definition at least sometimes greater care than a reasonable person would take in the circumstances (and so, a higher standard of care than negligence). The "fault" strict liability punishes, according to Gross, is falling below the standard of super care.

What is troubling about analyzing strict liability in this way is that our ordinary judgments do not seem to fit the analysis. We do not, for example, want to say that Baker should not have installed cruise control in his car.[46] Nor do we want to say that he should have had his cruise control checked more often than he did.[47] We do not even want to say that Baker was at fault in any way for using the cruise control on the day it stuck, since saying he *was* at fault for using it is, in effect, only another way of saying that he should not have used it. Except for the actual outcome, we have no reason to say that. In short, we do not think of Baker as someone who posed an "illegitimate" risk to others by his action, though we clearly see the risk he did in fact pose.

If those are our ordinary judgments, then Gross' talk of "illegitimate interests" is at least misleading. To say that someone intentionally undertook conduct to serve an illegitimate interest is to describe his conduct, as Gross does, as faulty; faulty not merely in the sense of failing to satisfy a technical legal requirement, but faulty in the sense of being what it should not be, law or no law. Yet, what makes Baker's case interesting is that, as in many other reported cases of strict liability, Baker's punishment seems to be for an intentional act that *legitimately* posed a threat of harm with which the law has concerned itself. Baker, though *without* fault, did something deserving punishment.

The disanalogy between negligence and strict liability is worth stressing. A law imposing criminal liability for negligence can be justified by a *natural* duty of reasonable care. Culpability for such crimes is still a function of evil mind – a mind not up to the standard of the ordinary reasonable mind. What makes strict liability so problematic for any theory of criminal law in which desert plays a significant part is that no corresponding natural duty of super care exists. Culpability for crimes of strict liability cannot be a function of evil mind, even in the low-grade way that negligent mind is. Baker's intentional act, turning on the cruise control that he had good reason to believe was safe, was not itself a blameworthy act. Had the cruise control worked as it gave every indication it would, his conduct would have been of no concern to the law. The law was concerned only with the unforeseen consequence of the act – the excessive speed caused by the cruise control getting stuck. This consequence, not even reasonably foreseeable, turned Baker's perfectly proper act into a crime.[48] Baker seems to have been punished for bad luck.

Had Baker exercised enough care, as he could have, he would have discovered the potential malfunction because that is what "exercising *enough* care" means when (as we are assuming) it is, at least in principle, possible to prevent the malfunction. What is important, however, is *not* that Baker could have prevented the malfunction had he exercised *super* care,[49] but that we do not normally expect people to exercise super care. The objective of strict liability statutes is not, or at least should not be, to make people super careful. Rather, the objective should be to get people to exercise *reasonable* care in a situation in which the law cannot easily recognize the difference between reasonable care and negligence. The law tries to achieve this objective by shifting the burden of error to those who make the error. To adopt a strict liability statute is, in effect, to adopt a policy that "punishment will rain upon the negligent who cannot be proved to be negligent and the non-negligent alike; so, act accordingly." Whether this policy works any better than imposing a rebuttable presumption of negligence is an empirical question about which we know far too little. That question, however, only addresses the wisdom of strict liability statutes. It is not directly relevant to whether one can deserve punishment for violating such a statute.

The problem posed by strict liability in the criminal law, then, is that of explaining how the objective of strict liability statutes can justify any punishment at all or, in other words, how there can justly be a crime without fault, a crime without even the low-grade evil mind of negligence. Gross avoided this problem only by treating failure to exercise super care as faulty conduct. That was a mistake. Failure to exercise super care is not a fault. Since the problem of punishing faultless conduct now seems unavoidable, we need a theory that explains how it is possible both to act without fault and to deserve punishment. Such a theory would make it unnecessary to find fault with Baker for not exercising super care, as Gross does. It would also show that Gross' analysis of criminal liability needs significant revision. Gross must give up the strong connection he makes between culpability and fault.[50]

Such a theory would also have more general implications for the theory of punishment. It would, for example, establish the limited usefulness of "reprobative" or "expressive" theories of punishment, those theories that try to understand punishment as blaming carried on by rougher means. We cannot be justly blamed for doing something without fault. If Baker, though without fault, deserved punishment, then we can, it seems, deserve punishment without deserving blame and, therefore, punishment cannot be conceptually equivalent to rough blaming. To be blameless is not the same as to be innocent. I shall now offer a theory explaining how faultless conduct can deserve punishment.

Culpability and "Super Care"

For Gross, the purpose of the criminal law is neither to punish all moral wrongs nor to punish only moral wrongs.[51] The use of concepts such as "culpability," "blame," "wrong," and "fault" in legal reasoning does not turn such reasoning into ordinary moral reasoning. The concepts have application well beyond morality. One can, for example, deserve nonmoral blame for playing cards badly as well as moral blame for cheating.[52] For Gross, the purpose of the criminal law is to prevent harm by the threat or application of punishment. The principles of criminal justice, including Gross' principle of culpability, are mere side constraints on that objective.[53] Moral principles have only a secondary role. They impose general limits on the principles of criminal justice.

To say that the purpose of criminal law is not to punish moral wrongs is, however, *not* to say that violating the criminal law is not always at least prima facie morally wrong. And Gross does not say that. Instead, he describes two "strong arguments" for the moral wrongness of lawbreaking, without endorsing either. One is a social contract argument: "[I]n a society in which general consent is necessary for the legitimate exercise of legal authority by government through law, there is as part of such consent a promise binding on each member of society to abide by the rules promulgated under legal authority."[54] The second argument appeals to fairness: Those who take the advantages derived from the burdensome obedience others accord the law — and those who merely receive such advantages without objection — should not disobey those rules merely because it is to their advantage to do so.[55] Both arguments assume that the criminal law in question is part of a relatively just legal system.[56] The assumption puts Gross close to contemporary retributivists.

But another assumption puts a wall between him and them. Gross assumes that he can provide a theory of criminal justice without committing himself to any analysis of the connection between lawbreaking and moral wrong. This assumption accounts for his indifference to the difference between social contract and fairness as alternative arguments for the moral wrongness of lawbreaking. The difference is significant. A social contract argument makes any punishment imposed in accordance with the law just simply because the criminal received what he bargained for. Under standard social contract theories, a promise to obey the law is a promise to take the law as it is, strict liability included. According to the fairness argument, on the other hand, only those punishments that are substantively fair are just. The choice between social contract and fairness is more than a choice between two ways of showing primary legal rules to be morally binding. The logic of the two arguments could affect the moral status of secondary legal rules as well.

Gross' principle of culpability seems to be a principle of fairness, not a mere term in the social contract. His failure to recognize this may perhaps be explained by another feature of his theory. He treats harm both as the *reason* for subjecting a class of acts to criminal liability and as a *measure* of their culpability. Had he more clearly distinguished the question of making an act criminal (where harm is central) from the question of degree of culpability (where it is not), he might have seen that measures of culpability other than harm are consistent with his general theory of criminal justice. One example of such a measure is the unfair advantage taken by doing what the law forbids.

To understand how the measure of culpability can be independent of the reason for making a class of acts culpable, we must examine Gross' principle of culpability. The principle may conveniently be broken into four subprinciples: (1) just prohibition; (2) just criminal liability; (3) just conviction; and (4) just punishment. These four principles, though convenient for our purposes, have no privileged status. Others might equally well summarize Gross' theory. We must now consider what these four principles are, how they are related to the principle of culpability, and what they have to tell us about strict liability.

The first principle, the principle of just prohibition, may be stated as follows: *Prohibiting a class of events is just only when (a) what is prohibited poses a threat of harm (or loss of advantage) with which the law justly concerns itself, (b) the threat cannot be controlled satisfactorily by any reasonable provision short of prohibition, and (c) the threat can be controlled satisfactorily by prohibition.* Two of the terms used need explanation. First, "event" is a catch-all that includes "conditions"[58] and "outcomes,"[59] as well as "acts" strictly so called. Second, Gross defines "harm" as "any untoward occurrence consisting in a violation of some interest of a person."[60] So, we must not read too much into the concept of "harm." For Gross, whatever the law seeks to prevent is "harm."

The principle of just prohibition guides any reasonably just legal system in limiting its citizens' liberty and in deciding whether the criminal law or other means are to be used to impose the limit in question. Like Gross' principle of culpability, this principle states only a necessary condition. Also like Gross' principle, it includes part of the "weighing-in-balance" Gross thought necessary to identify illegitimate interests. A proposed prohibition should do something law is supposed to do, do it better than less restrictive means, and do it satisfactorily, that is, at reasonable cost in money, liberty, and the like.

The principle of just prohibition is worth separating from the others because it identifies the decision to punish illegal acts as special lawmaking, though we often think of it as paradigmatic. Legislators need not prohibit at all. They can instead try to control a certain harm by taxes that discourage it, by public provision of some service such as free safety inspection that prevents it, or by some other means short of absolute prohibition. Even if legislators decide that they need to prohibit, it does not follow that what they should prohibit is a class of *acts*. Prohibition may be directed towards mere events. For example, being in the country without a passport may be a prohibited event, thus assuring that an alien may be deported even though he was brought into the country unconscious and without his prior consent. Distinguishing this first principle allows us to understand why prohibiting faultless conduct should not be controversial. We seem quite willing to prohibit even mere conditions[62] or outcomes.[63] So, prohibiting faultless *conduct* should pass without notice — provided there is no question of criminal liability.

The second principle, the principle of just criminal liability, might be stated as follows: *A prohibition is justly enforced by criminal liability only when (a) criminal liability is for violating a law satisfying the principle of just prohibition, (b) nothing short of criminal liability will ensure sufficient obedience to the law in question, (c) criminal liability will ensure sufficient obedience, and (d) criminal liability does not impose an unfair burden.*[64] Like the principle of just prohibition, this principle also includes a weighing-in-balance. This time, however, the weighing includes the cost of enforcement, including the cost of using the police, public prosecutors, and criminal courts. Because of these new costs, a proposal to use criminal liability to enforce a certain prohibition requires reasons beyond those put forward for the prohibition itself. Legislators should evaluate other methods of gaining compliance.[65]

Like the principle of just prohibition, this second principle leaves open the question whether liability is to be for an act or some other event. Though Gross says nothing to suggest that he would approve criminal liability merely for connection with an event, such liability is consistent both with actual practice and with Gross' conclusions (provided the liability does not include conviction or punishment). Criminal liability is not solely liability to conviction and punishment. Criminal liability also makes the act in question the concern of specific government agencies. So, for example, if I call the police because my neighbor is building a garage with one corner on my property, the police will tell me that, though she has violated my property rights and the city's zoning law, it is a civil matter about which they can do nothing. If, however, my neighbor falls dead drunk on my front lawn, no less inert than her garage, the police will happily take her down to the station for a night in jail and a morning appearance before a judge. Because public drunkenness is a crime, the police can interfere with, and the courts can at least look into, my neighbor's drunkenness, even if her condition was involuntary—for example, because she had a rare allergic reaction to the alcohol in her cough medicine. It is reasonable to make some events criminal just so the police can intervene.

The third principle, the principle of just conviction, may be stated as follows: *Conviction for a crime is just only when (a) the conviction is for some act or omission of the accused, (b) the act satisfies the definition of the crime, and (c) the act is not exempt under some morally required justification or excuse.* This principle limits criminal liability for events to police intervention and perhaps to prosecution and trial. Only what Gross calls "intentional acts" (to distinguish them from bodily reflexes) can make one culpable (that is, properly subject to conviction or punishment). This principle does not necessarily exclude from the criminal law status crimes such as vagrancy (even if their endorsement includes conviction as well as liability to arrest, investigation, and the like). The principle would, however, not allow conviction for a status crime unless the criminal's condition was in part the result of something he did.[66]

The principle of just conviction thus provides a basis for excuses concerned directly with the act in question, such as necessity or mistake of fact. Excuses concerned with the actor[67] rely on what Gross calls "the principle of responsibility" rather than on the principle of culpability.[68] The distinction between these two principles, though important for Gross elsewhere, need not detain us, provided we remember that criminal liability involves more than culpability.

Just conviction is in part a principle of legality; it connects conviction to the legal definition of the crime. But it does more than that. It identifies a part of the principle of culpability not directly concerned with harm (that is, maintenance of social order). The principle of just conviction requires exoneration whenever the accused has some justification or excuse sufficient to exempt him from conviction.[69] The principle does not require any weighing-in-balance, nor does it require provision for any justification or excuse except those that morality requires. If Gross had analyzed his principle as we have, he might have seen that weighing-in-balance should be relevant only to deciding general terms of criminal liability, not to deciding guilt or the maximum deserved punishment.

I have distinguished the crime's definition from the various excuses or justifications in part to clarify the relation between just criminal liability and just conviction. The police, prosecutors, and courts are set in motion if some reason exists to believe the definition of a crime has been satisfied, whether or not the actor has an excuse or justification. That is the extent of criminal liability under the second principle. The third principle becomes relevant only once that machinery is in motion. Justification or excuse becomes relevant only if the definition of some crime is satisfied.

I have also distinguished the crime's definition from the criminal's excuse or justification for another reason. The importance of the distinction is not limited to clarifying the relation between our second and third principles. Distinguishing the crime's definition from the various justifications or excuses is also more convenient and closer to everyday practice than combining them. A crime's definition can ordinarily be found in a statute book under the name of the crime itself, but only rarely will any of the justifications or excuses be found there. While debate over strict liability in the criminal law can be described as concerned with a question about the definition of crimes,[70] it seems simpler to think of the debate as concerned with such questions as whether non-negligent ignorance of a material fact should, in general, be a complete excuse.[71]

The fourth principle, the principle of just punishment, may be stated as follows: *Punishment is just only when (a) it does not exceed in severity the seriousness of the crime of which the accused has been convicted, and (b) the conviction itself is consistent with the principle of just conviction.* This last principle is a version of the traditional retributive principle that punishment should be proportioned to culpability.[72] Like the principle of just conviction, it makes no reference to the interests that the law serves. All that need be weighed in the balance is the seriousness of the crime. Though it is not easy to see the principle in Gross' formulation of the principle of culpability, he intends it to be there. For example, after noting that the principle of just proportion "serves as the foundation of every criminal sentence that is justifiable,"[73] Gross adds that it is "dictated by the same principle that does not allow punishment of the innocent, for any punishment in excess of what is deserved for the criminal conduct is punishment without guilt."[74]

The first two principles may be thought of as creating a certain practice, that of laying down the statutory rules, including provisions for penalties. The second two principles may likewise be thought of as regulating particular cases. Though the first two principles are relevant to the debate concerning the justice of strict liability, neither seems central to it. For example, no one objects to prohibiting speeding even if the crime's definition includes accidental speeding, as it did in Baker's case. We want people to avoid speeding, accidental or not. If merely prohibiting speeding will discourage it, why should we not prohibit it? We also want the police to be able to intervene to stop speeding even when the speeding is not intentional, reckless, or negligent. Speed kills — even when it is as accidental as Baker's was. So, no one should object to strict criminal liability if limited to police intervention to stop dangerous acts or events. Indeed, few people object even to issuing a ticket to someone like Baker and requiring him to give his excuse to a judge.

So, the first two principles may now be set aside, leaving the last two. Doubts about the correctness of strict liability begin only when, for example, the judge refused to accept Baker's excuse. That Baker should be *convicted* seems to bother many people, not his strict liability to police interference or trial. Those who object to Baker's conviction hold that, however minor the punishment, it is still too severe for faultless conduct. Baker's excuse should be sufficient to sustain a not-guilty verdict, just as insanity or automatism would.

But why? A conviction in itself implies only that Baker did what the law forbade and did so without a legally recognized justification or excuse. This implication seems to be no more than the literal truth. Baker *was* operating a speeding vehicle and had *no* justification or excuse under the statute. If conviction itself entailed some reprobation beyond the mere attribution to the accused of the act charged,[75] it would be relatively clear that convicting Baker would be wrong. People should not be reproved for faultless conduct. But, except for the conviction and fine, Baker was not reproved, condemned, or otherwise reprobated for what he did, however much the judge may have spoken ill of the speeding itself. This lack of condemnation is appropriate. Even though Baker *was* convicted under a criminal statute, it was not his fault that he was speeding. His offense was a mere technical violation.

Even putting truth aside, we can see a point to convicting Baker. Suppose, for example, that Baker's monthly visits to the mechanic do not prevent the cruise control from sticking several more times this year. Baker would pose a threat to other motorists on the road. Yet, unless he is convicted each time he is caught speeding, the criminal law cannot prevent him from driving his potentially dangerous vehicle. A sequence of not-guilty verdicts is not the proper basis for taking away someone's license. Of course, taking away

Baker's license would be, as Gross puts it "because of" his speeding, not "for" it. It would be a safety measure like quarantine, not a punishment like a fine or imprisonment.[76] We would, however, not tolerate taking his license even as a safety measure unless the taking were founded on a series of convictions.[77]

The principle of just *punishment* may seem peripheral to this analysis. If Baker deserves conviction, his punishment should be small because he is not very culpable. If, however, he does not deserve conviction, the principle of just punishment does not apply at all. The appeal to safety measures and the like to show that Baker deserves conviction[78] implies that strict liability cannot be justified as an attempt to prevent harm by threatening to punish according to the principle of culpability. So, it seems, the principle of just punishment need not even be mentioned in a chapter concerned with the justice of strict liability.

This argument may help to explain why the problem of strict liability has been so difficult. To accept the argument is to give up a promising approach to the problem. The approach is promising because the reverse of what the argument concludes seems to be true. The injustice of Baker's conviction depends on his deserving no punishment for what he did. If he deserves some punishment, his conviction would be just. If those opposed to strict liability could see why Baker *deserved* some punishment for his faultless act, they would have to agree that the law need not recognize his excuse. So, the principle of just punishment is not out of place here.[80] We must consider whether Baker deserved the punishment he received for his faultless act.

I shall proceed as follows: First, I shall show how the theory of criminal desert I have been defending allows a relatively straightforward application of the principle of just punishment to crimes of strict liability. Next, I shall apply the theory to Baker's case. Last, I shall consider some serious objections to what I have done. I intend none of this to be the last word on the subject. I only hope to demonstrate another promise of my approach.

Unfair Advantage as the Measure of Deserved Punishment

The principle of just punishment forbids us to punish a criminal more severely than the crime deserves and bids us to measure that desert by the crime's seriousness. The question, then, is how to measure seriousness. Gross' proposal is that we measure seriousness in large part by the harm the act risked, the harm in question being what the law sought to prevent by forbidding the conduct in question.[81] Chapter Three explained what is wrong with that approach. We shall therefore continue to follow our alternative: measuring seriousness by the unfair advantage the criminal gets by doing what the law forbids. This approach assumes that a law creates a system of expectation, cooperation, and sacrifice and that the harm, or more exactly, the "untoward occurrence," relevant to punishment is a function of the expectations, cooperation, and sacrifices so created. The harm the law seeks to prevent is neither the only harm the criminal does by breaking the law, nor even the primary consideration in determining culpability. If, for example, the accused used means the inadequacy of which was obvious to everyone but him, one might say that he in fact risked no harm in Gross' sense of the term, though he thought he did. We would nevertheless convict him of attempting the crime in question and impose some punishment. In such circumstances, talk of harm seems misleading. What is "untoward" about the occurrence is that, in doing what the law forbade, the accused received an advantage the law abiding did not receive.[82]

The importance of the distinction between harm and unfair advantage can be clarified by comparing Gross' theory with the theory I have been defending. Like most contemporary retributivists, Gross agrees (a) that the criminal law of a relatively just legal system tends to maintain a fair balance between the benefits and burdens of those subject to it and (b) that providing for punishment if someone disobeys the law in such a legal system is justified (in part at least) because providing for such punishment helps to assure that the law will be obeyed.[83] For these theorists, including Gross, statutory penalties should be set to create a "system of liability ensuring that those who commit crimes do not [too often] get away with them."[84] Crime cannot be "punished away." The long-run aim of punishment is only to prevent "the disintegration of the social order through a loss of respect for the rules."[85]

For Gross, punishment is proportioned to the seriousness of the crime when the punishment is sufficient, but not more severe than necessary, to serve that aim.[86] Punishment serves that aim by "not allowing those who break the law to get away with their crime."[87] What is deserved in punishment depends "not on what most people feel like seeing the perpetrator suffer, but rather upon what is defensible through reasoned argument."[88] For Gross, that argument would take into account the two factors that go into measuring culpability as he understands it: first, whether the actor intended the harm, consciously risked it, negligently but knowingly risked it, or risked it through lack of "super care;"[89] and, second, whether the act was harmful or posed an imminent danger of harm, created a serious risk of harm, or merely created a significant risk. For Gross, these factors are not relevant, as they would be for most retributivists, because justice so requires. Rather, they are relevant only because of their connection with preventing the disintegration of society. For Gross, apparently, the justifying aim of punishment as an institution should be closely mirrored in decisions about how much to punish particular criminals for their crimes.[90] In this respect, he is closer to Bentham than to most retributivists.

The difficulties inherent in *weighing* the factors that Gross thinks relevant are obvious. Yet, he does not explain how the weighing would be done.

Instead, he appeals to the market to show that the rational weighing of such diverse factors is possible.[91] Through the weighing necessary for just punishment involves judgments of value. Gross suggests that it is no more a matter of subjective feeling than is the judgment that, for example (and the example is mine), on a given day and in a given place, one melon is really worth less than one pound of gold. We can present reasons for the truth of that claim and, because the claim does not require any fine judgments, those reasons should be decisive. The weighing of factors necessary to proportion punishment to criminal desert is, for Gross, no less objective than the weighing necessary to make judgments of fair market value.

Gross' use of the market is limited to this offhand analogy. He does not use the market to *understand* the weighing that, on his analysis, determines the degree of culpability required. If he had, he might have seen that his position on proportioning punishment must either amount to the "intimidation" version of deterrence, which he rejects,[92] or simply measure the seriousness of the crime in terms of "unfair advantage." The only way to ensure that the criminal does not get away with his crime is to take back the advantage he has unfairly taken by committing the crime. Whether this will help to prevent the disintegration of society will depend a good deal on factors beyond those concerned with culpability.[93] I therefore suggest that we focus on unfair advantage rather than on Gross' list of factors and that we use the market more than Gross did.

Let us once again imagine a society in which anyone subject to the law may bid on a small number of licenses to do what the law forbids. Because the number of licenses would be determined in much the way the number of licenses to hunt a certain animal in a certain season is determined, by considering how much hunting can be done without leaving less to hunt in years to come,[95] this procedure takes due account of society's need for order. The penalties so determined should also be severe enough to satisfy Gross' concern that the criminal does not get away with his crime. They will generally be severe enough so that a potential criminal forced to choose between abiding by the law and suffering the penalty for a crime, would choose to abide by the law. And because the penalties so determined also correspond to the unfair advantage the criminal took by his crime (are explained in Chapter Four), they are what he deserves in punishment. So, if crimes of strict liability can be shown to take some advantage, but less than the advantage taken by the corresponding intentional, reckless, or negligent crime, it would follow that such crimes deserve some penalty, albeit a relatively light penalty.

Pricing the License

We must now formulate the appropriate licenses and estimate their relative value. Each license must specify the crime to be excused, for example, murder or speeding. "Crime," as used here, means the "harm" the law seeks to prevent. It is not, however, a synonym for *actus reus* because it includes the purpose or other state of mind required by the crime's statutory definition. For example, a statute may define burglary as "breaking and entering the house of another in the night, *with the intention* of committing a felony thereon." Under the statute, no crime is committed unless the entry is done "with the intention of committing a felony." The harm the law seeks to prevent is not breaking and entering itself, but breaking and entering for the purpose of committing a felony in the house.[96]

The license must also specify whether what it excuses is intentionally committing the crime, committing it recklessly, committing it negligently, or committing it without fault. Some crimes, such as speeding, can be committed without fault as well as negligently, recklessly, or intentionally. So, there are four ways of licensing the crime of speeding (in addition to pardoning the crime whatever the criminal's state of mind). Other crimes, such as manslaughter, can be committed intentionally, recklessly, or negligently, but not without fault. There is one less way to license such crimes. Still other crimes, such as murder, can only be committed intentionally or with gross recklessness. Such crimes can be licensed in even fewer ways.

Determining the relative value of licenses is not as simple as formulating them. The value of a license could be a mere artifact of the auction. For the auction to be a plausible analogue of our thinking about proportionate punishment, the procedures of the auction must be reasonably related to what we want to find out. They should, as much as possible, have their counterpart in any ordinary system of criminal law. Since our concern is the relative *unfair* advantage of committing a crime without fault, we must also take care to assure that the procedures are fair.

We can now determine the value of a license to commit a crime of strict liability relative to the value of a license to commit the same crime with an "evil mind." The auction will have bidders of at least four types (some of whom may be of more than one type). Each bidder will decide what to bid in a somewhat different way).[97]

The first type of bidder is one who *knows* his conduct will (if successful) do the harm the law forbids. The price that bidder is willing to pay for a license will depend on how much he values doing that harm. A would-be speeder might, for example, ask himself whether speeding is worth a certain amount of money. But the maximum he could rationally offer is not this amount, but this amount discounted to allow both for the probability that he will not need the license after all[98] and for the "transaction costs" (including the value of the time he must spend to get the license).

The second type of bidder is one who does not intend the harm the law forbids but knows that what he wants to do may very well result in that harm.

He knows he is negligently risking harm, but does not care enough to exercise reasonable care to avoid it. He is reckless. He, for example, may rapidly accelerate the car without bothering to check the speedometer. Such a bidder will not ask how much he values doing the harm the law forbids because he does not care whether he does the harm or not. Rather, he will ask how much he values doing what unreasonably risks that harm.

The third type of bidder is one who neither intends the harm the law forbids nor is indifferent to doing it. He does not *know* that his conduct will be criminal, as does the first type of bidder. Nor does he know that his conduct is likely to be criminal, as does the second type. This bidder thinks his conduct is reasonably safe. He does not know what more is required of him. If he did, he would do it. He has taken all the precautions he thinks reasonable to prevent the harm the law forbids and he does not expect to cause that harm. Nevertheless, he worries that he may not be taking all reasonable precautions. He is interested in a license to commit the crime because he recognizes the possibility of error and prefers to buy a license rather than bear the cost of looking for other reasonable precautions to take. An example of this type of bidder is the speeder who did not watch her speedometer more closely but would have if it had occurred to her. She is negligent. Like the reckless bidder, she will bid taking into account that her conduct will only risk the harm the law forbids, but she will not treat the risk as if it were the same risk taken by the reckless bidder. Insofar as the negligent bidder is careful, the risk of her doing a particular harm is less than it would have been had she not been careful. So, insofar as the negligent bidder believes herself to be careful, she will view the risk she runs as less than that of the reckless person and will bid accordingly.

The fourth type of bidder includes Baker. Like the negligent bidder, this type does not intend the harm the law forbids. Nor does he act in reckless disregard of the harm. He believes his conduct is reasonable. Indeed, he may have done more than a reasonable person would to prevent the harm. He nevertheless knows that what he does involves a risk of harm that the law forbids and that the risk could be avoided simply by avoiding a certain range of legal conduct. He wants a license to do what the law forbids because he, like the negligent bidder, does not want to pay the cost of reducing the risk further. He would rather pay the price of a license, if the price is not too high, than give up the legal conduct in question. Among such bidders, besides Baker, is the liquor seller who wants to go on selling liquor to people who look young but are not underage, yet does not want to do what is necessary to be sure customers are not in fact underage. For such a bidder, the cost of a license might approach, but would not exceed, the cost of being super careful in the relevant respects.

Although each of these bidders would like a license to do what the law forbids, what they are willing to pay is not likely to be the same. What they are willing to pay for a license is a function in part of the probability that they will use the license. That probability will vary with whether the bidder intends the crime, will merely risk the crime recklessly, will risk it negligently, or will risk it without fault. For example, if I *intend* to commit a certain crime, I will need a pardon unless my plans change or I escape detection. If I only *knowingly fail* to take reasonable precautions to prevent the harm the law forbids, I will be less likely to do the harm because we are in general less likely to do what we knowingly risk than what we intend. If I *unknowingly* fail to take reasonable precautions, I am even less likely to do the harm in question. How much less likely will depend upon how much care I have taken.[99] If, however, I neither intend to do the harm nor am negligent with respect to it, I am even less likely to need a pardon because part of what makes a certain degree of care reasonable is that it is more likely to prevent the harm in question than a lesser degree of care.

So, all else equal, there should be bidders even for licenses to commit crimes without fault. A license pardoning such a crime would be in demand because people sometimes do what the law forbids even though they have exercised reasonable care (Baker, for example). Such a license, however, would not be worth as much as a license pardoning the same crime committed negligently. One who believes that he needs a license for negligence is, all else equal, more likely to do what he should not than one who believes he merely needs a license to commit the same crime faultlessly. A license to be negligent is more useful than a license to risk the same harm without fault. So, a license to commit a certain crime without fault should be worth something, but not as much as a license to do the crime negligently, and by similar reasoning, recklessly or intentionally.

Objections

Possible objections to the foregoing argument are many. Some concern the fairness of the auction. Because I believe the auction, as imagined, will yield approximately the same outcome as any free market would, I believe as well that such objections will not withstand scrutiny. (I will say more about this in Chapter Ten.) Other objections, for example, those regarding the plausibility of treating punishment as corresponding to payment for a license, I have already answered in Chapter Six. I need not repeat those answers. I do, however, have more to say in defense of the analysis just given. No analysis is better than the understanding it imparts. If what I have said so far makes sense, it should help us understand why we punish crimes of strict liability as we do. If it does not help, other objections are more or less beside the point.

Consider Baker's case again. Under the analysis just given, Baker does not deserve punishment unless his lawbreaking constituted taking unfair advantage. Baker *had*, it seems, an advantage the law-abiding do not have. He operated his car at a speed well above the posted limit. He came to have that advantage by adopting a method of operating his car that he could easily have done without. He did not intend to speed or consciously take an unreasonable risk of speeding. Indeed, he did not even unknowingly take such a risk. He was, in other words, not guilty of intentional, reckless, or negligent speeding. However, since he was not punished as severely as he would have been had he been guilty of such speeding, the lack of intent, recklessness, or negligence is irrelevant — or, rather, is relevant only to the question of whether Baker actually took the advantage in question

Baker had an advantage the law-abiding do not have. But was it an *unfair* advantage? That it is an advantage the law-abiding do not have certainly suggests that it was unfair. After all, Baker's conviction supposedly occurred under a relatively just legal system and the laws of such a system generally distribute benefits and burdens fairly. If Baker did what the law said he should not have done, then, all else equal, he must have had an unfair advantage. But the critics of strict liability claim that strict liability makes all else less than equal because holding people strictly liable in the criminal law introduces an unfair burden of compliance into an otherwise just legal system.[100] Against this claim, we may now set the principles of just prohibition, just criminal liability, and just conviction. This chapter presented a justification for each of these principles and showed that some strict liability statutes could satisfy them all. Critics of strict liability must then either provide an argument for rejecting or amending one of these principles, show that no strict liability statute can satisfy them, or admit that strict liability statutes do not necessarily impose an unfair burden of compliance.

That brings us to the central question, whether Baker *took* the unfair advantage he seems to have had. We cannot avoid the question merely by talking of "having" an unfair advantage instead of "taking" it. To substitute "having" for "taking" would open wide the door to absolute liability. It would, as well, mean that punishment within the criminal law could not be characterized as a response to the criminal's *act*. One would need only to have the advantage to deserve the punishment, no matter how one came to have it. The arguments that have helped to revive retributivism, arguments contrasting punishment for acts with treatment for what one suffers, would have to be abandoned or at least recognized as far weaker than they seem to be. The distinction between "having" an advantage and "taking" it is so fundamental to my analysis that to abandon it would amount to abandoning the whole. We must show that Baker "took" the unfair advantage he had in a sense not to be mistaken for merely having the advantage. But how?

It is easy to understand how someone can negligently take an *object* without intending to. We have only to consider those circumstances in which someone found with a missing object might say, "I didn't mean to take it."

People generally say this honestly only when they did take it but without realizing what they were doing. They *mis*took it for something else or perhaps missed seeing it in what they did mean to take. When someone has not taken something, he does not say that he did not mean to. He says he did not take it. What then is the problem with saying that someone like Baker, by intentionally using his cruise control, set in motion a chain of events leading to his unintentionally taking an unfair advantage by speeding?

This is the problem: We hesitate to say that someone can *wrongfully* take *without fault* what he did not mean to take at all. It is as if "wrongfully take" and "fault" were conceptually coupled the way "cause" and "responsibility" often seem to be. Indeed, we might cast the problem in terms of "cause" and "responsibility." To "take" is to be "the cause" of the object's coming into one's possession, to be responsible for its being there. If such possession is wrongful and one has come into possession without fault, then one is not responsible for having it, not the cause of its being in one's possession, and, therefore, not the one who took it. "It just happened; so, don't blame me." If "take" means that one can only take unfair advantage intentionally, recklessly, or negligently, then certainly Baker did not "take" the unfair advantage in question, and there was no unfair advantage for which Baker deserves to be punished.

This way of stating what might be objectionable in strict liability is appealing. No one wants to be held responsible for what was no part of his plans, for what seems to spring from his act as the result of bad luck or divine malevolence. Perhaps this is just the feeling that underwrites thoughtful opposition to strict liability in both the criminal and civil law. But it is a feeling in need of an argument. On the one hand, moral theory includes a significant literature on "moral luck." It is now a respectable, though still controversial, view that people can be held morally responsible for more than they intended or even unreasonably risked.[101] On the other hand, the question remains why the law must adopt the exact standards of liability governing nonlegal activity. Has the law no concerns that might make strict liability morally permissible for it even if not permissible for morality as such?

In any event, the criminal law certainly seems to allow luck to have a substantial part in determining punishment in areas other than strict liability. For example, the difference between manslaughter and reckless driving is whether the reckless driver killed someone. Though whether a reckless driver kills someone is necessarily a matter of luck, even the *Model Penal Code* distinguishes between manslaughter and reckless conduct not resulting in death.[102] Leaving such differences to luck has been much criticized in this century. Indeed, Gross is among the critics. However, unlike some others, Gross is not afraid to draw the unattractive conclusion compelled by excluding luck. Gross expressly acknowledges that doing away with luck in setting penalties means that those who risk harm without actually doing it are just as blamable as those who take the same risk and actually do the harm, that most attempts should be punished as severely as the corresponding complete crime, and that one can commit murder without killing anyone so long as one fails only by chance.[103] These conclusions, while not counterintuitive enough to be decisive, are certainly sufficient to give pause.

Happily, there *is* an argument that should make such worries about luck unnecessary. We have only to show that "take" is not coupled with "fault" in the way supposed and the problem disappears. Showing this is not difficult. Consider, for example, the sleepwalker who goes into her neighbor's yard, takes an apple from the tree, and eats it. Undoubtedly, she took the apple. Yet, we would not punish her for theft, though we might punish the same physical taking done while awake. We would not even say the sleepwalker was at fault, though the apple was not hers to take. We would say she was not responsible for what she did. It was not her fault that she wrongfully took the apple. We thus have a clear example of wrongful taking without fault.[104]

This example may seem to be irrelevant because it involves taking an object rather than taking an unfair advantage. That, however, is not so. The example involves the unfair advantage of taking another's apple as well as taking the apple itself. Taking the apple is wrong because it is a taking of unfair advantage. We tacitly admitted that the sleepwalker took unfair advantage when we agreed that her taking the apple was wrong. Our conclusion that she should not be punished was not based on her *culpability* for the taking (whether of the apple or of the advantage), but on her *responsibility* as a person. In Gross' terms, we appealed not to the principle of culpability to excuse her, but to the principle of responsibility. There is no need to excuse under the principle of responsibility what does not deserve punishment under the principle of culpability. So, our analysis of why the sleepwalker should not be punished seems to work as well for taking unfair advantage as for taking the apple itself.

It will, perhaps, be contended that Baker's case is still not the same as the sleepwalker's. Although she was not responsible, she did in her sleep what she wanted to do and enjoyed the fruit of her wrongful conduct. Baker, on the other hand, did not enjoy speeding and did not want to speed, awake or asleep. He did everything in his power to stop the speeding as soon as he could.

These differences must be admitted. Yet, it is one thing to admit them and another to admit their relevance. That Baker did not enjoy speeding seems good reason to mitigate whatever penalty he deserves. It does not show, however, that he has taken no unfair advantage deserving punishment. After all, even someone who deliberately steals does not always enjoy what he steals. (Think, for example, of a thief who steals a stinking skunk thinking it a prize cat.) Unless the definition of a crime requires actual enjoyment, enjoyment should not be necessary for punishment. Introducing such a subjective standard would make proof of guilt much more difficult than it is. More to the point, it would amount to saying that, if a criminal fails at a crime in his own eyes or in ours, he should not be punished and perhaps should not even be convicted. Because I know of no respectable writer who has taken this position, I shall say no more about it.

It seems, then, that we can identify an unfair advantage that Baker did in fact take (though without fault). His speeding, though unintended, was a consequence of his act. The law forbade speeding. Others did what was necessary to obey the law, or if they broke the law (and were caught), suffered the prescribed punishment. Unless Baker is punished, he will have an advantage others do not have. To get some idea of the objective value of the license Baker took, we have only to imagine an auction in which licenses to do what Baker did are put up for bid. The advantage is, as we have seen, significant. While Baker may deserve no blame for what he did because it was not his fault, to treat him as if he had not broken the law would be unfair. He deserves to be punished for what he did. He was not innocent.

If this is right, then we need not distinguish, as Gross does, between strict liability in minor offenses and strict liability in felonies, provided penalties are proportioned so that persons satisfying the crime's definition in part without fault are punished less severely than those satisfying it intentionally, recklessly, or negligently. We need not, as Gross does, look beyond the letter of the law to find the harm the statute really intends to prevent. If the minimum penalty imposed by a particular statute is still too high, punishing the crime that severely would be unjust. The injustice involved is, however, not peculiar to crimes of strict liability. Proportion is a general condition of just punishment; the test of disproportionate punishment is much the same no matter what the criminal law in question.[105] On our analysis, whatever the wisdom of felony statutes imposing strict liability, such statutes can satisfy the principle of culpability in the same manner as statutes imposing strict liability for misdemeanors. Strict liability for felonies is, on our analysis, not the anomaly it is for Gross.

Notes

The National Endowment for the Humanities, Fellowship FB-22388-84, made work on this paper possible.

1. Joel Bishop, *New Criminal Law* 9th ed. (Chicago: T. H. Flood and Company, 1923), p. 192.

2. *State v. Baker*, 1 Kan. App. 2d 568, 571 P.2d 65, 66-67 (1977). What follows is an attempt to summarize the court's reasoning and to make sense

of it; not an attempt to provide an alternative interpretation of the facts or an alternative theory of liability.

3. *Baker*, 69.

4. Ibid.

5. *Kan. Stat. Ann.* 8-1336(a)(3) Supp. (1976).

6. Baker, 69.

7. "Criminal intent," of course, here includes both recklessness and negligence, as well as literal intent.

8. In Baker's case, the maximum punishment was a $500 fine and one month of confinement. *Kan. Stat. Ann.* 8-216, 21-4502 to -4503 (Supp. 1976).

9. Packer, for example, notes that "[t]he consensus can be summarily stated: to punish conduct without reference to the actor's state of mind is both inefficacious and unjust. . . . Consequently, on either a preventive or retributive theory of criminal punishment, the criminal sanction is inappropriate in the absence of mens rea." Herbert Packer, "Mens Rea and the Supreme Court," *Supreme Court Review* (1962): 109.

10. See, e.g., Richard Wasserstrom, "Strict Liability in the Criminal Law," *Stanford Law Review* 12 (July 1960): 731-745; Note, "Criminal Liability Without Fault: A Philosophical Perspective," *Columbia Law Review* 75 (December 1975): 1517-1577.

11. W. LaFave and A. Scott, *Criminal Law* 31, at 218 (1972).

12. See *Hill v. Baxter*, [1958] 1 All E.R. 193 (Q.B.); Williams, "Absolute Liability in Traffic Offenses," *Criminal Law Review* 1967 (April 1967), p. 201.

13. Ibid.

14. I am not certain that absolute liability in the criminal law can ever be excused, much less justified. My guess is that it cannot, in part at least, because the alternative of imposing strict liability seems to make absolute liability to conviction and punishment as unnecessary as it would be harsh. Nevertheless, strict liability, not absolute liability, is our concern now.

15. *Barnes v. State*, 12 Conn. 398 (1849) (accused convicted of unknowingly selling liquor to common drunkard); *Regina v. Woodrow*, 153 Eng. Rep. 907 (Ex. Ch. 1846) (tobacco dealer fined for possessing adulterated tobacco thought to be genuine).

16. *Model Penal Code* 2.05 (Tent. Draft No. 4, 1955).

17. *Model Penal Code* 2.05 (Official Draft & Revised Comments 1985).

18. See Jerome Hall, *Principles of Criminal Law* (Indianapolis: Bobbs-Merrill, 1960), pp. 342-351 (objecting to criminal liability for negligence for same reasons he objects to strict liability); H.L.A. Hart, *Punishment and Responsibility* (Oxford University Press: New York, 1968), pp. 177-184 (condemning what seems to be absolute liability); Glanville Williams, *Criminal Law: The General Part* (British Publications: Stevens and Sons, 1961), pp. 215-265.

19. Hyman Gross, *A Theory of Criminal Justice* (Oxford University Press: New York, 1979).

20. Gross, 344.

21. Gross, 373.

22. Ibid.

23. Ibid.

24. Criminal Code of 1961, *Ill. Rev. Stat.* ch 38 11-5 (1979). The maximum penalty for conviction of this misdemeanor is one year imprisonment. Compare 11-4 for which conviction is a felony punishable by 4 to 15 year imprisonment and a reasonable belief about age is an affirmative defense.

25. Gross, 365-367. For the same analysis of strict liability for serious crimes, see Joel Feinberg, *Doing and Deserving* (Princeton University Press: Princeton, New Jersey, 1970), pp. 224-225; George Fletcher, *Rethinking Criminal Law* (Boston: Brown, Little & Company, 1978), pp. 716-730. But see Williams, *Criminal Law*, 239- 245.

26. Gross, 365-67.

27. Gross, 357-61.

28. Ibid.

29. See above, notes 16-17 and accompanying text.

30. Gross, 344.

31. Gross, 352. Indeed, for Gross the proposal that we have "penal liability without fault to insure precautionary alertness" is simply a proposal to impose "absolute liability." It requires more precaution than otherwise reasonable if reasonable precaution is not enough to prevent the prohibited outcome. Since Gross believes absolute liability in the criminal law to be necessarily unjust, he lays down three conditions (discussed in the accompanying notes 34-37) for the imposition of strict liability to assure that the punished conduct will be faulty, even if excusable.

32. See, e.g., James Brady, "Strict Liability Offenses: A Justification," *Criminal Law Bulletin* 8 (April 1972): 217-227.

33. Gross, 346.

34. Ibid.

35. Gross, 357.

36. Gross, 357-358.

37. Gross, 358.

38. Gross, 346.

39. Ibid.

40. Ibid.

41. Gross, 80.

42. See above, notes 3-4 and accompanying text.

43. Gross, 346-347. Gross actually says that an act like Baker's "constitutes negligence per se." I have not adopted this usage because it is so unusual that it invites misunderstanding. Most often, "negligence per se"

does not refer to negligence as such but merely to imputed negligence — when violating a certain law amounts to negligence regardless of the circumstances. Imposing liability for negligence in such circumstances amounts to saying that "this act fell below the standard of reasonable care however reasonable it was." The effect of such an irrebuttable presumption of negligence is to impose strict liability. To be "on the safe side," people may have to be super careful. Sometimes, however, "negligence per se" means "self-evidently negligent." "Negligence per se" is, in this sense, simply actual negligence of the most obvious sort and, as far as I can tell, has nothing to do with strict liability.

44. The process in question is what a reasonable person would *do* in the circumstances.

45. The standard is outcome-oriented in the sense that the act's outcome is all that matters. The level of care is *sufficient* if it in fact prevents any "illegitimate" risk when prevention is possible and not "prohibitive." Otherwise, the level of care is not sufficient, however much the actor does.

46. If we wanted to say that Baker should not have installed the cruise control in his car, we would in effect want to prohibit cruise control altogether. According to Gross, this is not a proper aim of strict liability.

47. We are, of course, assuming that Baker had the cruise control checked reasonably often. The court did not suggest otherwise. The assumption allows us to reach our question, that is, how society justly can demand more of someone than what a reasonable person would do.

48. Baker's act was a "crime" in the sense that it was a minor offense punishable within the structure of the criminal law. "Crime" does *not* mean only "felony."

49. That Baker could have prevented the offense by exercising such care is simply another way of saying the offense is one of strict liability rather than of absolute liability.

50. Gross, 372.

51. Gross, 24.

52. Gross, 23.

53. Gross, 15 and 26. Gross' argument that acts can be culpable but not morally wrong seems uncharacteristically weak.

54. Gross, 14.

55. Gross, 15.

56. A just legal system is one either resting on free consent or so fairly arranged that it may invoke the principle of fairness.

57. Gross, 114-115.

58. An example of a "condition" would be having no visible means of support.

59. An example of an "outcome" could be Baker's speeding.

60. Gross, 115.

61. Gross, 122.

62. For example, we might prohibit the presence of noxious chemicals near residential land.

63. For example, we might require persons with a certain income to owe no less than a certain amount in taxes, whatever their deductions.

64. Gross, 139-140. Note that this condition would allow Gross to absorb the supposedly novel theory offered in J. Braithewaite and P. Pettit, *Not Just Deserts: A Republican Theory of Criminal Law* (Oxford: Clarendon Press, 1990).

65. Among the other methods are disqualification, strict inspection, tort liability, security bonds, and injunctions.

66. Gross, 145 and 348. If the vagrant quit his job, his condition would be the result of his own act and the principle would not prevent a conviction based on his status.

67. Insanity or extreme youth are examples of excuses that go to the actor.

68. Gross, 142.

69. Justifications and excuses should include those required by morality. Convictions obtained because the law failed to include such a required justification or excuse would be unjust. Gross, 138.

70. For example, should "knowingly" be read into the strict liability statute?

71. Cf. G. Fletcher, 683-698.

72. See, e.g., *Coker v. Georgia*, 433 U.S. 584, 592 (1977) (death sentence grossly disproportionate punishment for rape).

73. Gross, 436.

74. Ibid.

75. Cf. Gross, 460-461. Gross seems to say there can be no punishment without reprobation.

76. Gross, 461.

77. Even in a civil proceeding to revoke Baker's license, we would want to have each offense proved. (The practical difficulties of finding a civil alternative to strict liability should be weighed under the principle of just criminal liability, not under the principle of just conviction.)

78. Gross, 461.

79. Gross, 351.

80. The principle of just punishment would, however, probably be out of place in discussion with the wisdom, rather than the justice, of strict liability.

81. Gross, 77-88 (state of mind and legitimacy of interests also relevant to culpability); see also Gross, 446.

82. For a defense of this claim, see Chapter Five.

83. Gross, 400-401.

84. Gross, 401.

85. Gross, 403.

86. Gross, 438-445.

87. Gross, 439.

88. Gross, 440.

89. Gross, 77-88.

90. Gross, 446-447 (mirroring is necessary to preserve "our moral sensibilities"). Thus, near the end of his book, Gross takes back much of the independence from morality that he granted the law at the beginning.

91. Gross, 436-447. See also his response to this chapter, "Fringe Liability, Unfair Advantage, and the Price of Crime," *Wayne Law Review* 33 (Summer 1987): 1395-1411, esp. pp. 1406-1411.

92. Gross, 394-97.

93. How well the punishment is publicized, or the desperation of certain criminals, are examples of what I have in mind.

94. For example, the criminal who kills the wrong man or steals something he cannot sell or use does not benefit from his crime.

95. The analogy with game management is not as inapposite as it may seem at first. The criminal law aims at maintaining a certain level of social order (enough, as Gross puts it, to "prevent the disintegration of society"). That level of social order corresponds to the animal population of concern to game wardens. And just as game wardens allow hunters to kill a certain number of animals each year, so a society that is not willing to pay the price required to have less crime sets the rate of crime it will allow.

96. "Crime" as used in this section excludes only those states of mind or other circumstances that may affect the seriousness of the crime rather than whether the crime in question has or has not occurred.

97. Because the harm is the same whether the crime is done intentionally, recklessly, negligently, or faultlessly, we may assume hereafter the proportion between supply and demand is roughly the same for each type of license. For defense of this assumption, see Chapter Ten.

98. He might not need the license because he changed his mind, failed in the attempt, or escaped capture.

99. If I am rather dense about such things, my negligence may be as dangerous as someone else's recklessness, but the market price should, if I am rational, be determined by general tendencies, not by my special circumstances.

100. Gross, 346-348.

101. See, e.g., Thomas Nagel, "Moral Luck," in *Mortal Questions* (Cambridge: Cambridge University Press, 1979), 24-38; Robert Nozick, *Philosophical Explanations* (Cambridge, Massachusetts: Harvard Universtiy Press, 1981), 391-395.

102. *Compare Model Penal Code* 210.1, 210.4 (official Draft 1962) (provisions creating a felony of negligent homicide with 211.2 (provision creating misdemeanor of recklessly endangering another person).

103. Gross, 428-430.

104. Some may find this harsh, for it follows that sleepwalkers might be convicted of the theft if intention could be proved. I do not find this harsh so long as there is no liability to punishment. See my "Guilty But Insane?," *Social Theory and Practice* (Spring 1984): 1-24.

105. See Chapters Four, Five, and Six.

8

Sentencing: Must Justice Be Even-Handed?

A decade ago a distinguished federal judge, Marvin Frankel, published a sharp attack on the discretion judges had in setting criminal sentences. The attack included an anecdote drawn from a prison director's testimony before Congress several years earlier:

> Take, for instance, the cases of two men we received last spring. The first man had been convicted of cashing a check for $58.40. He was out of work at the time of his offense, and when his wife became ill and he needed money for rent, food, and doctor bills, he became the victim of temptation. He had no prior criminal record. The other man cashed a check for $35.20. He was also out of work and his wife had left him for another man. His prior record consisted of a drunk driving charge and a nonsupport charge. Our examination of these cases indicated no significant differences for sentencing purposes. But they appeared before different judges and the first man received 15 years in prison and the second man 30 days.[1]

The anecdote is disturbing (even if we suppose 15 years for forging a check for $58.40 not to be out of proportion to the crime). If either convict deserved the 15 years in prison, it was the second. He at least had a prior record of some sort (though not a "criminal" record). He had no family to support. He seems to have been less stable (witness the drunk driving and nonsupport). And, though he wrote the smaller check, the difference between the checks ($23.20) seems insignificant (supposing the statute not to distinguish, say, checks of more than $50 from checks of $50 or less). Could any reputable theory of punishment justify such a pattern of sentencing (even if it could justify such a difference in sentence for similar offenses by persons similarly situated)? The only relevant variable is (let us suppose) the luck of drawing one judge rather than another ("Lovable Larry" rather than "Maximum John"). Certainly something is wrong with a system of criminal justice making so much depend on so little. Justice should be more even-handed than that.

But the interesting question is not whether something is wrong. The interesting question is what is wrong. That question, unfortunately, is too large for us now. The question I want to consider is smaller but related: *Does the anecdote report an injustice?* If we find that it does, we have a partial answer to the large question. At least part of what is wrong with a system of criminal justice making so much depend on so little, is that it is unjust. If, instead, we find that the anecdote does not report an injustice, we still have done something worthwhile. While we would still have the large question waiting an answer, we would have a question much clarified by the exclusion of one likely answer. We would have learned something about how even-handed justice must be.

I shall argue that the anecdote does *not* report an injustice.

The Question: Context and Importance

Though every question leads some place, not every place is worth the trip. Why this question? Let me answer by putting the question in context. The context explains what makes the question worth asking.

When Frankel published his attack on judicial discretion in sentencing, rehabilitation (and incapacitation) dominated the practice of punishment. Judicial discretion was part of a system of "indeterminate sentencing," the historic (and, to a lesser degree, the logical) companion of rehabilitation. A sentence is indeterminate insofar as its term (and form) cannot be known before it is imposed (or carried out).

Rehabilitation and indeterminate sentencing come to be companions in this way: Because the legislature is furthest from the individual criminal, the legislature is least well placed to determine when a particular criminal will be rehabilitated. So (according to rehabilitation theory), the legislature should say as little as politically possible about sentences. A statutory provision of zero to life would be ideal. (California, for example, used to approximate this ideal.) Such broad statutory provision leaves room for judicial discretion. Because the trial judge can observe the particular criminal, and because he can receive the reports and advice of experts familiar with the particular criminal, the judge is better placed than the legislature to determine how long the criminal should remain in prison to be rehabilitated. But, because even the judge cannot know in advance how successful the prison's efforts to rehabilitate will be, even the judge's sentence should (according to rehabilitation theory) leave broad discretion to those in charge of "corrections." A judicial determination of zero to life would be ideal. In practice a sentence such as "1-5 years" or "not more than 20 years" was more likely. (But once again, California used to approximate the ideal.) The greater the indeterminacy of the judicial sentence, the greater the discretion left to the parole board. The parole board (according to rehabilitation theory) is best placed to evaluate a particular criminal's rehabilitation and so best placed to determine when his sentence should end. Insofar as the parole board has final say, the sentence is absolutely indeterminate. The criminal's sentence ends when the parole board ends it, and the criminal cannot know how long his sentence will be until that day.

Frankel's attack on judicial discretion in sentencing was part of a general attack on the indeterminate sentence. That may seem surprising. After all, the parole board provides a partial check on the discretion of judges. A criminal sentenced to 15 years might be out on parole in one (if the judge's sentence is by law no more than a maximum). The dramatic difference between the two sentences of the anecdote might (upon inspection of applicable law) turn out to be far less dramatic than it appears.

The generality of Frankel's attack is, however, not surprising once one knows his objection to judicial discretion. Frankel objects to judicial discretion for the same reason he objects to the parole board's discretion. He objects to the parole board's discretion because it produces "arbitrary" distinctions. The distinctions are not arbitrary in the sense of relying on no fixed standard. Rehabilitation is a fixed standard. The distinctions are arbitrary in the sense of relying on no *usable* standard. Frankel argues that even the parole board is in no position to ascertain rehabilitation. The best it can do is guess. While the single parole board eliminates variation due to differences in judges, it still produces variations which are in fact unjustifiable. Both parole board and judge must (Frankel explains) act arbitrarily because they have no way (given the limits of actual knowledge) to do what rehabilitation theory requires.[2]

Frankel does not make clear whether his objection to arbitrariness is practical or moral (or both). Frankel's discussion emphasizes such practical considerations as the absence of tests for rehabilitation, the inability of prison to supply what is necessary for rehabilitation, the tremendous emotional cost to prisoners of having their future depend upon the incomprehensible discretion of a parole board, and the way indeterminacy itself undermines rehabilitation. Express appeal to principles of justice (or the constitutional equivalent) is rare, curt, and almost apologetic. Yet Frankel's tone is one of moral outrage.

Frankel's attack came early. Today rehabilitation, whether thought of as a justification of what punishment is or as a program for what it should be, is widely discredited. The indeterminate sentence is disappearing from one state after another (or, at least, is being made much more determinate). Since 1975, at least 13 states (including California) have adopted some form of "presumptive sentencing" requiring a judge to give a certain statutorily determined sentence for the crime unless she is willing to state her reasons for giving a heavier or lighter sentence. Several states (including California) prescribe a specific (and relatively narrow) range of sentence for a particular crime, say, 4-to-6 years. At least 10 states (including California) have begun to phase out discretionary parole of prisoners.[3] In 1978, the National Conference of Commissioners on Uniform State Laws approved a "Model Sentencing and Corrections Act" in which rehabilitation is expressly excluded from the facts to be taken into account in setting the term of imprisonment. (Rehabilitation appears only in the last subdivision of the Act's statement of purpose — immediately following deterrence and incapacitation — with the proviso that participation in rehabilitation programs be "voluntary.")[4] The legal community has always treated the recommendations of the Commissioners with great respect. The Model Act both exemplifies and consolidates a major change in how we decide punishment.

The change has been defended under such interchangeable theoretical banners as "just deserts," "fair and certain punishment," and "equitable sentencing."[5] Those banners refer to a principle that itself goes virtually undefended (and indeed, unchallenged). Let us call it "the principle of equality in punishment." Here are two examples of its use. The first is from an important legal theorist, Andrew von Hirsch:

> It is likewise a basic principle of justice — although one widely ignored in practice in our criminal justice systems — that persons guilty of equally serious crimes should not be subjected to grossly unequal punishment.[6]

The second example of the principle's use in from an important Supreme Court case, *Furman v. Georgia*:

> When the punishment of death is inflicted in a trivial number of cases in which it is legally available, the conclusion is virtually inescapable that it is being inflicted arbitrarily. Indeed, it smacks of little more than a lottery system. . . . No one has yet suggested a rational basis that could differentiate in these terms the few who die from the many who go to prison.[7]

In the first example, von Hirsch is discussing one consequence of preventive detention of the guilty. Two people guilty of the same crime may end up serving widely differing sentences because one is adjudged dangerous while the other is not. In the second example, Justice Brennan is discussing the way receiving the death penalty for aggravated murder seems to depend upon where the case is tried, who happens to be on the jury, or who happens to be the judge. Two murderers perhaps differing only in the judge sentencing them may receive sentences as different as life and death. In both examples, there is a quiet leap from the fact of difference in sentence unjustified by difference in crime to a finding of injustice. Undefended is the assumption that the dependence of a particular sentence in part on factors other than the crime itself makes the sentence "arbitrary," unjustifiable, and so unjust.

The principle of equality in punishment seems to provide a powerful argument for sentencing reform. The principle can, however, be defended in two ways, that is, as a practical principle *or* as a moral one. The way it is defended will determine how powerful an argument it will provide. If defended only as a practical principle, it will be just one practical consideration among many. The principle could be ignored where other practical considerations (for example, incapacitation or the political desirability of decentralized sentencing) made ignoring it appealing. The principle would provide only a relatively weak argument for reform. If, however, the principle is defended as a moral principle, it could *not* be just one principle among many. It would be the kind of principle it appears to be in the two passages quoted above (a "side constraint"). It would permit reformers to push aside all but the most clear and pressing practical considerations.

Those who have adopted the slogan "*just deserts*," "*fair* and certain punishment," or *equitable* punishment" seem to believe the principle of equality in punishment to be a moral principle. If they are right, then (as von Hirsch suggests) all sorts of practices commonly accepted in our system of criminal justice may be fundamentally unjust and any movement to replace them with a system of "just deserts" is a crusade. If, on the other hand, the principle of equality in punishment is only a practical principle, then the movement for "just deserts" is only a movement. We may in good conscience debate the practical consequences of each reform, opposing the movement on this or that reform without necessarily committing ourselves to injustice.

So, the small question I posed at the beginning of this paper is important. If the anecdote reports an injustice, the principle of equality in punishment is (very likely) a moral principle and we are bound in conscience to root out the cause of that difference in sentences (unless some equally important moral principle stands in the way). But if the anecdote does not report an injustice, we have no reason to suppose the principle to be anything but a practical principle and we may consider whether rooting out the cause of such inequalities in sentence is worth the cost. Our question takes us to the center of the debate over "just deserts," to the ability of the principle of equality in punishment to provide a decisive argument for reform of sentencing.

Formulating the Principle of Equality in Punishment

The principle of equality in punishment might be stated as two propositions:

1. Persons convicted of equally serious crimes should receive the same punishment; and
2. Any difference between the punishment one person receives and that another receives should be fully accounted for by some (relevant) difference in the way the particular crimes were committed.

There is, I think, much to recommend this formulation. The principle so formulated sounds like a classic statement of retributivism and that theory of punishment supposedly underlies the defense of just deserts.[8] The principle so formulated fits comfortably much of what defenders of just deserts say about punishment. A few have even given the principle roughly this formulation.[9] Others certainly appear to rely on it. For example, Kenneth Kipnis recently argued that plea bargaining is unjust because plea bargaining generally takes into account considerations beside what the individual in question did wrong (for example, how he would fare in prison or how much he eased the prosecutor's burdens) and "those . . . individuals who are clearly guilty of certain serious specified wrongdoing deserve an officially administered punishment proportional to their wrongdoing."[10]

Nevertheless, though the principle so formulated has much to recommend it, we must reformulate it if we are to do justice to most of those defending just deserts. The principle as formulated is too strong for the work it is supposed to do. There are several grounds for varying sentence that, though widely accepted in even reformed practice, are ruled out by the principle as formulated. Most of these grounds are expressly recognized in the Model Act. The defense of each is at least plausible within a retributive framework.

Reformulating the principle will be worth the trouble. Most discussions of punishment, especially among philosophers and social scientists, seem to forget the details of the practice they are trying to understand, to sketch fine-boned abstractions where there are only hard-working peasants. Even a brief survey of the reasons for reformulating the principle should remind us of the complex realities of sentencing, should help us to see how special our question is, will reveal a certain shallowness in some reformers' understanding of both retributivism and practice, and might even dissolve any lingering suspicion that the principle (however formulated) is so nearly vacuous as to be of no concern to a practical person. A little charity now may foreclose large misunderstandings later. The properties of the reformulated principle are strikingly different from those of the principle as formulated now. Let us then describe the grounds for varying sentence the principle as formulated excluded (though it should not), point out how those excluded grounds can be fitted into a system of punishment consistent with retributivism, and consider what reasons there might be for fitting them in that way. Having done all that, we shall be ready to reformulate the principle, to see what that second formulation commits us to, and so, to return to our question.

Circumstances of Crime. Let us begin with the least controversial ground for varying sentence in a way inconsistent with the principle of equality in punishment as formulated, "circumstances of the crime." "Circumstances" as used here is supposed to be somewhat vague. It includes all those facts about the crime itself or the criminal not technically elements of the crime with which the criminal is actually charged but still somehow closely connected. Any doubts should be resolved in favor of inclusion. (Inclusion in the category does not entail justifiable appeal to the circumstance in question but merely its being appropriate to take up the justification of appeal to it here rather than elsewhere.) Though vague, the notion of "circumstance" (as here defined) is not so vague as to fit nothing or everything. The fact that a criminal was born is not a circumstance of the crime. The fact is not *closely* connected with the crime (though, of course, it is connected). The fact that someone robbed using a loaded gun makes the crime armed robbery (supposing the usual statutory scheme). The fact is also not a circumstance of the crime. It is not because it is an element of the crime. But the fact that the victim was especially vulnerable or that the criminal did the robbery simply for excitement, does not make him guilty of any other crime (again supposing the usual statutory scheme). Such facts are mere circumstances of the crime (as here defined). They make the crime or criminal worse without changing the crime with which it is proper to charge him. Such facts are (as we say) "aggravating circumstances." Similarly, the fact that someone treated his victim with remarkable courtesy or robbed only to feed his family, does not make his armed robbery any less armed robbery. Like aggravating circumstances, such facts are mere circumstances of the crime. They tell us something good about the crime or criminal without changing the crime he is guilty of. They are (as we say) "mitigating circumstances."

Both aggravating and mitigating circumstances (of the crime) may be facts about the crime itself or facts about the criminal somehow closely connected to the crime. To sentence taking into account those circumstances that are facts about the crime (rather than the criminal) is consistent with the principle of equality in punishment as formulated. Though such facts are not officially elements of the crime, they may be thought of as unofficial elements of it. They are facts about the *way* the crime was committed and so are included in the principle as formulated. That the victim was especially vulnerable or that the robber was remarkably courteous are examples of such circumstances.

The principle needs to be reformulated not to allow for such circumstances but to allow for those aggravating and mitigating circumstances that are facts about the *criminal* rather than the crime (though still somehow closely connected with the crime). The criminal's motive is the best example of such a fact. Why should a criminal's motive make his crime better or worse? Why should a criminal deserve a harsher sentence for a robbery exactly like another just because he robbed for the excitement of it and another robbed to feed his family? The criminal's motive (unlike his intention) is not, strictly speaking, a fact about the way the crime was committed. The criminal's motive simply is the reason he did what he did. While the principle of equality in punishment seems to rule out such aggravating and mitigating circumstances, the Model Act (and common practice) provide for them.[11] Is there something wrong with the principle as formulated or with the Model Act (and common practice)? The answer, I think, is obvious. There is something wrong with the principle as formulated.

Making a case for treating as mitigating circumstances certain facts about the criminal closely connected with the crime is easy. Retribution does not require "an eye for an eye" even if it allows for it. Clemency is not inconsistent with retribution. Just as a debt may be wiped out by being forgiven as well as by being paid, so the criminal's justly deserved punishment may be forgiven instead of being exacted. The law (we might say) is made for the general case; clemency for certain kinds of exception.[12] We may not be able to forgive everyone for everything without breaking through the web of concepts to which retribution belongs. But we certainly can forgive some crimes sometimes without doing that.

We might think of sentencing as having two stages. The first stage satisfies the principle of equality in punishment as formulated. At that stage the judge tries to determine the punishment appropriate to the *crime*. That stage is strictly retributive. At the second stage, the judge looks beyond the crime. The question posed in this stage is whether there is any reason to depart from strict retribution.[13] Departing from strict retribution is not abandoning retribution as the central concept in punishment. It is no more abandoning retribution than recognizing that it is sometimes morally permissible to break a promise is abandoning the principle that promises should be kept. If the robber who robbed to feed his family deserves a certain punishment for what he did, he may yet deserve some clemency for the circumstances that made him do it. Such a man should not (we might say) be punished as if he were a common criminal. Though his crime was common enough, his motive was not. We should allow for that when setting his sentence.

If there is a problem about taking into account the circumstances of the crime, it is with treating some of these as "ordinary" *aggravating* circumstances. Why should a criminal's sentence be higher just because she did what she did for a bad motive? For the supporter of rehabilitation or incapacitation, there is, of course, a ready answer. The bad motive is evidence that the criminal will need more rehabilitation than she would need if she had acted from a good motive. But, for the retributivist (and deterrent theorist), the answer is harder to find. The business of the criminal law is, for the retributivist, the punishment of acts, and motives are not acts (or even elements of acts the way intentions are). The evil we "annul" by punishing the crime is the same whatever the motive for the act. So, the criminal's bad motive cannot be a reason for giving her a sentence above what she deserves for her act. Facts about the criminal may, however, be reasons for *not* mitigating the otherwise just sentence (even when there are some mitigating circumstances). "Second-stage" aggravating circumstances work in a narrower range than "first-stage" aggravating circumstances. The Model Act seems to recognize the distinction. While the Act expressly makes an offense's being "committed to gratify the defendant's desire for pleasure or excitement" an aggravating circumstance, its general "principles of sentencing" provide that "the sentence imposed should be no greater than that deserved for the offense committed."[14] Let us call such second-stage circumstances "special" aggravating circumstances to distinguish them from the "ordinary" aggravating circumstances of the first-stage of sentencing.

Recent Conduct. Perhaps, this first ground for varying sentence (the circumstances of the criminal closely connected with the crime) may be included under the principle as formulated by stretching the phrase "the *way* the particular crimes were committed" to the breaking point. There is a sense in which doing an act with a certain motive is a certain way of doing the act (though the sense seems Pickwickian). However that may be, the second ground for varying sentence is clearly beyond the reach of the principle as formulated no matter how far stretched. That second ground is the criminal's recent conduct, apart from the crime itself, up to the instant of sentencing (or, for short, his "recent conduct"). This second ground is more or less the complement of the first. It is just as vague. "Recent" may be thought to include the five or ten years before the crime. "Conduct" includes the sort of activity (rather than mere circumstances) that might be the concern of the criminal law.

Just as the first ground provided both mitigating and aggravating factors to consider when setting sentence, so does the second. The Model Act recognizes two sorts of recent conduct as "mitigating factors": that "before his detection, the defendant compensated or made a good faith attempt to compensate the victim of criminal conduct for the damage or injury the victim sustained"; and that "the defendant assisted authorities to uncover offenses committed by other persons or to detect or apprehend other persons who had committed offenses."[15] The Model Act also recognizes two sorts of recent conduct as "aggravating factors": that "the defendant has a recent history of convictions or criminal behavior"; and that "the defendant has a recent history of unwillingness to comply with the conditions of a sentence involving supervision in the community."[16] Though such grounds for varying sentence have no connection with the crime itself, they are as easy to fit into a retributive framework as the first sort we discussed.

Let us begin with mitigating factors. That a criminal should, before detection, attempt to undo the harm he did by his crime seems to be a reason for treating him less harshly than he would otherwise deserve. That he has made himself useful to his fellow citizens by helping to uncover the crimes of others also seems to be a reason for treating him less harshly. But the two reasons differ. The first is moral; the second, practical.

The criminal who voluntarily undertakes to make restitution before detection may show thereby that he genuinely repents his crime. He could, of course, have shown even more repentance, for example, by turning himself in to the police and confessing (rather than waiting to be detected). Even so, the criminal who only undertakes restitution is as uncommon as the criminal who robs only to feed his family. His conduct invokes our clemency as a recognition of his (regenerating) character. He cannot undo his crime without punishment or clemency. But he certainly can give us reason to show clemency. Clemency in response to his repentance would affirm the rightness of that repentance (and so, the wrongness of his crime). Such clemency would (it seems) do neither more nor less justice than would giving him the punishment his act deserves. Clemency here is nevertheless morally better than strict retribution because affirming the rightness of his repentance supports morality in a way simply ignoring his repentance would not. If repentance is morally good, we should (all else equal) do what we can to encourage it. Clemency in this case is one way to encourage repentance. There are, of course, other ways. We could, for example, praise him for his repentance, or reward him for it by finding him a job after he serves his sentence. If there is nothing morally wrong in taking such considerations into account where the choice of means of doing what we should is left to our discretion, there is nothing morally wrong with showing clemency in response to genuine repentance.

The criminal who tells on others to reduce her own sentence, does not show repentance. There is nothing morally praiseworthy in what she does (though the consequences are good). She is, if anything, morally worse than the criminal who refuses to tell on her fellows out of some notion of honor among thieves. How then can the "snitch" deserve clemency? The answer is simple. She can win our clemency by making herself useful to us. Our benefit is as good a reason as any for us to forgive her. The criminal owes both a private and a public "debt." The private "debt" is for the wrong she did her victim; the public "debt," for breaking the law. We are, of course, *not* in position to forgive the *private* "debt." Only the victim is in position to do that. For that reason, the victim has a right to sue for restitution or damages whatever punishment the court imposes (though the right is ordinarily empty). But the victim has no right either to forgive the criminal for breaking the law or to require the court to forego clemency. Punishment is independent of private wrong. Punishment pays a *public* "debt." The court can show clemency because breaking the law is a public wrong and the court, acting for the public, has the right to forgive what public order has suffered (supposing the law so to provide). Retribution is a theory of public "debt." If there is an objection to showing clemency to those who make themselves especially useful to the public, the objection is not retributive. The logic of "debt" leaves open the grounds of forgiveness.[17]

We may now turn to aggravating factors. How does taking account in sentencing of the recent bad conduct of the criminal (apart from his crime) fit into a retributive framework? The argument for recognizing certain recent conduct as a reason for a harsher sentence runs into the same problem as the argument for recognizing certain circumstances of the crime as a reason for harsher sentence. We can understand such aggravating factors either as reasons for not mitigating what we would otherwise mitigate (*special* aggravating factors) or as reasons for making a sentence harsher than it would be even when there are no mitigating factors (*ordinary* aggravating factors). If we understand the criminal's recent conduct in the first way, there is no problem. That a criminal has a recent history of convictions suggests that he is likely to commit other crimes as soon as soon as he leaves prison. That he has a recent history of parole violations suggests that he is likely to violate parole again. If we were thinking of lowering the criminal's otherwise deserved sentence because of some mitigating factor, such aggravating factors certainly should give us reason to reconsider. Such facts suggest that the criminal does not deserve clemency at all or that our clemency should not take the form of probation or parole.

If, however, we understand the criminal's recent bad conduct as not merely undermining mitigation but as providing (positive) reasons for raising the sentence (even where there are no mitigating factors), there is a problem. The recent conduct we are talking about (other crimes and parole violations) are either offenses for which the criminal has already been punished once or offenses of which she has never been proved guilty. It is hard to see how treating such conduct in the way suggested is consistent with retribution. The criminal wipes out her "debt" by serving her term (or by being forgiven). Having wiped out her "debt," she cannot now still be "charged interest." (And that seems true even if what is involved is only past revocation of parole for some violation. The revocation pays the "debt" the violation created.) If, on the other hand, the criminal has never been convicted of the crime in question, treating that unproved crime as an ordinary aggravating factor of the crime proved against her, while not exactly inconsistent with retribution, does seem inconsistent with a *just* system of retribution. It amounts to saying that once convicted of one crime, a criminal may be presumed guilty of others for which there is some evidence.

The Model Act's principles of sentencing seem to rule out treating conduct not related to the crime as ordinary aggravating factors.[18] Treating such conduct as ordinary aggravating factors would allow for a sentence more severe than the *crime* deserves.

Present Circumstances. That brings us to the third ground for varying sentence not recognized in the principle of equality in punishment as formulated, "the present circumstances of the criminal." By "present circumstances," I mean circumstances (excluding conduct) obtaining at about the time of sentencing. That a criminal is polite during the sentencing hearing is not a present circumstance because his politeness is an aspect of his (recent) conduct. But that a criminal looks dangerous, though arguably not a good reason to give him a sentence different from what he would otherwise receive, *is* a present circumstance.

That present circumstances may be reasons for mitigating the otherwise deserved sentence for a past crime seems quite uncontroversial. Who would not think it appropriate to give less than two-years imprisonment to an old embezzler dying of cancer even though one would give the two-year sentence to the ordinary embezzler guilty of a crime indistinguishable from his? Who would not show some mercy to a woman who deserves a year in prison for a theft, if she has an infant still nursing and no family to whom she might entrust it? The two examples are, of course, not equally inconsistent with the principle of equality in punishment as formulated. The first may be brought under the principle (at some cost). Because the old embezzler is dying of cancer, a two-year sentence is in effect a sentence of life imprisonment (with considerably more inconvenience than would be likely if he were healthy). So, though a sentence of two-years imprisonment is, for him, technically the "same punishment" as the ordinary embezzler's sentence of two year, it is not the equivalent in severity. If we are willing to read the "same" of the principle's proposition 1 as "equivalent," we can make the principle as formulated cover this case of mitigation. But the cost will be high. We shall then be forced to treat a criminal's special talent for adapting to prison life as an aggravating circumstance (though *perhaps* a special one). Only a longer sentence for him would be equivalent to a two-year sentence for the ordinary criminal.[19]

Whether we bring the first example under the principle as formulated or not, we cannot bring the second under it. At least part of the reason we are willing to reduce the sentence the woman deserves for her theft is that we do not want to separate her infant from its mother. That a prison sentence will place an unusual burden upon *others* seems a relevant mitigating factor. Why (even if we have the "right") should we cause serious harm to others just to "collect" the full "debt" owed us if we can get most of what we are "owed" while doing far less harm? The principle of equality in punishment as formulated rules out such questions. But, given the other grounds for mitigation, such questions seem entirely in place in setting sentence.

Curiously, the Model Act makes no express provision for such mitigating factors. If it makes provision at all, it does so obliquely. The list of mitigating factors includes a catch-all "any other factor consistent with the purposes of the Article and the principles of sentencing."[20] The second purpose of the Article is "to assure the fair treatment of all defendants by eliminating unjustified disparities in sentencing."[21] So, the "disparities" we are considering now (the lighter sentence for the dying embezzler or the thief with a nursing infant) may be "justified" by present circumstances (though, in a sense, not "fair" because less than strictly deserved for the crime). The Act's "principles of sentencing" provide in part that "[the] sentence imposed should be the least severe measure necessary to achieve the purpose [sic] for which the sentence is imposed" and that "[sentences] not involving confinement" should be preferred unless [confinement is necessary to protect society, avoid deprecating the seriousness of the offense, or provide a particularly effective deterrent; less restrictive measures have failed in the past; or some other purpose of the Act can only be fulfilled by confinement]."[22] Clemency for the dying embezzler or the thief with the nursing infant (say, probation rather than imprisonment) seems to be allowed given these principles (and, supposing neither the embezzler nor the thief to have a long history of criminal conduct, their present circumstances seem to assure that the lesser punishment will not deprecate the seriousness of their crimes, fail to provide a particularly effective deterrent, and the like).[23]

Miscellaneous. There are three other grounds we might suppose relevant to setting sentence (given the grounds already shown to be relevant): deterrence, prediction of the criminal's conduct after sentencing, and the burden exacting the sentence would place on society. All three do indeed have a place in the Model Act. Deterrence (as noted above) appears in the Act's "principles of sentencing" as a reason for choosing to confine someone when the preferred course would otherwise be something "less severe." (I am, I must admit, curious about how a judge is to make such determinations.) The Act treats the deterrent effect of confinement as entirely unproblematic. In the same place in the "principles of sentencing," the criminal's future conduct appears as a reason for confining only when the prediction is based upon "a long history of criminal conduct." The actual unreliability of other sorts of evidence rather than any principled objection seems to be behind that strict limiting of the evidence upon which the prediction may be based. Both deterrence and predicted future conduct provide only *special* aggravating factors. They are reasons for not mitigating what otherwise would be mitigated. That, of course, is not surprising.

The Model Act's treatment of the last ground *is* surprising. The Act makes provision for taking into account the burden exacting the sentence would place on society in a way both different and enlightening. The Act creates a commission to establish "sentencing guidelines" in addition to those the Act itself supplies. The commission is supposed to take account of (among other matters) "the available resources of the department [of corrections]."[24] The Act thus recognizes that individual judges are in no position to decide the effect what they do will have upon the prisons (since they cannot control what other judges will be doing).

Creating a sentencing commission with power to vary standard sentences to take account of prison conditions assures that two criminals sentenced at *different* times may receive widely differing sentences though their crimes and circumstances are otherwise the same. The Model Act assumes that "deserved punishment" for a particular crime is relative to the punishment for other crimes, that there is no "natural tariff" for any particular crime, and so that the scale may be expanded or contracted to take into account such social conditions as overcrowding of prisons. Such a view is consistent with what most defenders of retributivism have argued.

Procedural and Substantive Justice

If the foregoing arguments are at all convincing, then we should reformulate the principle of equality in punishment in something like the following way:

1'. Persons convicted of equally serious crimes should receive the same punishment unless there is good reason to give one of them a different punishment;

2'. There is good reason to give one of two persons convicted of equally serious crimes a punishment different from that the other receives if, and only if, there is a relevant difference (a) in the circumstances of their crimes, (b) in their recent conduct, (c) in their present circumstances, (d) in (reliable) predictions of their conduct after sentencing, (e) in the deterrent effect their sentences will have on others, or (f) in the burden exacting their punishment would impose on society; and

3'. Any difference between the punishment one person receives for the crime of which he is convicted and the punishment another receives for the crime of which he is convicted should be fully accounted for (a) by some relevant difference in the seriousness of the crimes, (b) by some relevant difference in good reasons for giving a punishment *less* than that the seriousness of the crime (considered alone) makes proper, or (c) by some combination of these.

The principle of equality in punishment so formulated seems to be a sensible moral principle. Propositions 1' – 3' take care of retribution; propositions 2' and 3' take care of clemency. The reformulation makes the movement from rehabilitation to retribution look more like a reversal of priorities within a settled scheme than a revolution. (Rehabilitation now counts far less in calculating "burden" of exacting punishment.) The principle may even seem little more than the penal version of "treating equals equally, unequals unequally." It is not. The principle is significantly stronger than that. Proposition 3' does not allow punishment to be *enhanced* beyond what the act deserves (even for good reason).

Does the principle as reformulated rule out the difference in sentence the anecdote reports? A difference in judges is not among the six sorts of good reason proposition 3' allows for a sentence "less than that the seriousness of the crime (considered alone) makes proper." Indeed, a difference in judges is a fundamentally different sort of "reason." The six sorts of good reason proposition 3' allows (those listed in proposition 2') are all reasons a judge could (however unwisely) take into account while setting sentence. But a difference in judges is not such a reason. "I sentence you to 15 years imprisonment rather than to 30 days in part because I am Maximum John, not Lovable Larry," helps to explain the sentence but does not tell us anything about the judge's reasons. So, it may seem the principle (even as reformulated) obviously rules out disparities like that the anecdote reports. Let us see.

Suppose that two judges have deliberated independently in cases indistinguishable in terms of the reformulated principle, that their judgments are not corrupted by ignorance, conflict of interest, or the like, that each justifies his decision by appeal to the principle of equality in punishment as reformulated, that the justification is made in good faith, and that nevertheless the sentences in the two cases differ as reported in Frankel's anecdote. Suppose too that the sentence of 15 years is unusually high in that jurisdiction for a crime of that seriousness accompanied by such mitigating factors (but not beyond what the crime itself deserves).[25] Last, suppose that the sentence of 30 days falls somewhere between average and unusually low for a crime of that seriousness accompanied by such mitigating (and aggravating) factors. What can we say?

No doubt one thing we can say is that the two judges are not working under a procedure like those the defenders of just deserts favor. The procedure the two judges are working under is relatively unreliable. Different judges following the same rules in similar cases can get quite different results without error (something not possible under the Model Act or similar reformed procedure). That much seems certain. But can we say as well that the sentence of 15 years is unjust (given the sentence of 30 days)? The question raises two distinct issues. The first is the justice of the particular act, sentencing this person to 15 years (given the sentence of 30 days in a similar case). The second issue is the justice of a practice in which such acts occur. The two issues are distinct because there is a difference between the justness of a procedure ("formal justice") and the justness of a particular act whatever the justness of the procedure under which it occurs ("substantive justice"). A just procedure may do (substantive) injustice, and an unjust procedure may do substantive justice.

The distinction between formal and substantive justice, though commonly made, is not commonly made in the same way. So, for convenience, let us make it this way: A particular procedure is just (let us say) if, and only if, it is not unjust. Procedural justice is simply the absence of procedural injustice. A procedure is unjust if (a) it is a procedure for settling questions of substantive justice (that term to be explained soon), (b) rational persons may be subject to the procedure against their will, and (c) there is at least one alternative procedure available that all rational persons would prefer, all things considered (the willingness of others to support the procedure in question being among the things to consider). Why understand procedural justice in this way?

Procedural justice is, it seems, a special case of fairness, that is, fairness in a procedure for deciding claims of (substantive) justice. Where there is no question of substantive justice, there can be no procedural justice or injustice either. Hence, clause (a).

Procedural justice is, however, fairness only in a *certain* kind of procedure, that is, a procedure that does not make a rational person's consent a condition of her participation. Procedural justice is a virtue of a procedure to which some parties may be made to submit. A procedure cannot be unjust if the parties must agree to submit to it (supposing the agreement not to result from coercion, fraud, or the like). An ordinary contract providing for arbitration of disputes may be fair or unfair, not just or unjust. Hence, clause (b).

A procedure satisfying both clause (a) and clause (b) can still be just. The first two clauses of our definition provide no standard of justness. Clause (c) does. The standard is supposed to recognize a variety of facts about procedural justice. A procedure may be just under some circumstances and unjust under others. (For example, flipping a coin may be a just procedure for deciding between parties having equal claim to some indivisible good but not for deciding whether to imprison or put on probation.) What is just procedure seems to depend in part upon the alternatives available and in part upon what rational persons subject to a procedure may wish to accomplish. Clause (c) tries to recognize all that by treating the standard of justness as the result of a "social contract" or "universal legislation." The standard of justness is what all rational persons subject to it are willing to accept (given the alternatives and what they wish to accomplish).

Substantive justice is, in contrast, a virtue of states of affairs. A certain social arrangement is just insofar as each member of the society has the goods (and evils) the rules of justice assign to him. A sentence is just in substance (whether the procedure is just or not) if the punishment assigned is what the rules of justice permit (or require). This way of understanding substantive justice has one curious consequence. A *procedure* might be *substantively* just (or unjust). That is to say, a procedure might – simply by its existence – create a state of affairs permitted (or forbidden) by the rules of justice. The use of well-paid juries might, for example, contribute to a just distribution of wealth as well as to fair trials. Such substantive justice in procedures is, I think, not germane to the argument for reform of sentencing. I shall therefore ignore it in what follows.

This definition of substantive justice is, of course, empty without some characterization of "rules of justice." For our purposes, the rules of justice are best characterized on analogy with "procedural justice." A rule of justice is (let us say) an enforceable rule all rational persons subject to it would prefer to any alternative, all things considered. The things to consider include the alternatives available and what others would be willing to accept. The consideration may be done from some theoretically privileged position ("the original position," "a cool hour," or the like) or in some less idealized way. The rule must, however, be one all rational persons can support. A rule not all can support is not a rule of justice (though it may yet be a just rule, that is, a rule permitted by a rule of justice).

A rule of justice is also an enforceable rule. If a rule is enforceable, it is at least morally permissible to claim something under it (where "claim" means "demand" or "invoke one's right" rather than "request" or "beg"); and it may be morally permissible to use force oneself or to call upon others to use force to exact what the rule requires. (There may be, in other words, degrees or kinds of enforceability.) Enforceability (in this sense) distinguishes rules of justice (those stating rights) from the rest of morality. Justice is enforceable. Rules of moral decency, goodness, or excellence are not. For our purposes, praising and blaming are not means of enforcement (strictly speaking). Their power to obtain conduct is more like that of speaking the truth than like applying force. Praising and blaming may be appropriate both in support of rules of justice and in support of other moral rules (and, indeed, even in support of rules that are morally indifferent). So, though the principle of equality in punishment (as reformulated) is a moral principle, it is not exactly a rule of justice. Proposition 1' (together with 3') constitutes a rule of justice insofar as it states the maximum just punishment. A criminal has a right not to be punished more than proposition 1' (with 3') allows. But the principle is not a rule of justice insofar as it provides for clemency. Proposition 2' (with 3') is not enforceable. A criminal has no right to punishment less than he deserves for his crime (even though there may be no injustice in imposing less).

A procedure can be just and yet do injustice because, though preferable to any alternative available, the procedure may still allow action to be taken with less than full information, in situations tending to deflect judgment, or under rules permitting incorrectable error. A just procedure is not necessarily a perfect procedure.

A Lottery of Judges?

Though distinct for this reason, procedural and substantive justice are still equally relevant to our original question. The anecdote reports an injustice whether what it reports is that someone was subjected to an unjust procedure and suffered as a result or that he was subjected to a just procedure that misfired in some way (and he suffered as a result). So, let us now consider the two issues our question raises, beginning with substantive justice.

The prospects of an argument establishing substantive injustice are not promising. The sentence of 15 years is (we have assumed) what the criminal deserves for his crime. (If it were not, the sentence would be out of proportion to his crime, cruel as well as unusual, unjust *whatever others get for the same crime*, and so irrelevant to *our* question.) An argument from substantive injustice would, it seems, have to provide a rule of justice *requiring* us to forgive certain crimes in part or in whole (under certain circumstances) whatever the legal rules of clemency happen to be and whatever good reasons there are for having them that way. The principle of equality in punishment is not such a rule of justice (since it states what justice permits in punishment, not what it requires in clemency).

That morality may include rules *directing* us to forgive under certain circumstances (whatever our laws happen to say) seems likely enough. The law may, for example, require us to report a crime conscience tells us to forget. The difficulty is in supposing such moral directives to be rules of *justice* (in our sense). If such directives are rules of justice, then the *minimum* they permit in enforcement is *claims* of forgiveness. Even that minimum seems too much. While it makes sense to think of a criminal pleading with us to turn a blind eye, it does not make sense (or, at least, the same sense) to think of him *demanding* that we turn a blind eye (in the absence of some special legal rule requiring clemency under the circumstances). Someone may deserve clemency for what he is, has suffered, has done, will suffer, or will do, just as he may deserve punishment for his crime. The difficulty is explaining why that deserving should be a matter of justice rather than of some weaker moral consideration. I know of no argument for substantive injustice that meets this difficulty for sentencing (much less one that overcomes it). Even the Model Act, when stating the "purposes of sentencing," "principles of sentencing," and "mitigating and aggravating factors," exchanges "shall" for "should" and "may."

Procedural injustice, not substantive injustice, provides the reformers' arguments from justice. There are, I think, at least four distinguishable arguments for the claim that any procedure allowing such disparities as the anecdote reports is unjust. Let us call them "the argument from unequal treatment," "the argument from lawlessness," "the argument from possible bias," and "the argument from chance." None of these arguments is without serious flaw. Let us take them in order.

Unequal Treatment. The argument from unequal treatment may be stated in this way: Any unreformed sentencing procedure allows equals to be treated unequally. For example, unreformed procedure allows two people differing only in the judge before whom they come to receive quite different sentences though the cases are otherwise indistinguishable. The principle that equals be treated equally (and unequals unequally) is (so the argument runs) a principle of justice applying to second-order acts like choosing this sentencing procedure as well as to first-order acts like sentencing these persons. To adopt or maintain a procedure like that reported in the anecdote is to act in violation of that principle of justice (the choice of the procedure amounting to choosing to treat equals unequally). The judges do not necessarily act unjustly considered one by one. They may do what justice requires insofar as that is possible under a procedure providing so little coordination between judges. Those who act unjustly are those who adopt or maintain the procedure as a whole (that is, the legislature or society). A procedure that cannot be adopted or maintained without violating a rule of justice is an unjust procedure. So (the argument concludes), an unreformed sentencing procedure is unjust.

The argument from unequal treatment rests on at least four assumptions. To uncover those assumptions is to show the argument to beg the question. The argument assumes, first, that the principle that equals be treated equally (and unequals unequally) is a principle of justice. But the principle may or may not be a principle of justice. That depends on how the principle is filled in. The principle is formal ("equal" not being self-defining). Our discussion of the principle of equality in punishment has already suggested that if "equal" includes all facts about a person (except her crime), there is at least one departure from the principle of equal treatment that justice almost requires. If two people are exactly alike except for the crime each has committed, the principle of equality in punishment makes *differing* treatment just. Our discussion also suggested that two persons may be "equal" in that they committed the same crime and yet, because of circumstances unrelated to the crime (for example, a young child to look after or overcrowded prisons), may justly be treated unequally.

The argument from unequal treatment therefore rests as well on an assumption about *which* acts, circumstances, and the like are relevant to being "equal" and which are not. In particular, the argument assumes that standing before Maximum John rather than Lovable Larry is irrelevant to what one should receive in punishment. The argument assumes that it is not just for a *procedure* to determine punishment in part by the accident of judicial assignment. The argument seems to apply the same standard to procedure as to judicial reasoning. There is, we have noted, something (procedurally) unjust in a judge citing his being himself as a reason for his sentence. His sentence would (in that respect) be arbitrary (since being oneself is a reason for any sentence if it is a reason for this one).

But we are not now concerned with such reason-giving. We are concerned with a procedure that lets judicial assignment have a major effect on sentence (though each judge abides by the principle of equality in punishment). That difference in concern is important because the procedure in question could have a justification (whereas the judge's arbitrariness cannot). To the question, "Why did I get 15 years rather than 30 days?" we ("society") must answer, "Because you got Maximum John rather than Lovable Larry." But to the question, "Why should my sentence depend on something like that?" we could answer, "Because there is no better procedure available." If what we answer were in fact true, the procedure, though treating equals unequally (in some sense), would not be unjust. It would not be because there would be no rational alternative to it. Such a justification might even be defensible under the principle of equality in punishment (as reformulated) — as it would be, for example, if the cost of equal punishment in such cases were more than society could reasonably bear.

So, the argument from unequal treatment must rest upon a third assumption. The argument must assume that there is a better procedure available, one that reduces differences in sentence attributable simply to assignment of judges and does so at reasonable cost. Since there seem to be such alternatives available (the various reformed procedures), the question of cost is crucial. A procedure is not unjust in itself. The alternatives available, the conditions under which the procedure must operate, and the aims of the rational persons subject to it are all relevant to whether a procedure is just or not. In sentencing reform, the costs are not all on one side. The switch from unreformed to reformed sentencing would certainly have costs (as well as benefits). Unreformed procedure allows a *judge* to take into account all those factors specified in the principle of equality in punishment (as reformulated). All proposed reforms restrict a judge's power to do that (restricting that power in order to coordinate the sentencing of otherwise independent judges). The proposed reforms also have other costs, for example, loss of judicial flexibility, increased complexity of the sentencing process, and multiplication of grounds for appeal. Rational persons might well disagree about the existence of an alternative *preferable* to unreformed practice. And, if that is so, then (given our understanding of what makes a procedure just) unreformed procedure is not unjust simply because there are reasonable alternatives.

So, the third assumption must rest upon a fourth. The third assumption is justified only if there is some reason to ignore such costs of reform. The only reason for ignoring such costs is, I think, that maintenance of un-reformed practice is itself unjust (under the circumstances). There is (the argument from unequal treatment must assume) a rule of justice that (under the circumstances) prohibits choosing unreformed procedure. That, it seems, is what the argument must assume if it is to prove what it set out to prove. But it cannot assume that. It cannot because that is exactly what the argument set out to prove. The argument therefore begs the question. The remaining arguments (whatever their faults) do not do that.

Lawlessness. The second argument, the argument from lawlessness, tries to show that a recognized rule of justice (other than equal treatment) requires us to prefer reformed to unreformed sentencing procedure. The argument goes something like this: Under an unreformed procedure, the judge is free (within wide limits) to do as he thinks best. He is not bound by rules (within those limits). He need not state his reasons for a particular sentence. His sentences are not generally subject to appeal. His sentencing power is, in these respects, lawless or tyrannical. A lawless or tyrannical system of punishment is (the argument concludes) unjust.

The argument depends upon at least three confusions. First, the argument confuses "freedom *within* rules" with "freedom *from* rules." The argument assumes that insofar as a decision is not determined by rules, it is lawless or tyrannical (and so unjust). While a *system* in which every decision depends upon the ruler's arbitrary will is tyrannical and (in a sense) lawless, a system in which only certain decisions are left to certain officials' "discretion" is not to that degree tyrannical or lawless. Tyranny and lawlessness are not matters of degree. A *system of laws* excludes tyranny and lawlessness (in the sense relevant here). The claim that there is tyranny or lawlessness if rules do not determine everything, seems to commit a fallacy of composition. If tyranny and lawlessness are systematic notions, they cannot be applied to parts of a system without risk of equivocation. To say that either a system of rules determines every act under it or some acts under it are lawless (or tyrannical) is like saying that either a man is fat in every cell or he is not a fat man. It makes as much sense to talk of tyranny *within* rules as to talk of the tyranny *of* rules.

A second confusion obscures this first one. The argument from lawless-ness confuses freedom within rules ("discretion") with arbitrary power. The argument assumes that, if the relevant statute does not determine the exact sentence, the judge is free within the statutory bounds (of unreformed practice) to do as he wishes. The argument misses the possibility that the judge may yet be constrained by various principles, policies, or standards (whether these are understood as part of the law, part of the judge's craft, or as practical constraints). At a minimum the judge is supposed to do justice within the law. He is not free to do whatever he likes. His sentencing power is not arbitrary (that is, without fixed standard).

If the judge's sentencing power nevertheless seems arbitrary, that is because of a third confusion. The argument also confuses the absence of appeal with arbitrariness. While this last confusion rests upon a solid enough point, it rests too much on that one point. The absence of appeal means that error correctable on appeal will go uncorrected (and so, that arbitrariness may go uncorrected too). That is certainly true. But arbitrariness is more than the possibility that arbitrariness will go uncorrected on appeal. Arbitrariness is the absence of fixed (and proper) standards in judgment. If the absence of appeal were all there were to arbitrariness, then every decision of the Supreme Court would be an indisputable example of the exercise of arbitrary power (and so, for the purposes of this argument, unjust). That, of course, is absurd (whatever one's legal theory).

If the example of the Supreme Court does not seem to address quite the right worry, consider it further. There are ways of holding judges to a standard beside reversing them on appeal, for example, by close public scrutiny of their work, by threat of impeachment (or recall), and by selecting judges for whom justice is a firm habit of mind. The Supreme Court is not an arbitrary power in part at least because of constraints such as these. The same may be true of any judge making a decision from which there is no appeal. While unreformed sentencing procedures make little use of such means of control, merely listing them makes evident the mistake of assuming that absence of appeal is equivalent to arbitrary power. The sentencing power of judges under unreformed procedures is great, but it is not therefore arbitrary. It may be greater than is wise, but it is not therefore unjust.

Possible Bias. The third argument, the argument from possible bias, picks up where the argument from lawlessness leaves off: The sentencing power of judges is (the argument begins) great. Such power leaves much room for bias, prejudice, and ignorance and for the abuses of power they encourage. Such power makes it likely that some criminals who would have received light sentences under a reformed procedure will receive heavy sentences under unreformed procedure. No one wants to suffer a heavy sentence rather than a light one just because of the bias, prejudice, or ignorance of his judge. No one would support such a procedure if there were a better alternative. There is a better alternative, as the existence of various reform procedures proves. So (the argument concludes), the unreformed sentencing procedure is unjust because it leaves room for bias, prejudice, and ignorance when it is possible to exclude them.

This argument (unlike the argument from lawlessness) does not claim judges have arbitrary power, only that the great power they do have (especially in the absence of appeal) leaves room for bias, prejudice, and ignorance to work. The claim must be admitted. The argument then builds upon that claim the conclusion that the procedure is unjust. The claim is not enough to bear that conclusion. The mere possibility of (substantively) unjust acts is not enough to make a procedure unjust. If it were, then our whole legal system would be unjust. Even the fact of unjust acts under a procedure now and then does not make the procedure unjust. Every human institution is open to abuse. The argument must assume that there is an alternative, that the alternative reduces the abuses, and that it does so at a cost all rational persons prefer to the costs of continued subjection to unreformed procedure. The assumption is necessarily that strong. Any assumption weaker than that would leave the choice between reformed and unreformed sentencing procedure a choice between just procedures.

A procedure is, we said, unjust only if there is an available alternative *all* rational persons would prefer (all things considered). Where rational persons disagree about whether it is better to bear the costs of the procedure in question or some alternative (assuming they agree about what the costs are), the procedure is not unjust. Yet, as noted earlier, there certainly are grounds upon which rational persons may disagree about whether the costs of reform are worth it. For example, not everyone will agree that delay owing to complexity of reformed procedure is worth the increased predictability of sentences the more complex procedure produces. The argument from possible bias is an important argument. But, as it stands, the argument does not show unreformed procedure to be unjust (though it does provide a good reason to look for an alternative). The argument cannot show unreformed procedure to be unjust without showing what is not true, that there are decisive grounds for preferring the costs of reformed procedure to the cost of unreformed procedure. The importance of the argument from possible bias is that it shows one cost of unreformed procedure to be more bias-caused substantive injustice than under reformed procedure. That, of course, is quite different from showing the unreformed procedure to be unjust.

Chance. The last argument we shall discuss, the argument from chance, is at once the most interesting and the most complicated. The argument combines elements of all the other arguments discussed so far (while avoiding the errors of each). The argument may be put this way:

If a single agency sentences differently in exactly similar cases, at least one of the sentences must be unjust (because it is harm imposed in violation of some rule of justice). At least one of the sentences must be unjust because the distribution of punishments in question cannot correspond to what any rule of justice requires or permits. It cannot because, if a single agency gives two people different sentences when their cases are identical, the distribution has *no* fixed standard. Now (the argument continues) procedural justice requires a fixed standard even in the granting of clemency. While justice does not require clemency, it does require that clemency be given justly (that is, without any violation of a right). Particular sentences may or may not be arbitrary, biased, or substantively unjust and yet the overall distribution of sentences may still be the work of "chance" (that is, a distribution according to no fixed standard of justice or clemency). No rational person (the argument assumes) wants to suffer harm by chance, at least where the chance is not voluntarily taken and can be eliminated at reasonable cost. So, there must be a rule of justice forbidding distributing by chance involuntary harm under such conditions. But, the anecdote reports a case of just such forbidden harm. The criminal receiving the heavier sentence would not have received it had he too been assigned the other judge. The heavier sentence is a harm. The harm is the result of chance (the chance assignment of this judge rather than that). The chance was not voluntarily taken. A criminal (let us agree for purposes of the argument) does not "bring the punishment upon himself" in the same sense as, say, he might voluntarily accept a plea bargain. And, most important, the effect of chance can be eliminated at reasonable cost. Whatever our opinion of sentencing reform, we must admit that the cost of reform is not un-reasonable (that is, not so high that no rational person could accept it). So (the argument concludes), the anecdote reports an injustice.

The argument begins with an observation about the distribution of punish-ments, that is, about a certain state of affairs. The argument thus begins with substantive justice. The argument does not, however, overlook the distinc-tion between justice and clemency we made so much of during our discus-sion of substantive justice. The argument does not assume that the person receiving the greater punishment has a right to less punishment (and that the sentence is unjust because the sentence violates the rule of justice creating that "right"). The argument merely assumes that it is possible to give someone what she deserves for her act and still harm her unjustly. The injustice consists in giving her the punishment she justly deserves but giving it to her by chance rather than for any proper reason. The right violated is a procedural right and it is violated even though the criminal gets only what justice permits.

The argument from chance may appear to be open to an obvious objection. If the criminal receives only what justice permits (the objection runs), there is no injustice to her. And, if there is no injustice to her, how can there be any injustice at all? The objection, though obvious, is not sound. The criminal receiving a sentence she deserves for her crime, still suffers harm (all the punishment beyond what she might otherwise have suffered). If the harm is imposed by a procedure violating some rule of justice, then she has been done an injustice (even if the harm is "poetic justice"). The objection fails to take *procedural* justice seriously.[26]

There are, however, two other objections which, if less obvious, are more telling. The first concerns the identity of that single agency. The argument must assume a single agency doing the sentencing. If there is more than one agency, we cannot conclude that there is no fixed standard just because there are different sentences in like cases. Where there is more than one agency, we can at best conclude that there is no fixed standard *or* that there is more than one interpretation of such a standard. The difference is important. No one supposes any injustice if, say, in cases otherwise indistinguishable, a criminal tried under an Illinois statute receives a much heavier sentence than a criminal tried under an identical Wyoming statute. That there are two agencies (Illinois' courts and Wyoming's courts) bars the inference. Where there is more than one agency, there can be good reason for each interpretation and good reason for there being more than one interpretation. That there is only one agency doing the sentencing allows the inference to chance. Without the assumption of a single agency, the argument from chance cannot begin. What then is that single agency?

If there is a natural candidate for that single agency, it is the courts. Now, under reformed procedure, there is often such an agency, for example, a court of appeals. The moment a jurisdiction permits "disparity" to be grounds for appealing sentence, the court of appeals becomes the single agency responsible for reconciling differing sentences. The argument from chance then makes the reconciliation of sentences a matter of justice. But, what happens under reformed procedure is irrelevant here. The anecdote dates from a time when there was no such appellate review (or anything like it). The anecdote is supposed to provide an argument for reforms such as appellate review. The argument from chance is supposed to be that argument. What happens then if we try to apply the argument from chance to unreformed practice? The argument does not work. Two judges operating under an unreformed procedure are not a single agency. For example, each judge of the anecdote can say that he treats equals equally, that the anecdote reports only a difference between his interpretation of the principle of equality in punishment and that of another judge, and that there is no (procedural) injustice in mere diversity of interpretation. His sentence is (he might add) just in substance because (as we have assumed) it is not more than what justice allows for the crime. The same is true of the other judge's sentence. If there is an injustice, it is (he might say) in adopting or maintaining a procedure that leaves judges to work with so little coordination (that is, as separate agencies). That injustice, however, if it is an injustice, is not an injustice in what the courts do. It is not an injustice in any agency that sentences. It is an injustice in what the legislature did.

The legislature, of course, is a single agency. So, the argument from chance might be recast as an argument to prove that adopting (or maintaining) unreformed procedure (rather than imposing this or that sentence) is the unjust act. While I am not sure the argument can be recast in that way without converting it into the argument from unequal treatment we already discarded, I shall not pursue that point. Any recasting that did not convert the argument from chance into the argument from unequal treatment would, I think, still leave unaddressed the second objection I have to the argument.

The argument also assumes that all rational persons take a certain attitude toward chance. They will not (the argument assumes) support a procedure distributing harm in part by chance unless either the risk of harm is voluntarily assumed in each case or the chance of harm cannot be eliminated at reasonable cost. The assumption, as stated, is ambiguous. The assumption is, I think, correct if the harm in question is understood to be *added* to what is (otherwise) just. The assumption so interpreted would explain the limitation we thought it proper to put upon the use of aggravating factors in sentencing. If, however, the harm in question is understood to be *deducted* from what is (otherwise) just, the assumption is *not* correct. The attitude of rational persons toward good fortune is not symmetrical with their attitude toward misfortune. We mind suffering misfortune. We do not mind "suffering" good fortune ourselves. If we mind good fortune at all, we mind our neighbors "suffering" it when we do not. If there is a basis for rejecting "clemency by chance," the basis is, it seems, envy.

For some, just pointing out envy as the basis for rejecting "clemency by chance" may be enough to discredit the argument from chance. (Envy, thanks to Rawls, has of late been in particularly bad odor.) For others, perhaps, envy may be as good a reason as any, if all rational persons agree as a result. For us, however, it is only necessary to show that rational persons do not all agree in rejecting "clemency by chance." The simplest way to do that is to provide an example of "clemency by chance" which seems (to most people at least) nothing to complain of. The examples are many. I shall provide one.

The Romans used to punish mutiny by death, but they did not punish all mutineers by death. When a whole unit mutinied, they did not (as we might) punish only the leaders or (as the envious might wish) punish each for his act without exception. Instead, the Romans put to death one in ten of the mutineers. Which one was left to chance. The mutinous unit might be lined up and ordered to count off by tens, every tenth man being executed on the spot. To this practice we owe our word "decimation." Decimation, though perhaps harsh, is not so harsh as executing all or so foolish as punishing none. It is far simpler than trying, before imposing sentence, to determine what exactly each mutineer did. And, though the only distinction between those who live and those who die is literally chance (the "lottery" of which Justice Brennan complained), I know of no writer who thinks decimation unjust.

Indeed, it would be easy to argue for the justice of decimation. Decimation is consistent with the principle of equality in punishment (as reformulated). The principle allows the social burden of exacting punishment to count as a good reason for showing clemency. We can well imagine the People and Senate of Rome adopting decimation (a) because executing all mutineers would be a waste of good soldiers, (b) because executing some would provide a sufficient deterrent to mutiny, and (c) because selecting by lot those who will be put to death is the least expensive way to decide to whom clemency should be shown. Provided one does not think the death penalty unjust or out of proportion to mutiny, what rule of justice could one invoke against such an argument?

The example may not appear decisive. If decimation is just (as it appears to be), perhaps (it might be said) the way to understand how it can be just is to understand decimation itself as the penalty. Every member of the unit (it might be said) suffers *that* equally (because he suffers an equal chance of execution). Decimation is then (it might be concluded) not an example of the just distribution of clemency by chance. Indeed, decimation is an example of justice *without* clemency.

While I do not deny such an understanding is possible, I do deny it will do the argument from chance any good. Punishment under an unreformed sentencing procedure can be "understood" in the same way. The two criminals of the anecdote had the same chance of coming before Lovable Larry rather than Maximum John. The punishment each suffered (we might say) was the chance-of-getting-30-days-or-15-years (rather than the sentence actually imposed). If the argument from chance is to remain an argument for reform, it cannot be saved in this way.

Conclusion

The purpose of this chapter was not to discredit the movement for reform of sentencing. The major reforms can, I think, easily be defended without appeal to justice. The reformers' practical arguments, though not so powerful that no rational person can remain unconvinced, are still powerful enough to convince most people who take the time to wrestle with them.

The purpose of this chapter was both more limited and more benign. The purpose was to discredit arguments purporting to show sentencing reform to be a matter of justice (as well as of good sense). I undertook to discredit those argumentsWhatever because, if they showed what they purported to show, they showed as well that we have no choice but to reform (or do injustice) and that there are procrustean constraints on what those reforms can be. If, for example, adopting sentencing guidelines is a matter of justice, it is not open to us to balance ordinary administrative costs against degree of specificity. If adopting such guidelines is a matter of justice, the guidelines have to be specific enough to rule out all "disparities" in sentencing that can be ruled out without reasonable cost. If, however, this chapter has accomplished its purpose, reformers have room for maneuver here they would not otherwise have — and we have a theory of sentencing consistent with the main outlines of the theory of criminal desert for which we have been arguing.

This chapter does not, of course, *demonstrate* that sentencing reform is not a matter of justice. To do that, I would have had to refute *every* argument for the claim (and to prove that I had refuted them all). I certainly have not done that. I have only refuted the arguments I discovered after looking over the literature of reform. I may have overlooked a good argument. There may even be a good argument reformers have not yet invented. If there are such arguments, then this chapter only poses the question with which it began in clearer form. But that too is worthwhile. And, until someone comes forward with some new argument from justice, we are entitled to our conclusion: The anecdote may report a system of punishment not serving (strict) retribution, deterrence, or rehabilitation, but it does not report an injustice. Justice need not be so even-handed as the anecdote suggests.

Notes

Work on this chapter was supported in part by an Organized Research Grant from Illinois State University (June, 1981).

1. Marvin E. Frankel, *Criminal Sentences: Law without Order* (New York: Hill and Wang, 1972), pp. 21-22.

2. Ibid., especially pp. 38 and 48-49.

3. George B. Merry, "Seeking Nationwide Sentence to Fit the Crime: States Move toward More Uniform System of Justice," *Christian Science Monitor* (June 1, 1981), p. 12. For an older (but more scholarly) discussion, see Marvin Zalman, "The Rise and Fall of the Indeterminate Sentence [Parts I and II]," *Wayne Law Review* 24 (November 1977): 45-94.

4. Sec. 3-102(5) and Sec. 3-101, in Harvey S. Perlman and Carol G. Stebbins, "Implementing an Equitable Sentencing System: The Uniform Commissioners' Model Sentencing and Corrections Act," *Virginia Law Review* 65 (November 1979): 1175-1285. Much of the Model Act is included in Appendix I of that article, pp. 1270-84. All citations of the Act here are in that Appendix.

5. Ibid., pp. 1176-83. Some reformers recognize that such banners merely proclaim "retribution" in a softer but not theoretically distinct way. See, for

example, Andrew von Hirsch, *Doing Justice: The Choice of Punishment* (New York: Hill and Wang, 1976), pp. 45-46.

6. Andrew von Hirsch, "Prediction of Criminal Conduct and Preventative Confinement of Convicted Persons," *Buffalo Law Review* 21 (Spring 1972): 751.

7. *Furman v. Georgia*, 408 U.S. 238 (1972), p. 293 (Justice Brennan concurring).

8. See, for example, Edmond L. Pincoffs, *The Rationale of Legal Punishment* (New York: Humanities Press, Inc., 1966), pp. 2-16. Pincoffs states the theory of retribution in three propositions: (i) The only acceptable reason for punishing a man is that he has committed a crime; (ii) The only acceptable reason for punishing a man in a given manner and degree is that the punishment is "equal" to the crime; (iii) Whoever commits a crime must be punished in accordance with his desert [that is, as his act deserves].

9. Richard G. Singer, *Just Deserts: Sentencing Based on Equality and Desert* (Cambridge: Bollinger Pub. Co., 1979), p. 35.

10. Kenneth Kipnis, "Criminal Justice and the Negotiated Plea," *Ethics* 86 (January 1976): 93-106, especially 101-102.

11. Sec. 3-108(8) and Sec. 3-109(7).

12. See, for example, Herbert Morris, "Persons and Punishment," *The Monist* 52 (October 1968): 475-501; Claudia Card, "On Mercy," *Philosophical Review* 81 (April 1972): 182-207; and Hyman Gross, *A Theory of Criminal Justice* (New York: Oxford University Press, 1979), pp. 436-456.

13. For more about these two stages and their place in a general theory of retributive punishment, see Chapter Four.

14. Sec. 3-109(7). But see *Fair and Certain Punishment: Report of the Twentieth Century Fund Task Force on Criminal Sentencing* (New York: McGraw-Hill Book Company, 1976), pp. 19-29, which recommends so-called "presumptive sentencing." The presumptive sentence is the sentence the crime deserves if there are no mitigating or aggravating circumstances. Mitigating factors permit reduction of sentence down to a specified limit. Aggravating factors permit increase in sentence up to a certain limit. The range is not supposed to be wide. Such an arrangement appears to ignore the distinction made here between "ordinary" and "special" aggravating factors. The *Report's* list of aggravating factors, however, includes only one factor that is *not* a circumstance of the crime. That factor is eccentric ("defendant has threatened witness or has a history of violence against witnesses"), p. 44. So perhaps the ignoring is more apparent than real.

15. Sec. 3-108(6) and (10).

16. Sec. 3-109(1) and (8).

17. It is perhaps worth remarking that the notion of "clemency" employed here does not work like Card's "mercy." Mercy, for her, is a moral virtue. "Clemency" (as used here) may as well be the manifestation of prudence,

selfishness, or whim as of virtue. For Card, mercy is a response to *personal* desert, p. 192. Clemency (as used here) is lessening of deserved punishment for whatever reason (personal desert being only one possibility among many). Nevertheless, whether we speak of mercy or clemency, we have a refutation of Kipnis' claim that plea bargaining is unjust because the criminal gets less than he deserves for his crime. Card and I are agreed that justice allows (but does not require) forgiving. Kipnis seems to have missed the fact that the logic of "debt" (that is, of retribution) does not make forgiving for reasons independent of the crime unjust. Kipnis is, of course, not the first to miss that. Kant's attitude toward clemency is the classic example of what can happen when we miss the possibility of forgiving. Immanuel Kant, *The Metaphysical Elements of Justice* (Indianapolis: Liberal Arts Library, 1965), pp. 102 and 107-108.

18. The argument does not show that a *statute* may not expressly make a second conviction a more serious crime than the first. The argument shows only that the first conviction (and subsequent punishment) does not make the second offense worse (though it may make the criminal in question a less likely candidate for mitigation). The argument for a "repeat offender" statute is conceptually distinct from the argument for making something an aggravating factor. Compare Gross, pp. 455-456, and von Hirsch, pp. 84-88. Having said that, I must admit to a certain unease about defending *both* retribution and repeat offender statutes. How can what has been annulled still count? See Chapter Six.

19. Card attributes the desire to enhance a sentence to take account of a criminal's special advantages to "envy" and rejects such enhancement because "envy is perverse," pp. 199-200.

20. Sec. 3-108 (12).

21. Sec. 3-101(2).

22. Sec. 3-102(3) and (4).

23. Though most writers on punishment treat imprisonment as the ordinary punishment and probation as exceptional, the Act seems to do the opposite. In this the Act is faithful to current practice in the United States. My example here is then less realistic than I could wish. Still, the realism of the example does not, I think, affect the point I make here. For clemency, the relevant starting point is not the ordinary punishment but the deserved punishment. There is no necessary connection between them. (A number of courts, I must admit, have said otherwise. See Bruce W. Gilchrist, "Note: Disproportionality in Sentences of Imprisonment," *Columbia Law Review* 79 (October 1979): 1119-66, especially 1154-61). The deserved punishment is what the act deserves, that is, what the statute provides before taking up aggravating and mitigating factors not circumstances of the crime. The ordinary punishment is a function not only of what the act deserves but of what other circumstances and conduct ordinarily accompany the act. (The

provisions of the Model Act's "principles of sentencing" I cited all refer to conduct or circumstances apart from the crime.) The statutory penalty for the crime is always a "fair" punishment for the act (unless it is "cruel and unusual"). It is fair even if it is, taking everything into account, too harsh. In other words, justice does not require clemency, though it allows or even recommends it.

24. Sec. 3-115(b) (4). The sentencing commission would also seem to be the logical agency (apart from the legislature itself) to make reliable judgments of deterrence. Why does the Model Act not treat deterrence as it treats social burden of exacting sentence?

25. If the sentence were beyond what the crime itself deserved, the sentence would be subject to Constitutional attack as "disproportionate" (or "cruel and unusual"). The question of disparity would be foreclosed. So, that "but" introduces an assumption inherent in our topic all along.

26. Cf. my "Racial Quotas, Weights, and Real Possibilities," *Social Theory and Practice* 7 (Spring 1981): 49-84.

PART THREE

Replies to Some Objections

9

Criminal Desert,
Harm, and Fairness

This chapter begins by comparing von Hirsch's theory of criminal desert with what I have called "the fairness theory." This, in effect, is a brief summary of the argument so far. The body of the chapter defends the fairness theory against five objections recently made against it by von Hirsch and Gross. The objections are variations on the charge that the fairness theory is implausible, incoherent, or otherwise fundamentally flawed.

Some Preliminaries

There are important points of agreement between von Hirsch and me. We agree that desert, not the likely consequences of punishing, should set the upper limit on a particular sentence and should, in addition, be the primary determinant of how much below the upper limit the actual sentence falls. We agree as well that the statutory penalty should likewise be determined by considering what crimes of that kind deserve, not by considering what punishing crimes of that kind this or that way would accomplish. We are, in other words, both retributivists.[1]

The points of disagreement are, however, at least as important as these points of agreement. Von Hirsch treats punishment as ordinary blaming carried on by rougher means, that is, he accepts (what he calls) "a condemnatory theory of punishment." I do not. Von Hirsch thinks moral desert should be the primary determinant of the upper and lower ends of the punishment scale, what he conveniently calls "the anchoring points." I think simple moral desert has much less to do with determining the anchoring points. Most important, perhaps, von Hirsch holds that deserved legal punishment for a crime is best conceived as a complex function of the harm the act did or risked, the criminal's mental state, and any excusing conditions. I hold that deserved legal punishment is better conceived as a simple function of the unfair advantage one takes by committing the crime in question, whatever the harm actually done or risked.

Von Hirsch, in short, accepts a form of *lex talionis* – a humane form, to be sure, but still a form of retributivism connecting the harm associated with the crime directly with the deserved punishment. For von Hirsch, the principles of criminal justice are pretty much the same principles that would apply in circumstances if no statute applied. Von Hirsch is a respresentative of what again seems the majority view among retributivists.

I, in contrast, may represent a dwindling remnant. For me, deserved punishment is a function of the criminal law itself, not something to be determined by considering how much we would blame or otherwise respond harshly to the act in question if no law prohibited it. So, the particular disagreements between von Hirsch and me are not accidental. They are symptoms of a more fundamental divergence of theory.

Some Advantages of Unfair Advantage

If it is fair to say that Von Hirsch came to the theory of punishment from "below," that is, by way of the law and practice, then it is also fair to say that I came to it from "above," that is, by way of political philosophy and ethics. This difference in origin may explain an important difference in approach. Von Hirsch has devoted himself primarily to showing that his theory fits the *core* of the criminal law well enough to allow legislators, sentencing commissions, and the like to move from judgments of relative gravity for crimes like murder, fraud, and theft to judgments of deserved punishment. He has had little, if anything, to say about crimes of strict liability, victimless crimes, insanity, or even attempts. His only work at all near the periphery of the criminal law concerns recidivism. Most of my work in theory of punishment is quite different.[2] I have dealt extensively with the core of the criminal law in only three papers, one on rape, one on sentencing, and one on setting statutory penalties in general.[3] And, even in these papers, the periphery is much in evidence.

My approach may, I fear, have had some unfortunate side-effects. A theorist with no interest in attempts, for example, may skip my paper on that subject, even if she is concerned with the general question of setting penalties. Criminologists, sentencing commissions, and the like may do the same for another reason. They are not likely to be concerned about what even few theorists dispute.

Still, however unfortunate the side-effects, my approach is better for theory than von Hirsch's. Most theories of punishment do pretty well with the core of the criminal law. Theories that do not are dismissed, almost before they can be stated, as "utopian" or "against common sense." If we want to learn anything from comparing *lex talionis* with the fairness theory, we should, it seems, look to the periphery of the criminal law. Only there are we likely to find the crucial tests by which one theory can show itself better than another.

The fairness theory does much better at such tests than *lex talionis* (even in von Hirsch's sophisticated version). I need not rehearse here all the arguments made earlier.[4] I shall, however, give one brief example to recall those arguments to mind.

Recidivism as a Crucial Test

Legislators can take account of recidivism in at least two ways: (a) by *sentencing provisions* that make conviction of a previous crime an aggravating circumstance of the present crime; or (b) by *recividist statutes* that make a certain sequence of convictions itself a separate crime (or transform the present conviction into conviction of a much more serious crime). Von Hirsch and I seem to agree that recidivism may be treated as an aggravating circumstance only for purposes of negating otherwise deserved leniency. Unlike brutality or breach of trust, recidivism is not properly a *positive* aggravating circumstance. A "three-time loser" is, all else equal, merely less deserving of leniency than a first offender.

Though we seem to agree on that, I think it fair to point out that von Hirsch has some difficulty getting even this out of his theory of punishment. A good part of one chapter of *Past or Future Crimes* candidly reports the false trails by which he eventually reached his present position. One of those false trails leads to the view that recidivism implies defiance and defiance, being blamable in itself, provides grounds for treating recidivism as a positive aggravating circumstance. The chapter ends with the admission that "[operationalizing] a desert system in a sentencing grid [makes it] uncertain whether a premium or a discount is involved.[5]

That chapter strikes me as a triumph of good instincts over bad theory. But, more important here is how little von Hirsch has to say about recidivist *statutes*. These are only addressed in a short footnote at the end of the chapter. The note explains what "habitual offender laws" typically do and then concludes that "[from] what I have said in this chapter, it should be evident that I do *not* support such drastic measures for repeat offenders."[6]

No doubt von Hirsch exiled recidivist statutes to a footnote because their use is relatively rare in the criminal law, not at all like treating recidivism as negating otherwise deserved leniency. The footnote nonetheless suggests (what von Hirsch has said more clearly elsewhere):[7] his theory does not allow him to conceptualize the crime such statutes punish. He does not know what to make of a "recidivist premium" that exceeds the maximum penalty for the "underlying crime." Either such statutes are equivalent to sentencing provisions (that is, mere prohibitions of leniency) or they are insupportable. He sees no other alternative. Though recidivist statutes remain relatively common both in the United States and elsewhere, they are, as far as he is concerned, morally unjustifiable — unjustifiable *not* simply as a matter of empirical fact but *in principle*.

How important is von Hirsch's admission that his theory cannot conceptualize the crime recidivist statutes punish? If no other theory could do better, the admission would not matter. All theories are imperfect. They win adherents by beating the competition. Von Hirsch's theory could beat the competition even if it shared an imperfection with them. If, however, another theory did not share that imperfection, his admission could be important. We would have a relevant test if his theory failed while another passed. Of course, one failure need not be decisive, especially if the failure does not involve the core of the criminal law. But, joined with many others, even if equally peripheral, such a failure would give the alternative an important advantage and, all else equal, should be decisive.

Can any other theory do better than von Hirsch's? The fairness theory of criminal desert certainly can. According to this theory, the criminal law creates a cooperative practice. Some people forbear doing what they would otherwise do because the law has given them reasonable assurance that others will do the same (and everyone will be better off if everyone abstains). Such cooperation imposes burdens insofar as people do not do what they would otherwise do. Anyone who breaks a law does not bear the same burden the rest do. Unless punished, the lawbreaker will, in effect, get away with doing less than.his fair share. He will have an advantage the law-abiding do not. The advantage is what the criminal law may take back by punishing the criminal for his crime.

The advantage bears no necessary relation to the harm the criminal actually did. For example, she may have done great damage and only committed theft; or no damage at all even though she attempted murder. According to the fairness theory, the damage a criminal actually does is between her and her victim, a private matter to be settled by civil suit or the moral equivalent. Her *crime* consists only in the unfair advantage she *necessarily* took over the law-abiding simply by breaking the law in question. The measure of punishment due is the relative value of *that* unfair advantage. The greater the advantage, the greater the punishment should be.

If this advantage could not be gauged, the fairness theory would be empty. But the advantage can readily be gauged by imagining a reasonably efficient market in which licenses corresponding to particular crimes are bought and sold. Each license would be a pardon-in-advance for a particular instance of a particular crime. The terms of the license would track the statutory or common-law definition of the crime in question (rather than describe the crime as it actually turned out). We are, in other words, to imagine each crime as taking a license for which deserved punishment is fair payment. That way of imagining crime has a long pedigree within retributivism. The other details of the market, though important, need not be repeated. What is important now is how the fairness theory leads us to an understanding of recidivist statutes von Hirsch's theory does not.

The fairness theory of criminal desert is consistent with any theory of punishment that presupposes criminals who are more or less rational, laws that can be followed or not as potential criminals choose, and penalties that can provide a potential criminal with a good (though not necessarily decisive) reason for not doing what she might otherwise do. The fairness theory as such includes no claims about the purpose of punishment as an instatition. The statutory penalty can be a fair price for a crime whether the purpose of attaching set penalties to prohibited acts is to frighten off potential criminals, to help convicted criminals appreciate the wrongness of what they did, to maintain social consensus about the wrongness of particular acts, or to accomplish some combination of these or other objectives. The fairness theory also includes no claims about what justifies having a system of criminal law, what gives the state a right to punish, or whether there is any moral duty to punish. The fairness theory would measure criminal desert in exactly the same way whether having a system of criminal law is justified by necessity, by the consent of the governed, by considerations of natural justice, or by some combination of these or other considerations. The fairness theory also includes no claim about which acts should be made criminal. It would measure criminal desert in the same way whether the criminal law were limited to prohibiting immoral acts, acts that threaten important interests of individuals, or acts it might be useful to prohibit or require. The fairness theory is, in other words, only a small part of punishment theory.

The fairness theory nonetheless does explain (in part at least) why a particular criminal deserves to be punished. The explanation is more or less independent of any particular theory of the purpose or justification of criminal law and any theory of criminal legislation. For example, according to the fairness theory, a recidivist deserves punishment, if he does, because committing a crime after he has been convicted of others takes a ("second order") advantage a first offender would not take just by committing the same "underlying" crime. The advantage is analogous to going back for seconds when not everyone has had a first helping. There is nothing wrong with going back for seconds (and hence, nothing to punish as a distinct crime) unless taking that advantage is against "the rules." But if it is against the rules (as it would be once there is a recidivist statute), taking that advantage is unfair and so there is something to deserve punishment. *How much* punishment will depend on the market value of the license to be a recidivist compared to the market value of other licenses, especially the license to commit the underlying crime. Chapter Six showed that the market value of such a license could only be a small faction of the market value of the underlying crime.

That conclusion is not too far from von Hirsch's. We both think that some of today's recidivist statutes impose undeserved punishment. My conclusion nonetheless differs significantly from his in at least three ways:

First, I have shown that the "recidivist premium" might be deserved even if the criminal receives no leniency with respect to the underlying crime. Punishing recidivism can punish a different crime. That was precisely what von Hirsch could not show.

Second, I have shown this without considering whether recidivism is *in itself* blameworthy. All that matters for fairness-based desert is that being able to "go back for seconds" is an advantage when others are not allowed to do the same. Whether the state should prohibit criminals from "going back for seconds" is an independent question. Unlike von Hirsch's condemnatory theory, or other forms of *lex talionis*, a fairness theory need not assume that the criteria for criminalizing an act must be similar to the criteria for deciding how much to punish the act *once criminalized*. The fairness theory allows the unfair advantage of committing a crime to have little to do with the unfairness (if any) of doing the act were it not a crime.

Third, because I need not consider whether recidivism is blameworthy in itself, or otherwise harmful apart from the law prohibiting it, I can explain the relevance of claims typically used to defend recidivist statutes, for example, that recidivist statutes help to incapacitate repeat offenders or that they deter the otherwise undeterrable. While the

defenders of recidivist statutes do not seem to have the evidence to make good such claims, surely, all else equal, any theory that (like von

Hirsch's) rules such claims irrelevant *in principle* is inferior to one that (like mine) can at least explain their potential relevance.

Von Hirsch's Objections to the Fairness Theory

The disagreement between von Hirsh and me is not, I think, primarily about what people should do. "My seven easy steps to a fitting penalty"[8] differ little from his description of how sentencing commissions work under his guidance.[9] Our disagreement is more abstract. It is primarily about how best to *conceptualize* what people should do. I claim that fairness-based desert provides a better conceptualization of the criminal law than does criminal-desert-as-ordinary-blameworthiness. Von Hirsch explicitly argues the opposite. Though abstract, the disagreement is important. It is when we cannot adequately conceptualize what we are doing that we are most likely to make a mess of it. When the concepts in question concern punishment, making a mess very likely means doing injustice.

Because his first book, *Doing Justice*, was friendly to the fairness theory[10], von Hirsch's present opposition deserves great respect. If the fairness theory is flawed, who is more likely to know what those flaws are than a former friend? Von Hirsch has three objections to the theory: (a) that it is inapplicable without "a heroic belief in the justice of the underlying social arrangements"; (b) that many crimes do not literally provide any advantage to their perpetrators; and (c) that the institution of punishment is easier to accept than the fairness theory upon which it is supposed to rest.[11] Let us consider these objections in this order.

Social Injustice. Von Hirsch's first objection may be understood in one of three ways. It may, first, be understood as claiming that just punishment under the fairness theory is inconceivable apart from a perfectly just society. So understood, the objection would assume that taking unfair advantage is impossible except where *all* advantages are distributed fairly. This form of the objection need not detain us. It is, I think, obvious that some criminals can take unfair advantage even in a less than perfect society. For example, a middle-class college student who beats up drunks in a city park "for kicks" seems a clear case of someone who takes unfair advantage — even in a society as imperfect as my own. If most of those whom he passed on the way to the park were as indifferent to the law as he is, he would not dare to leave his own neighborhood. His criminal activity depends in part on few others being equally lawless.

So, the fairness theory need not assume the truly heroic belief that any actual society is perfectly just. That brings us to a second way of understanding the objection from social injustice. The problem with the fairness theory (it might be said) is not that it assumes a perfectly just society but merely that it assumes *more* social justice than most actual societies can manage. So understood, von Hirsch's first objection presupposes an answer to the question, *When is a particular society not just enough for the fairness theory to apply?* Neither Von Hirsch nor anyone else making this objection actually answers the question.[12] That is surprising. The question is not hard to answer.

The fairness theory necessarily conceives the criminal law as a practice in which each subject can rationally participate in part at least because he expects to benefit from other subjects doing the same. Each subject's participation must benefit others while being a burden to him; otherwise, failing to do his part would not necessily be taking *advantage*. Each subject must participate (in part at least) because he expects others to do the same; otherwise, we could not properly speak of a failure to participate as taking *unfair* advantage. The fairness theory thus conceives the criminal law as a cooperative practice — or, as von Hirsch puts it, a system of mutually beneficial rules. The theory does not apply if a society's criminal law cannot be conceived in this way.

What would a society have to be for its criminal law *not* to be a cooperative practice at all? Its criminal law would have to be so disadvantageous that each (rational) subject would prefer to do without it even if the alternative were no criminal law whatever. The law would have to endure as an alien imposition, something to be obeyed almost entirely from fear of its penalties (or, in some science-fiction world, because of will-breaking drugs, hypnotic control, or the like). Subjects would have to be held under close guard, intimidated by harsh penalties, or otherwise forcibly kept from immediate revolt. Obeying the law would have to be rational only because, and only while, subjects lacked the resources to disobey safely.

A century ago, such a state of subjection might have been described as "utter slavery." Today, we are more likely to think of Hitler's concentration camps. Either way, I see nothing heroic in the belief that most societies differ fundamentally from such subjection. Our second way of understanding von Hirsch's objection from social injustice thus seems no better than the first. It does, however, suggest a third. According to this third way of understanding the objection, the criminal law may be a practice from which *most* subjects benefit overall. The problem is that too many *criminals* do not benefit (or benefit enough).

Though society as a whole is relatively just, "pockets of injustice" hold most criminals. According to this third form of the objection, the fairness theory requires heroic belief in social justice because a system of criminal justice in a society like ours would be unworkable if every criminal (or even most) had to take unfair advantage to deserve punishment. Most crimes in fact move the society toward a fairer distribution of benefits or burdens (or, at least, do not disturb the balance).

This third form of the objection depends on the empirical claim that most criminals do not take unfair advantage. The evidence for this claim seems to be that most societies do in fact have pockets of injustice and criminals do in fact come from them in disproportionate numbers. The evidence is, of course, suggestive. But, by itself, it proves nothing. Missing is the link between the evidence and the conclusion. How does an origin in a pocket of injustice assure that the criminal will not take unfair advantage?

The one person who seems to have taken this question seriously, James Sterba, recently argued that the fairness theory is committed to excusing from punishment only

> . . . persons who engage in criminal activity that (1) is undertaken after other options for achieving reasonable progress toward a just society have proven ineffective or too costly for those whom they are intended to benefit and that (2) involves only minimal violations of the moral rights of others.[13]

I find this principle of excuse both workable and morally attractive. The principle would, for example, excuse the starving mother who steals bread to feed her family—provided she cannot obtain bread legally and she uses no more force than necessary. The principle would *not* excuse the poor robber whose victims are poor people. Such a criminal does not bring a just society closer. Nor would the principle excuse the poor robber who uses force when he could simply shoplift. He has violated the moral rights of others more than necessay to make the distribution of benefits and burdens more just. The principle would also not excuse the shoplifter who could instead have applied for welfare or taken a low-paying job. Such a criminal has also violated the moral rights of others more than was necessary. He cannot excuse his conduct by appeal to the injustice he has suffered because he has not simply engaged in self-help against that injustice. He has helped himself by taking an advantage he could not happily allow everyone else to take. He has, in other words, taken unfair advantage.

My impression is that most criminals belong to this excuseless class even in such oppressive societies as the Union of South Africa, China, or Iran. In most societies, I would, I think, have no trouble showing almost any criminal how his crime took unfair advantage. I need only show him that, though he may be a victim of injustice, his crime did nothing to make society more just overall and then ask him to consider how much worse his life would be if all police were fired, the courts closed, the prisons emptied, the law books burned, and everyone allowed the same license he took. Hobbes is a text for explaining the law to criminals.

So much for the objection from social injustice.

No literal advantage. Von Hirsch's second objection to the fairness theory is that many crimes do not literally provide any advantage to their perpetrators. A crime could, he admits, literally provide the criminal an advantage if, but only if, "the act of disregarding mutually beneficial rules *itself* constitutes the advantage."[14] He dismisses this possibility for two reasons. First, he has already (mistakenly) dismissed the claim that the criminal law can usefully be understood as a system of mutually advantageous rules. Second, even if the criminal law could be so understood, the fairness theory could not, he thinks, explain why the unfair advantage should not be taken back by some other means, for example, by formal censure and compensation rather than by punishment. The problem for the fairness theory is, he thinks, that unlike compensation, "[punishment] does not in any literal sense restore the fair distribution of social benefits that the wrongful act has disrupted."[15] So, unless punishment is, as von Hirsch holds, the appropriate form of censure, what could be its point?

We may, I think, dispose of this second objection without returning to the question of social injustice. The act of disregarding the criminal law can literally constitute an advantage. If it could not, we could not imagine rational people in a free market paying good money to have the corresponding license. Punishment can also literally take back the unfair advantage if it returns the criminal to a position — with respect to the law — no better than he would have been in had he not committed the crime. He would return to such a position if he paid a fair "price" for breaking the law. A fine, time in prison, probation, or even a suspended sentence is literally a "price" (that is, a burden one would not freely accept except to get a benefit in return). So, if punishment is fairly proportioned to the unfair advantage committing the crime takes, the punishment will literally take back the advantage.

Punishment may, of course, leave the criminal with his loot (if there is any) and other contingent advantages his crime produced. Such "profits" are not the crime itself, according to the fairnes theory, and so are not the proper subject of punishment. Like injury to the victim, such contingent "profits" belong to the civil law. So, as von Hirsch says, the fairness theory does not explain why we punish *rather than* compensate the victim. The fairness theory instead treats compensation as a natural companion to punishment, not as an alternative to it. The fairness theory leaves to the justification of the criminal law any explanation of why we should have a system of criminal law rather than just tort law and to the theory of criminal legislation the explanation of why this or that particular wrong should be a crime as well as (or instead of) a tort.

Von Hirsh is also correct in saying that the fairness theory will not itself explain why we punish rather than merely censure criminals — *if* censure is here understood as a substitute for punishment. The reason is, of course, again, that, being only a theory of criminal desert, the fairness theory cannot give answers appropriate to a theory of justification. If, however, censure is understood as a kind of punishment, von Hirsh is mistaken in his claim. The fairness theory (at least as I understand it) puts three constraints on the choice of anchoring points: (1) the scale must include no inhumane penalty, (2) the penalties for less serious crimes must not exceed the penalties for more serious ones, and (3) the choice of anchoring points must not threaten the desired level of social order (either by setting penalties too low to discourage crime enough or by setting them so high that punishment is likely to be too infrequent to discourage crime enough).[16] The fairness theory will therefore condemn substituting a reasonable scale of formal censure for our present scale of penalties if (as seems probable) the substitution would reduce social order too much.

That, I think, answers the objection from lack of literal advantage as von Hirsch stated it. Yet, I am uneasy. Von Hirsch knows that punishment and formal censure or compensation are not mutually exclusive alternatives. A sentencing judge may solemnly reprove a criminal before passing sentence; and my experience is that such consuring is common. While it *is* uncommon for a victim of crime to seek compensation from the criminal, that seems to be because criminals are generally proof against collection, not because the law does not recognize the difference between undoing private harm and undoing the advantage of committing the crime. Why then does von Hirsch complain (albeit unjustly) that the fairness theory cannot explain why we punish *rather than* censure or compensate?

Dubious assumptions. Von Hirsch's third objection to the fairness theory is that the fairness theory is too "arcane." The condemnatory theory, he asserts, "rests on much simpler [and so, less dubious] ideas."[17] These simpler ideas he summarizes in this way:

> Prevention explains why the state should impose painful material consequences on victimizing conduct. Reprobation for wrongdoing explains why that sanction should take a condemnatory form. These two ideas of prevention and reprobation cannot be collapsed into one another. Both ideas are used in practical and moral discourse in everyday life.[18]

Von Hirsch and I are, of course, agreed that preventing objectionable activity is a good reason for the state to make the activity a crime if taxation, censure, or other less drastic means of control cannot keep it in check. Though von Hirsch's language suggests that criminal conduct must "victimize," I shall assume he recognizes that many forms of criminal activity have no victim (that is, no one who suffers as a result of the particular crime). I shall also assume von Hirsch recognizes that some acts are made criminal to bring about a good effect rather than to protect potential victims. (Think, for example, of laws requiring the reporting of crime or giving aid in an emergency.) Our disagreement thus seems the narrow one of whether the concept von Hirsch variously calls "condemnation," "reprobation," "blaming," and "censure" provides a simpler, less arcane, or less dubious analysis of criminal desert than does fairness.

Von Hirsch does not explicitly identify his reasons for believing the fairness theory to be too arcane or dubious, but the context suggests that his first two objections in fact state those reasons. If so, I have done all I can to show the fairness theory not to be arcane. What then remains to von Hirsch's third objection is the claim that the condemnatory theory is nonetheless less dubious. The only way finally to dispose of that claim is to show that the condemnatory theory is *relatively* more dubious than the fairness theory. Space, however, will only allow me to point out a sufficient number of serious problems to destroy any presumption in favor of the condemnatory theory. I shall now do that.

One problem of the condemnatory theory is that it does not — contrary to what von Hirsch says — draw on ideas used in everyday discourse. Three *words* are used every day — "blame" "censure," and "condemn." The verb "reprobate" is rare even among legal theorists (though its doublet "reprove"

is common enough). Of the three words used in every day discourse, two—
"blame" and "censure"—are used solely for *verbal* acts (as, indeed, the
dictionary says "reprobate" and "reprove" should be).

To blame someone is to speak ill of her (or at least judge her to deserve
such a bad report). In ordinary practice, to blame someone is *never* to hit
her, to cut off her allowance, or otherwise to punish her. We do, of course,
sometimes treat someone badly *because* we blame her for something. We
may, for example, refuse to have anything to do with her for a while (or
forever). We do not, however, treat her badly *as part of* blaming her. The bad
treatment seems to be justified, when it is, because blaming is not the only
response that is appropriate (rather than that mere blaming is not enough).
The wrongdoer may, for example, have revealed herself to be a person with
whom we should not associate (whatever she may in fact have done).

Censuring is also merely verbal. The difference between "censure" and its
doublet "censor" is precisely that censuring involves words only while today
censoring includes acts like seizing books. In this respect, "censure," not
"censor," is closer to their common root. The Roman censors from whose
office of keeping morals we get our word "censor," had no power to punish,
only the power to reprove.

"Blame," "censure," and "reprobate" thus seem out of place in a theory
of punishment involving anything more than harsh words. That leaves "condemning." It may seem that "condemning" at least names a physical act. For
example, sinners (it is said) are condemned to burn in hell; and, in the United
States, to condemn property is to take it for public use. Certainly, the root
of "condemn"—the same as "damage," "damnation," and "indemnify"—
suggests something more than mere words. Yet, it seems to me, in each case
where "condemn" seems to refer to an act, it in fact refers to words of a
special type, that is, a speech-act, rather than an act much like punishing.
The condemnation of sinners occurs on *judgment* day, not in the eternity that
follows. To condemn property, strictly speaking, is to transfer title and set
the damages the owner must receive in compensation rather than actually to
take physical possession from the owner. And so on.

"Condemn" also has another disadvantage. Unlike "blaming," "censuring," and "reprobating," most examples of "condemning" come from the law
(or such lawlike contexts as the Last Judgment). The central legal usage is
in sentences like "I now condemn you to twenty years in prison." That usage
is perhaps more easily understood as assessment of the "damages" owed for
the crime than as reproof. The condemnatory theory of punishment has a
problem identifying the ordinary practice from which its simple ideas come.
It seems to be living on borrowed simplicity.

That is not the end of the theory's problems. If we put aside "condemn,"
we can identify a class of everyday ideas to which von Hirsch may be thought
to refer. These are singularly inappropriate for constructing a theory of

criminal desert. Blaming, censuring, and reprobating are, as already noted, verbal acts not much like the physical acts associated with punishing. The condemnatory theory needs to explain how blaming, censuring, and reprobating transmute into punishment *without* also changing their nature. Von Hirsch provides no explanation. I don't think anyone else has either.[19]

The reason no one has, I think, is that no one can. Blaming, censuring, and reprobating are all related to shaming. They are in fact the most common means by which we shame people. Shaming is not the same as punishing. Punishment is typically centralized. When it is not, one person's act of punishment still preempts that of others. We think it unjust for a criminal to be punished twice for the same crime. Shaming, however, is typically decentralized and not preemptive. That I have reproved you as you deserve for what you did does not preclude others from doing the same. Indeed, if you deserve blame at all, everyone could justly do the same as I.[20]

Shaming may also involve a different conception of seriousness than punishment does. Surveys asking people to rank crimes according to "seriousness" have produced scales differing in significant respects from the ranking in any actual system of criminal law. For example, one study found that "*assault* with a gun on a policeman" ranked eleventh most serious while "*assassination* of a political official" ranked fifteenth.[21] Von Hirsch thinks such peculiar rankings may derive from "factual error."[22] Perhaps they do. But he cites no study showing that. The studies I have seen suggest that, if such peculiar rankings do derive from factual error, the error is one police officers share with college students, the rich, and the poor.[23] I would therefore suggest another explanation: The studies accurately report the ranking of crimes according to blameworthiness. They are in fact evidence against the thesis that punishment is blaming carried on by harsher means. One reason for accepting this explanation instead of von Hirsch's is that the studies involved generally do not ask respondents to rank crimes according to how much they should be punished. "Seriousness" is left undefined.

Feinberg revived the condemnatory theory two decades ago (in part at least) to explain the "infamy" that generally accompanies punishment but not other equally harsh treatment.[24] Punishment imports blame, he suggested. Other forms of harsh treatment do not. That seems a sensible suggestion. But the simplest explanation of this difference between punishment and other harsh treatment is *not* that punishment is blaming carried on by harsher means (as Feinberg, von Hirsch, and far too many others have concluded). The simplest explanation is that punishment imports blame because conviction of a crime ordinarily means being proved to have engaged in exceedingly blameworthy conduct. The best inference from the mere fact that someone has been punished is that she did something blameworthy (and the more severe the punishment, the more blameworthy the act). The inference is, however, not irrebuttable; and when rebutted, punishment loses its infamy (without necessarily ceasing to seem just). So, for example, law schools stopped automatically denying felons admission after the federal government sent a significant number of conscientious young men to prison for violation of the draft laws.

The law schools did not necessarily change their rules of admission because they thought the draft-resisters had been unjustly punished. They seem to have changed them, in large part at least, because conviction of a felony no longer seemed to justify automatic inference from an applicant's criminality to his unfitness to practice law. The law schools were, in other words, reminded that felonies other than murder, embezzlement, fraud, theft, and the like exist. The publicity concerning draft resistance reminded them of the periphery of the criminal law they had forgotten. The condemnatory theory's appeal seems to depend on a similar forgetting of what lies beyond the criminal law's core. The connection between punishment and blame is not as close as the condemnatory theory requires.

Two Gross Objections

Von Hirsch is not the only critic of the fairness theory, nor are his objections the only ones being made. I should therefore like to discuss two objections of another important critic, Hyman Gross. A comparison of Gross's objections with von Hirsch's will, I think, reveal a pattern of misunderstanding, suggest how many other objections might also be refuted, and incidently clear von Hirsh of the charge of mere carelessness. Gross has recently argued: (a) that the institution of punishment is itself inconsistent with the existence of a cooperative practice of which criminals could take unfair advantage; and (b) that the unfairness theory seems to justify criminalizing all acts of unfairness, not simply those already part of the criminal law.[25] Let's take these objections in order.

Punishment as inconsistent with cooperation. Gross, like von Hirsch, has trouble identifying the unfair advantage the criminal must literally take if the fairness theory is to be more than a metaphor. His concern is, however, different from von Hirsch's. We might put Gross' objection this way. Suppose I benefit from the criminal law but commit a crime. I would take unfair advantage if, but only if, I were exempt from punishment. "If I were king, for example, it might be said that I was taking unfair advantage of my position as a sovereign immune from [punishment by] the law when I refuse to obey it."[26] If, however, I am merely an ordinary subject not exempt from punishment, my crime does not (according to this objection) take unfair advantage. My crime is simply a move in a game for which the game itself provides a response. Playing by the rules cannot be unfair.

This objection rests on the assumption that violating the rules of a practice cannot be unfair if the practice provides a fair penalty. That assumption is,

I think, correct when violating the rules is certain to be detected and punished. When punishment is *certain* to follow violation of the rule, the punishment in fact operates like a price system. You must pay for whatever you get. The assumption can, I think, also be correct in a system in which many violations go undetected, *provided* the penalties are sufficiently high to take into account the probability of not being caught. The penalties would, in other words, have to be high enough that any violation would have a net expected utility (for the actor) of zero or less. Given penalties that high, a violation could not take unfair advantage. The violation could not take advantage at all.

Some deterrentists may think of punishment in this way, but no one should. In no actual society is punishment for crime certain or the statutory penalty high enough to keep the expected utility of crime zero or less. Why? The reason is obvious. Many crimes — for example, theft or burglary — are seldom solved. So, a single-minded policy of setting penalties high enough to keep the expected utility of crime from being positive would produce a penalty scale of almost unimaginable severity.

I therefore see nothing odd about comparing the ordinary subject of the criminal law to Gross' sovereign. For each such subject — that is, all of us more or less — the expected utility of doing without the criminal law will be negative. We are all better off with the criminal law than without it, even if having it means having to do as it says. The utility of any crime for which the criminal receives all the punishment she deserves may, in retrospect, also be zero or less. Just punishment should leave the criminal with no unfair advantage. Nonetheless, the *expected* utility of any particular crime can still be *positive* for *some* subjects (assuming, of course, that the corresponding statute is not unnecessary). The utility can be positive even in retrospect because a just punishment can take back the crime's unfair advantage *only if* the criminal can be caught, convicted, and subjected to punishment. Any potential criminal who has a good chance of escaping detection, capture, or conviction may rationally commit a crime. If he does and escapes punishment, he may have a (net) advantage the law-abiding do not. So, our society cannot depend on just punishment alone to maintain order. Potential criminals, that is, all of us more or less, must cooperate to maintain order or we shall all be much worse off.

Though many critics, including Gross and von Hirsch, find thinking of the criminal law as a cooperative practice hopelessly unrealistic, I find it closer to reality than any alternative. Gross, for example, expressly declares his position to be that "[the] bottom line is not allowing people to get away with crimes . . . [so more] serious crimes require a harsher response to allay suspicions of partial impunity."[27] Is it realistic to expect to allay the *suspicion* of *partial* impunity?

It is not, of course — and Gross knows it. By the end of the paper from which the quoted passage comes, Gross has taken a position much more like von Hirsch's. The primary determinant of deserved punishment should be how harmful the crime is (its "culpability"). Other considerations such as state of mind and the criminal's excuses are relevant too. Overall, punishment should be avoided whenever not clearly necessary. "Impunity" all but disappears from Gross's vocabulary.[28] (I shall say more about this shift from impunity to other factors below.)

Criminalizing all unfairness. Gross states his second objection this way: "If punishment is warranted by unfair advantage taken through some unlawful act, why should that warrant not apply generally throughout the law, so that civil liability as well as criminal will have punishment as a consequence?"[29]

This objection, like von Hirsch's second, rests on a misunderstanding of what the fairness theory is. The fairness theory is (I repeat) a theory of criminal desert, not a full theory of punishment. Since the fairness theory is only a theory of criminal desert, it has nothing to say about what justifies penal institutions or what acts should be made punishable. It only answers questions about *how much* to punish acts that have already been made criminal. Hence, Gross' objection seems irrelevant.

The distinctions on which this response rests are now so common that I may seem to have missed altogether the force of Gross' objection. We can, I think, imagine Gross replying as follows: Why should the fairness theory have nothing to say about what should be punished? Surely, our reasons for making a class of acts punishable will be reflected in how much we think it proper to punish particular instances of that class. If a theory of criminal desert is not also a theory of legislation, deserved punishment might sometimes defeat the purpose of making an act criminal. So, any theory of criminal desert that is not also a theory of legislation is, for that reason alone, inadequate.

This imagined reply is, I think, correct insofar as it rests on two methodological claims: (1) that, all else equal, a theory explaining all of punishment with only one principle is better than one that needs a second principle to explain criminal desert; and (2) that, all else equal, a theory of criminal desert that has a tendency to serve the purposes of criminal liability is better than one that has a tendency to defeat them. Though correct in its methodology, the reply is nonetheless mistaken about the *relative* adequacy of the fairness theory.

That the fairness theory is not, like most theories of criminal desert, also a theory of legislation is not an arbitrary feature of the theory. It is a deduction from its own assumptions. The theory assumes that the criminal law is itself a cooperative practice. When the criminal law is not such a practice, the theory does not apply. But when the criminal law is such a practice, the theory need not inquire into what the law's subjects are trying to do (except perhaps to determine that it is morally permissible). Their purposes do not make the criminal law any more or less a cooperative practice. The fairness theory is, then, more or less independent of the theory of legislation.

Because the fairness theory is only a theory of criminal desert, it will be consistent with any general theory of punishment having a place for criminal desert (provided, of course, the theory does not purport to apply under extreme conditions like those of a concentration camp). Since no theory of *punishment* is without its important opponents, the fairness theory's limited domain is a strength rather than a weakness. Not only does it make it immune to the sort of attack we are now considering, it may also help to explain why principles that seem to justify the institution of punishment or to explain why certain acts should be punished, are so unsatisfactory as measures of criminal desert.[30]

That the fairness theory has a tendency to defeat the purposes of punishment under any theory to which it is joined also seems to me, on balance, a strength. On the one hand, a simple-minded pursuit of some general purpose is likely to lead to injustice or, at the least, to results quite contrary to common sense. On the other hand, a more sophisticated pursuit of the same general purpose is likely to lead to compromises much like those the fairness theory requires. Consider, for example, how Gross's impunity theory compares with the fairness theory when the question is how much to punish theft.

Theft is a crime, according to Gross, because we believe theft would be too common if the only responses to it were less drastic (for example, civil liability). We punish theft to allay any suspicion that a thief can get advantage from her crime. For purposes of argument, assume that only one theft in a hundred is solved (a quite plausible assumption in the United States). So, allaying any suspicion of impunity would seem to require that each thief we catch be given a penalty equal to one hundred times the expected utility of the crime she committed (the expected utility not including the prospect of punishment).

If we were simple-minded, we might stop here, writing the appropriate penalty into the statute books, say, fifty years for theft. But we are not simple-minded. We know that the penalty for theft must fit in with penalties for other crimes, including the most serious, murder.

Let's assume that nine out of ten murders are solved (and the murderers captured, convicted, and punished). Allaying suspicion of impunity for murder would require that murderers be given a penalty equal to about 1.1 times the expected utility of the murder. The expected utility of any particular murder is *not*, however, likely to be a hundred times that of a particular theft. So, we have a problem. We must make the penalty for theft severe enough to allay all suspicion of impunity. We must do the same for murder. But, we probably cannot do both. Suppose, for example, that our jurisdiction has no capital punishment or any inhumane penalty. Suppose too that the average criminal cannot expect to live much more than fifty years from the date of his crime. No matter how high we set the penalty for murder, a thief faced with capture unless he kills his pursuer will be able to kill his pursuer with at least partial impunity. He cannot serve out two consecutive fifty year terms (and concurrent terms are as good as impunity for one of the crimes). What then should be the punishment for theft?

Gross has an answer to that question (as we noted earlier). But the answer compromises simple-minded impunity in much the way the fairness theory would. The compromise breaks the tight connection between the purpose of punishing and the amount of punishment a crime deserves. The compromise also opens the way for thinking of the criminal law as in part a cooperative practice. My impression is that every plausible theory of punishment must include a theory of criminal desert with such compromising features. I therefore conclude that, on balance, the fairness theory is about as likely to be consistent with achieving the purpose of punishment according to a particular theory as any plausible version of that theory would be.[31]

Conclusions

I have now refuted five objections to the fairness theory. I think these constitute a fair sample of the objections now being made. The refutations have relied on standard distinctions like that between a theory of legislation and a theory of criminal desert. I do not believe I have said anything here that those I criticize could not have thought themselves. I am therefore left wondering why those making the objections did not reformulate them to take account of what would almost certainly be said in response. Is there a deeper issue that both they and I have missed?

Notes

This paper was originally prepared for the Jerusalem Conference on Justice in Punishment (March, 1988). I should like to thank Paul Gomberg and Don Scheid for helpful comments on the first draft.

1. See Chapter Two, n. 26.
2. Chapters Five, Six, and Seven are a good indication of my interests. See also "Guilty But Insane?," *Social Theory and Practice* 10 (Spring 1984): 1-23; and "Death, Deterrence, and the Method of Common Sense," *Social Theory and Practice* 7 (Summer 1981): 145-178.
3. "Setting Penalties: What Does Rape Deserve?," *Law and Philosophy* 3 (April 1984): 62-111; Chapter Eight; and Chapter Four.

4. Most of these arguments are to be found in Chapter Three.

5. Andrew von Hirsch, *Past or Future Crimes* (New Brunswick, New Jersey: Rutgers University Press, 1985), p. 91.

6. Ibid.

7. See, for example, Andrew von Hirsch, "Desert and Previous Convictions in Setencing," *Minnesota Law Review* 65 (April 1981): 591-634, esp. p. 619 n. 64: "If the offender has a very large number of convictions, there may be an understandable desire to begin to respond more severely. But that would have to rest, in my view, on utilitarian notions (e.g., the notion that harsher measures need to be tried when lesser ones have failed so often before . . .), rather than on the idea of the offender deserving more punishment . . . "

8. Chapter Four.

9. *Past or Future Crimes*, pp. 74-76. One example will suggest the flavor of this whole section: "At least so far as typical crimes of theft, force, and fraud are concerned, one can develop a rough assessment of their consequences using the legal definition of the crime and available common knowledge of its probable effects," p. 74.

10. Andrew von Hirsch, *Doing Justice: The Choice of Punishment* (New York: Hill and Wang, 1976), pp. 47-49.

11. *Past or Future Crimes*, pp. 58-59.

12. See, especially, Jeffrie Murphy's seminal paper, "Marxism and Retribution," *Philosophy and Public Affairs* 2 (Spring 1973): 217-43. I ignore here Murphy's psychological complaint that it is unfair to punish the poor for committing crimes in a society that makes clear to the poor how much they are missing. I ignore it for two reasons. First, most of the poor do not commit crimes; so, most of the poor are among those the crimes of the poor take unfair advantage of. Second, Murphy's argument seems to rest on a particularly mechanical view of the connection between temptation and action or desire and responsibility.

13. James. P. Sterba, "Is There A Rationale For Punishment?," *American Journal of Jurisprudence* 29 (1984): 29-43, esp. 43. Those who do not understand why justification of punishment seems so divorced from political philosophy would do well to read Sterba carefully. His conditions for just punishment are so weak that almost any state is likely to satisfy them in most cases. Though political theory and punishment theory are not unrelated, their relation is, it seems, so weak that the theory of political justification is unlikely to tell us anything interesting about punishment.

14. *Past or Future Crimes*, p. 58.

15. Ibid.

16. Chapter Four.

17. *Past or Future Crimes*, p. 59 (and again, p. 36).

18. Ibid.

19. See, for example, Sanford H. Kadish, "Complicity, Cause and Blame: A Study in the Interpretation of Doctrine," *California Law Review* 73 (1985): 323-410. As the title suggests, the purpose of the article is to use the concept of blame to explain complicity doctrine. Kadish in fact devotes a whole section of the paper (pp. 329-336) to explicating the concept of blame. Yet, no where does he even ask why the principles of blaming should be the same as those of punishing. He merely begins with the undefended claim that blame is "a concept that reaches so deeply into the jurisprudence of the criminal law that no account of the law can succeed without explicating its meaning and its role," p. 329. My point is nonetheless an old one. See, for example, H.L.A. Hart, *Law, Liberty, and Morality* (New York: Vintage Press, 1963), pp. 65-66.

20. How then do I explain the difference between my analysis of shame and that Herbert Morris gives in *On Guilt and Innocence* (Berkeley: University of California Press, 1976), pp. 59-63? Morris there distinguishes *between* blame *and* shame, arguing that blame and guilt are more alike than either is like shame. Perhaps because I am not concerned with shame as such, but with *how* we shame, I find shaming to be much more like blaming than either is like punishment. Perhaps too, Morris (in that paper), Gross, von Hirsch, Kadish, and others are working with a philosophical model of blaming (blaming as a kind of punishment) whereas I am simply drawing on etymology and ordinary nonphilosophical usage. Certainly, something strange is going on. Morris expressly distinguishes between blaming and punishing in his more recent "A Paternalistic Theory of Punishment," *American Philosophical Quarterly* 18 (October 1981): 263-271. For example, "Because of this relationship, punishment is connected with the good that I have described in a way that blame and disapproval by themselves are not," p. 266. For another analysis of blaming close to mine, see William Kneale, *The Responsibility of Criminals* (Oxford: Oxford University Press, 1967), pp. 25-30.

21. Peter H. Rossi et al., "The Seriousness of Crimes: Normative Structure and Individual Differences," *American Sociological Review* 39 (April 1974): 224-37, esp. pp. 228-29.

22. *Past or Future Crimes*, p. 65.

23. V. Lee Hamilton and Steve Rytina, "Social Consensus on Norms of Justice: Should the Punishment Fit the Crime?," *American Journal of Sociology* 85 (1980): 1117-44.

24. Joel Feinberg, *Doing and Deserving* (Princeton University Press: Princeton, New Jersey, 1970), pp. 95-98.

25. Hyman Gross, "Fringe Liability, Unfair Advantage, and the Price of Crime," *Wayne Law Review* 33 (Summer 1987): 1395-1411. Though he makes other arguments as well, they need not concern us.

26. "Fringe Liability," p. 1403.

27. Ibid., p. 1405.

28. Ibid., pp. 1410-1411.

29. Ibid., p. 1404.

30. See, for example, D.A. Duff's disappointing discussion of setting penalties in his generally impressive *Trials and punishments* (Cambridge: Cambridge University Press, 1985), especially pp. 279-281.

31. Theorists generally seem disappointed when someone else's theory of punishment shows signs of such compromise. Note, for example, Jeffrey H. Reiman, "Justice, Civilization, and the Death Penalty: Answering van den Haag," *Philosophy and Public Affairs* 14 (Spring 1985): 115-148. He there criticizes me for only taking account of cost to the victim "halfheartedly," pp. 120-121, n. 10. Like other critics of the fairness theory, he also suggests problems and then doesn't wait for an answer.

10

Using the Market to Measure Deserved Punishment: A Final Defense

That the criminal law is in some respects analogous to a market seems uncontroversial. Prosecutors often talk of a particular crime as having a "price" (the statutory penalty) and of punishment as paying that price. Defense attorneys sometimes talk of the "going rate" for this or that crime. Scholars have compared the penalty scale to a price or tariff system. The concept of fairness seems as much at home in the criminal law as in the market.

But the disanalogies between market and criminal law seem at least as uncontroversial as the analogies. The market sells things we are willing to let people buy; the criminal law "sells" just those "things" that (all else equal) we would rather people *not* "buy." Price is generally not intended as a disincentive or sanction, only as a way to recover cost or to achieve profit. Punishment, in contrast, is emphatically a disincentive or sanction.

So dramatic are the disanalogies that any attempt to use a market to measure deserved punishment may seem foredoomed, an intriguing possibility cursed at conception.[1] This supposed curse may explain why few legal theorists have used the market to understand deserved punishment and why even those few have not tried to use the market to measure it.[2] Still, though the curse may explain what happened, it cannot justify it. I have now worked with the analogy between market and criminal law in four chapters (Three, Five, Six and Seven). The results have, I think, been good. Each chapter took up some difficult problem in the theory of punishment and showed that the analogy helps to provide an analysis of the problem at least as good as any alternative.

Yet, each of those chapters, though successful in its own terms, may seem open to a criticism I could not reasonably take up within its scope. The criticism might be put this way: "Your market is like a magician's hat. The rabbits you pull out are simply the rabbits you put in."[3] The purpose of this

234

paper is to dispose of that criticism. I shall try to show that the model I used to measure deserved punishment is more than a way to work out the consequences of certain more or less arbitrary assumptions, that in fact it provides a means of gauging at least one important vector of just legal punishment.

The Criminal Law as a Cooperative Practice

My concern here is *how much to punish criminals* under the laws of a relatively just society — what we might call "the theory of proportion in just or deserved criminal punishment" — *not* the definition (or meaning) of punishment, its purpose (or function) as an institution, or its justification. What I shall say should be consistent with a wide range of what are generally called "theories of punishment." On my view, the amount of legal punishment a particular crime (or class of crimes) can legally deserve should be the same whether or not condemnation is part of punishment's definition, whether punishment's purpose is to prevent harmful acts or to vindicate the law, or whether punishment is justified by its extrinsic effects or because of what it is. What I shall say should also be consistent with a wide range of theories concerning what the criminal law should prohibit (or require), what we have called "theories of criminal legislation" (including theories of excuse or justification). On my view, a theory of proportion in punishment should be much the same whether, for example, the criminal law justifiably does no more than protect individual liberty or instead is obliged to protect public morals or help bring about the millenium.

The theory of proportion in (criminal) punishment is, as I understand it, primarily a function of two essential features of any adequate theory of just criminal punishment: (a) a certain *structure* of rules and (b) a certain *relationship* between those rules and the society they govern. I shall now summarize these essential features one at a time, beginning with the structure of rules. My purpose in so doing is not to state my theory of proportion in full or to defend it against every objection. My purpose is simply to remind the reader of what went before and so lay a foundation for what follows.

On my view, the theory of proportion in punishment presupposes a system of rules (a system of criminal law) meeting (something like) the following five now standard conditions: *First*, there are "primary" rules that prohibit certain acts, the "crimes." The rules may also require certain acts (and then *not* doing any one of those acts would also be a crime). *Second*, the rules apply to beings with the power to follow the rules or not as they choose and capable of choosing which on the basis of reasons. We may call such beings "rational agents" or "persons." *Third*, there are "secondary" rules establishing procedures for inflicting specified undesirable consequences ("penalties") upon any person who does not do as the "primary" rules say (a consequence being undesirable if those subject to the rule would generally consider the prospect of suffering the consequence a good reason not to do an otherwise desirable act). *Fourth*, these rules, both primary and secondary, are (in general at least) known to those subject to them. *Fifth*, and last, imposing a penalty is justified (in part at least) by showing that the person upon whom it is to be imposed committed a crime for which the penalty is a specified response.

Such a system of rules is, I think, what most legal theorists accept as the basic structure of the criminal law. Disputes are likely to break out only over claims that having such a system is the *same* as having a system of criminal law. Some theorists might, for example, require *as well* that the penalty be justified *only* by the criminal's having done the crime or that the penalty be imposed in part at least as an emphatic denunciation of what the criminal did. Such disputes belong to the theory of definition. They need not concern us. However they turn out, the criminal law will, at a minimum, satisfy these five conditions.[4]

Though such disputes need not concern us, a related one must. Some writers, most notably Barbara Wootton, seem to reject one or more of these conditions.[5] On my view, such writers must be taken as proposing an alternative to criminal punishment rather than simply as trying to provide a theory of it. Taking them this way is, I think, consistent with what they themselves generally say.[6]

Though, on my view, the theory of proportion in punishment is a function of the structure of criminal law as just described, it is not *simply* a function of that. The theory also presupposes a society that satisfies at least three other conditions. Any legal punishment imposed in a society not satisfying these additional conditions is likely to be a "mere penalty" rather than carrying the moral condemnation legal theorists have generally been at pains to preserve (if not explain) — or, if more than that, to carry moral condemnation only for reasons entirely independent of the act's being against the law. The three conditions are:

1. The society must be so organized that those subject to the criminal law are better off with the criminal law than without it. The subjects of the criminal law must justifiably prefer the criminal law as it actually is to the condition they would be in if all criminal laws were repealed, the courts closed, and enforcement ceased. Ordinary morality, social pressure, taxation, self-help, civil liability, and the like must not be enough to keep undesirable activity within tolerable limits.
2. The society must include a substantial number of persons ("potential criminals") who would sometimes choose to break the law if the penalty for the crime or the probability of suffering the penalty were sufficiently low.

3. The society must lack the power (or will) to make criminal activity so expensive, risky, or otherwise undesirable that almost no one could rationally choose to commit a crime. The society must depend in part on voluntary obedience to law to preserve a social order from which even potential criminals benefit.

In a society meeting these three conditions, the criminal law will be (in part at least) a cooperative practice. The benefits each gets from the practice as a whole will depend in part on the voluntary cooperation of others. Each subject's obedience to the law will help assure to others the benefits that she herself derives from their obedience. Each will be better off if the others obey, even if she too must obey, and each could sometimes benefit by disobeying so long as not too many others do the same.

Insofar as the criminal law is a cooperative practice, each subject will be in a position to take advantage of others by disobeying the law when disobeying seems to her advantage. The advantage so taken would be unfair (insofar as the practice in question is both just and cooperative). One indication of unfairness is that the person taking the advantage could not rationally allow all others relevantly like her to do the same.

A theory of proportion in (criminal) punishment does not apply in any society whatever. The penalties imposed in such a radically unjust society as a concentration camp or slave galley could be correct (under some rule), effective (in obtaining an institutional objective), and efficient (even perhaps according to a utilitarian calculus). Some of those penalties might even be morally deserved (supposing morality to provide at least a broad range of permissible responses to the moral wrong involved); they might, that is, be deserved even if the society in question had no rule on the subject. But the penalties so imposed could not be deserved as *legal* penalties. Whether or not "punishment" can have its ordinary use in such a society, the concept of *deserved criminal punishment* could not.

The reason that it could not is, on my view, that criminal punishment can be deserved only if, and only insofar as, it takes back (or cancels) the unfair advantage the criminal takes by breaking a particular criminal law (whatever other advantages or disadvantages may accompany his act). In a concentration camp, there are no fellow cooperators of whom one can take unfair advantage by *breaking a camp rule*, hence no possibility of deserved *criminal* punishment.

We could, I agree, talk of deterrence, revenge, training, condemnation, and perhaps even education. Since each of these categories includes a principle of proportion, we *could* find a use for "deserved punishment" even in a concentration camp—just as we can find a use for "deserved punishment" when explaining why we kicked a dog. But such uses are easily distinguishable from the use of "deserved punishment" characteristic of criminal law.

Now, someone might object that even in a concentration camp we can sometimes find a use for "deserved punishment" much like that characteristic of the criminal law. If, for example, one camp inmate steals food from another, we could say being made to go without food for a day would be what such a thief deserves for what he did while being hung up by his wrists for a day was too severe.

I have two responses to this objection. One is that I find the example upon which it rests much less convincing than the abstract claim itself. I am not sure why that is. But I suspect the reason I find the example unconvincing is that it explicitly treats the camp rules as in the same moral category as the rules of a relatively just legal system — when they are not. Showing that would, however, take us too far into legal theory. My second response makes such a digression unncessary.

My second response is that, even if I agreed that we could find in a concentration camp a use of "deserved punishment" much like that characteristic of the criminal law, that would show only that a concentration camp is still enough like ordinary life for ordinary *moral* categories to apply. Our judgments of desert there would be judgments of simple moral desert, not of criminal desert. They would be the same whether or not the camp rules punished the theft of food.

My stress on the cooperative aspect of the criminal law may seem utopian. After all (it might be said), surely a society much like ours, with so many poor and disaffected, cannot satisfy the three conditions laid down above. Since I have dealt with this objection at length in Chapter Nine, I shall simply restate my conclusion here: Though our society is, at best, only relatively just, most of those subject to the criminal law are still better off than they would be without any criminal law whatever. Perhaps only those without food and shelter, huddling in alleys at night in bad neighborhoods, are no better off than they would be if all criminal statutes were repealed, the criminal courts closed, and the police disbanded. Those who do not benefit from the criminal law can deserve punishment only insofar as their offenses are immoral as well as illegal. They could, for example, deserve punishment for murder but not for sleeping in the park.

Deserved Punishment Through a Fair Market for Crime

We are now ready to understand the fundamental rightness of the analogy between the criminal law and the market. A market can provide a model of justly proportioned punishment because each penalty in a relatively just system of criminal law should correspond to the price a license to commit the crime would bring in a relatively fair market in a society in most ways like that to which the system of criminal law actually applies. The market, insofar as it is a fair procedure about which we know a great deal, is a way to help us fit together the various considerations we think go into just criminal punishment.

What might such a model look like? While there seem to be many possibilities, I shall continue to use the auction. So, let us imagine once again a society much like ours but having the practice of allowing anyone subject to the criminal law to bid on a small number of licenses to do what the law forbids. These licenses may be thought of as "pardons in advance," "immunities," "privileges," or a currency by which one may "pay one's debt to society." The terms of the license would correspond to the terms in which the law defines the crime. The number of licenses would have to be decided in much the way the number of licenses to hunt a certain animal in a certain season is decided. The number of licenses to commit a crime put up for auction should be the maximum (taking into account unavoidable poaching) consistent with maintaining the desired level of social order.

From society's perspective, all that matters will be "harm," that is, activities or outcomes the society wants to avoid. From society's perspective, for example, the intentional killing of another human being ("murder") and the accidental killing of another as the result of reckless conduct ("involuntary manslaughter" or "reckless homicide") involve the same harm, homicide.

Justice, however, requires us to consider more than society's perspective. We should not punish a criminal more severely than she deserves, even if society would benefit. Criminal desert seems in part to depend on what the criminal gains by her crime — not, I hasten to add, what she gains more or less incidentally by what she did (for example, $750 from a theft or the delight of seeing her enemy dead as the result of murder or manslaughter), but what she gains just by the crime itself, just by the act-as-breaking-a-specific law. What she gets simply by breaking the law is a certain advantage those obeying the law in question necessarily do not get. The advantage is a liberty to do what others cannot. We can represent that liberty by exactly the same licenses we use to represent the amount of crime society was willing to tolerate. The liberty ought to have a fair market price. If it does, the liberty is literally an advantage, that is, an advantage having a more or less objective value even someone who would not want that advantage can recognize. This objective value is the measure of deserved criminal punishment. Whether it is also the measure of the moral gravity of the act so licensed, all things considered, is an open question. All I claim is that it corresponds to the moral gravity of the act as a violation of a particular law of the legal system in question.

Some writers have supposed that what I have called "the value of liberty" must depend on some unknown calculus of *degree* of liberty or *degree* of self-restraint requiring interpersonal comparisons before deserved punishment can be determined.[7] That is not so. We can use an auction like the one we are imagining without knowing what makes a particular license valuable to a particular purchaser (or even *how* valuable it is to her). Whatever her motive for buying, she will (if rational) pay the price she does in part because she wants the license and in part because she cannot get it for less. She will not pay significantly more than what is necessary to outbid the competition (however valuable the license is to her). She will not because to do so would be a waste of money.

All we are entitled to conclude from her purchase is that the license is worth at least that much to her. The actual price she pays will be determined (in part at least) by individual judgments (hers and others) of how much liberty the license provides, how much restraint one will no longer have to exercise, and so on. Since such judgments are possible even if the liberty or self-restraint of one person is incommensurable with that of another, the market provides a mechanism that combines the values of different persons *without* presupposing any independent calculus.

What I have just said applies to all markets more or less. Yet, I should point out that my concern here is only a certain family of market models, those including only "market fundamentals," not those including as well such "technical factors" as crowd psychology. Though technical factors are not irrelevant to punishment, they belong to its empirical study. Crowd psychology may, for example, explain why the statutory penalty for some crimes changes so frequently while most remain unchanged. Crowd psychology will, however, tell us little about how much punishment is deserved. Technical factors are more or less independent of underlying value and, as we have understood unfair advantage, its price should be determined by its underlying value, not by any mere accident of market fluctuation.

The market allows us to combine the different values of different persons without presupposing any independent calculus. It also allows us to combine the social perspective characteristic of utilitarian theories of punishment with the criminal's perspective characteristic of traditional retributive theories. Indeed, it will even allow us to bring in something of the law-abiding person's perspective typical of recent condemnatory theories. We can, for example, imagine "protective associations" of public-spirited individuals who buy licenses in order to keep them out of the hands of would-be criminals. When I first wrote about these philanthropic associations, I thought they would have a decisive impact on the auction, keeping prices from falling too low.[8] Later I realized that any effect such associations could have would be short-lived. They could prevent would-be criminals from conspiring to keep prices low. They could not, however, actually hold prices at any level for very long. Their function in the auction would be much like that of market-makers at a stock exchange (or of the "insurance companies" discussed below). In the long-run, the price of any license will be a function only of social supply and criminal demand.

That being so, the price of licenses should be a good *index* of the advantage criminals in our society unfairly take by doing the forbidden act (provided the auction is itself a fair means of setting price). The penalties will then be assigned according to this index, the anchoring points being set by considerations of deterrence, humaneness, and the like (as explained in Chapters Two and Four). Because this procedure takes due account of society's need for order, the penalties so determined should be severe enough to provide adequate (but far from complete) deterrence. And because a penalty so determined also corresponds to the unfair advantage a criminal takes by his crime, the penalty should be what he deserves in (criminal) punishment for what he did.

Of course, all this assumes that tinkering with market rules would not allow us to vary results so much that the model would be useless in practice. We have now reached the question this Chapter is supposed to answer: Are the conclusions drawn from our auction as secure as any economist's or instead mere artifacts of assumptions having just and plausible alternatives from which they would not follow?

The importance of the question is obvious. The answer is less so. We cannot, I think, actually *prove* that our conclusions are not mere artifacts. To prove that, we would have to exclude an indefinitely large number of possible ways of tinkering with the assumptions. That is more or less impossible. The best we can do is make a case for the stability of our conclusions. We can do that in part just by explaining why certain seemingly attractive alternatives to the auction as we have imagined it are in fact unjust, implausible, or equivalent in effect to our version of the auction. But, in part too, we can make our case by so choosing alternatives that, considering them one by one, we build up a picture of the auction that suggests that our conclusion will be stable over the whole range of just and plausible assumptions, a picture explaining why undiscussed alternatives are no more likely to threaten our conclusions than those already discussed. If we choose carefully, discussing even relatively few alternatives should be enough to make us reasonably confident of the conclusions our model yields.

We can identify at least four ways the auction might be made to yield relative prices different from those likely to follow from the auction as we have imagined it. One way is to apportion licenses among the various "mental states" in some special way, for example, by setting aside many fewer licenses for manslaughter than for murder. Since supply is ordinarily an important determinant of auction price, differing apportionments of licenses could well produce radically different selling prices. A second way all else could be made unequal is by astute choice of procedures controlling what happens if someone commits a crime without a license. If, for example, we treat unlicensed murder too leniently, there would be no demand for licenses to commit murder and such licenses would be worth nothing. A third way to make all else less than equal is to tinker with how licenses are to be paid for. If different sorts of license could be paid for in different ways or at different times, that too might affect demand and so the relative selling price. A fourth way all else might be made less than equal is by varying the usefulness of licenses in some special way. For example, if licenses had to be used within a certain period of time, licenses the buyer could know would be needed during that period would be worth more than licenses the buyer could not know would be needed.

These are, I think, the principal ways in which we might find just and plausible alternatives to the market as we would imagine it. Let us examine them one at a time, beginning with apportionment. And, to avoid distracting detail, let us focus discussion on one relatively easy question, why murder deserves more punishment than involuntary manslaughter.[9]

Mental States

We have assumed that licenses must be rationed to preserve the desired level of social order. Rationing generates the first set of possible threats to the stability of any conclusion we might draw. If our concern is social order, then (it may seem) the number of licenses for a particular "kind" of crime, say, killing someone, should be independent of the mental state of the killer. Killing does the same "harm" whether done intentionally, recklessly, negligently, or even without fault. So, if a society cannot tolerate more than a certain amount of a certain harm (in our case, homicide), society's purposes in licensing will not distinguish between whether the crime is intentional, reckless, or negligent. And so (it may seem), the society need not concern itself with what "mental element" goes with the crime (beyond what is necessary to satisfy the crime's definition). All licenses for any particular crime should be "all-purpose"; or, if they must specify mental state, the mental state specified should be a matter of indifference (except insofar as relevant to maximizing return from sales).

Though this reasoning may seem plausible, it is not. The assumption that the society should be indifferent to who buys a license (or to the "mental state" required for its use) will not stand examination. Suppose, for example, that someone who buys a license to murder is ten times more likely to use it than someone who buys a license to commit involuntary manslaughter. Selling ten murder licenses would probably have about ten times the bad effect selling the same number of manslaughter licenses would. No society much like ours could plausibly be supposed to allow consequences such as that.

Supposing (something like) a ten-to-one ratio should not itself be rejected. The buyer of a murder license has control over when he will need it in a way the holder of a manslaughter license does not. People's intentions are a much better guide to what they will do than what they risk is. Only if the procedures of the auction compensated somehow for this simple fact about human action would it be possible to reject the supposition of differing effect. Later, I shall show that certain initially attractive devices that might compensate for such a differential are unattractive or ineffective. But, for now, let us suppose there are no such devices. It would then not be plausible to expect the society we are imagining to leave to the market the determination whether what is sold is one license to commit murder or one license to commit manslaughter. To preserve the required level of social order, the society would have to fix the number of one type of license it will treat as equivalent to one of the other type for purposes of calculating how many of each it can safely issue.

Having fixed the "exchange rate" between types of license, our imagined society will have to decide how to apportion licenses among the various types. Should it offer 500 licenses to commit murder and 5000 to commit manslaughter? 100 to commit murder and 4000 to commit manslaughter? Or what? Because (as we are now supposing) the effect on social order will be the same whichever of these ratios the society adopts, the obvious answer is, "Leave it to the market. Apportion licenses so as to produce the greatest return from sales."

Though the obvious answer, we must reject it. Leaving even this rationing decision to the market would be unsatisfactory both for our purposes and for those of our imagined society. The demand for a certain type of license, say, licenses to murder, might be so great that, though used ten times as often as licenses to commit manslaughter, they would in fact bring more than ten times the price of those licenses even if almost all the licenses to kill offered for sale were licenses to murder. Given such a pattern of demand, leaving apportionment to the market would mean, in effect, that involuntary manslaughter could not be licensed while murder could be. Such a result would leave us with no way to fix the price of manslaughter licenses. We would know that murder licenses were worth more. But we would not know whether a manslaughter license was worth anything at all.

That, of course, is a reason for *us* to reject market-controlled apportionment, not a reason for our imagined society to. But there is a reason for the society to reject it too. Such apportionment could amount to licensing the morally worse crimes (for example, murder) while categorically forbidding morally less bad ones (for example, manslaughter). That result would be both unjust and something a society much like ours could not plausibly be supposed to tolerate. So, we must suppose the society of our auction to offer some licenses of each type, even though so doing will not produce the greatest return from sales. Indeed, to avoid begging any questions, we should apportion licenses so that the ratio of satisfied to unsatisfied demand (holding price constant) is about the same for each type of license involving the same harm.

Punishing Poaching

Another threat to conclusions drawn from the auction arises from the possibility of committing crimes without the appropriate license. "Poaching" cannot be ruled out, either by definition or factual assumption.

If we defined terms so that no one could *in principle* poach, we would also make licensing a crime like manslaughter *logically* incoherent. To say no one could poach is either to rule out certain actions (for example, unlicensed homicide) or to rule out certain descriptions of such actions (for example, "unlicensed homicide"). Either way, if a crime like unlicensed manslaughter were impossible, then licensed manslaughter would be impossible too. If I cannot commit manslaughter without a license, I can avoid committing the crime simply by not getting a license. So, to commit the crime, I would have to plan ahead enough to obtain a license. I would have to plan on committing homicide. I would deliberately have to put myself in position to kill someone (without justification or excuse). If I then committed the homicide, the homicide I committed would be intential homicide, not involuntary manslaughter. My manslaughter license would be useless because it is a necessary means to the crime it pardons.

That is the implausible consequence of assuming that acts like unlicensed homicide are actually impossible. If instead we assume that unlicensed crimes are only legally impossible, the result is stranger yet. Legal impossibility rules out a certain legal description of an act, not any particular physical act as such. So, if poaching is merely legally impossible, no one can poach even if he kills and has no license.

We must admit then that there could be poaching. Might we still assume that there *would* (as a matter of fact) be none? The answer, I think, is that we cannot plausibly assume that. What society was ever so law-abiding? While no society has actually undertaken to license crime in the way we are imagining, it seems probable that, even in a society that did, a significant number of people would try to get something for nothing. So, we must assume that in any society much like ours, including the one we are imagining, not only *could* there be poaching, but that there *would* be a significant amount.

Assuming significant poaching has important consequences. Poaching must be kept in check if there is to be any legal order at all. If poaching is to be kept in check, it must, it seems, be punished. Indeed, it must be punished so severely that buying a license seems a bargain in comparison. Yet, as soon as we allow poaching to be punished, we face a dilemma. Either we punish all unlicensed commissions of harm with *equal* severity whether the crime was intentional, reckless, or whatever, or we *proportion* the punishment taking into account the criminal's "mental state." Both alternatives seem troubling, though not in the same way. We face a dilemma.

To proportion punishment to seriousness of crime, including the criminal's mental state, *seems* to beg questions our auction was to answer. The greater the punishment in prospect, the more (all else equal) one should be willing to pay to be exempt from it. So, if unlicensed murder is punished more severely than unlicensed manslaughter, a license to murder would (all else equal) automatically be worth more than a license to commit manslaughter. Though punishing poaching in this way would automatically yield the difference between murder and manslaughter we want, it would do so with suspicious ease. So, to avoid seeming to beg the question, we must assume that our imagined society punishes all unlicensed doing of the same harm the same way whatever the criminal's mental state.

That throws us on the dilemma's other horn. Punishing the same all those who do the same harm without a license, without regard to mental state, *seems* so harsh as to be unjust. Is it? The problem is not the harsh penalties as such. We are not, I take it, much bothered that harsh penalties should fall upon those who, though they know they could buy a license to commit a certain crime intentionally, nonetheless intentionally commit the crime without first obtaining the license. Such persons have knowingly risked punishment for poaching when they could have escaped that risk simply by paying a fair price for a license to commit the underlying crime. We should, I think, be content to let them suffer what they knowingly risked. Any concern we have should be saved for those who do not know that they are committing a crime until too late—for example, someone who kills his child while playfully pulling the trigger on a gun he thought was empty. Such criminals literally "do not know what they do" until they have done it. The stiff penalty for poaching seems unjust for them (if it does) in part at least because such "innocents" do not have the same chance to avoid their crimes that intentional criminals have to avoid theirs.

If *that* is our concern, then we have nothing to be concerned about. The ordinary principles of criminal legislation should prevent such injustice in at least one of two related ways. The first way depends on what crimes can be committed without the intention to do the act. Only a small class of crimes should be punished if committed without intention. Crimes that one could commit at any time or any place are not of that class. What should be necessary is that the crime result from some narrowly circumscribed activity, for example, playing with a gun, that one can avoid without much difficulty. The risky activity should be one the actor undertakes "voluntarily." The risks should be so well known that the actor cannot reasonably claim ignorance of them. Where these conditions are satisfied, the criminal cannot claim that he did not have fair notice of the need for reasonable care or of the probability that he would need a license to avoid criminal liability. He would have a fair opportunity to avoid the crime. If he is nonetheless caught poaching, the fault is his. He has no cause to complain of the law. Where these conditions are not met, he could not be justly convicted of the crime and the question of just punishment would be foreclosed.[10]

The other way our imagined society escapes the charge of harshness for punishing poaching the same whatever the criminal's mental state, involves the basic structure of the society we are imagining. We are supposing a relatively just society (since the notion of just punishment seems to make little sense outside such a society). We may suppose that in a relatively just society (almost) no one guilty of a crime like involuntary manslaughter would lack the price of a license (whether or not there are enough licenses to go around). We may suppose this for two reasons. First, in a relatively just society, wealth would be relatively widely distributed. Insofar as this condition is met, anyone not able to get a license would have lost out in a fair competition and so have been *fairly* denied the opportunity to commit the crime with a license. Second, as we already noted, the conduct a relatively just society would (on pain of punishment) hold to a standard of reasonable care should be so limited that anyone who cannot afford the necessary license can easily avoid the risk of committing the crime until he can afford it. The killer we have supposed might, for example, abstain from pretending to fire his gun at others or instead take greater care to check the firing chamber. Punishing him severely for poaching when he might easily either have bought the appropriate license or taken the appropriate precautions does not seem unduly harsh.

Those who find such a criminal's punishment, though not unduly harsh, still a bit much, may be tempted to lessen the harshness further by allowing a criminal to buy (or at least bid on) a license for the crime in question for a reasonable time *after* he knows (or at least should know) he has committed the crime. For intentional crimes like murder, such a "grace period" would begin quite early, that is, at about the time the potential criminal begins his preparations. For a crime like involuntary manslaughter, however, the grace period would begin rather late, that is, at about the time the crime actually occurs. The grace period would give criminals ample opportunity to buy the needed license.

As with most temptations, this one is less tempting once we think it through. If adopted, the suggested grace period would radically change the calculations setting the price at which licenses for nonintentional crimes would sell. It would actually reverse the ranking of intentional and nonintentional crimes.

Someone who knows himself likely to commit a crime like manslaughter would — unlike someone planning a crime like murder — have little incentive to buy a license before the crime. He could buy it after the crime during the grace period at about the same price he would pay if he bought it earlier. In the meantime, he would have the use of his money. For this reason, the price of licenses for crimes like manslaughter would largely be set by what those who have committed the crime would bid. Such bidders would not limit what they bid to what the crime was worth compared to other alternatives, as murderers still would. Unlike would-be murderers, these bidders could no longer avoid their crime. For them, the only relevant fact would be the relative severity of the penalty for poaching (suitably reduced for the possibility of escaping detection, capture, or conviction). Since licenses for intentional crimes like murder would still be determined taking into account the value of alternatives to committing the crime, and since the penalty for unlicensed murder would still be the same as for unlicensed manslaughter, the grace period we are assuming would assure that murder licenses sell for *less* than manslaughter licenses.

That implausible result is, I think, reason enough to reject any such grace period. But there is another. Our purpose is to use each license to measure the unfair advantage a criminal takes by the corresponding crime. The effect of any grace period much like the one we have been considering must be to make the price of licenses for crimes like manslaughter a measure of nothing more than the penalty in view once the criminal has poached. To assume a grace period is in effect to give up the interesting enterprise on which we have embarked for one in which we do indeed pull from a hat only the rabbit we put in — and the wrong rabbit at that!

Payment

Licenses must be paid for sooner or later. There seem to be only two options we need to consider (all others more or less mixing their features). One option is making the potential criminal pay for the license as soon as he has won the bidding (as is the practice at ordinary auctions). We might call this the "pay now" option. The other, what we might call the "pay later" option, is to make him pay only when he has to use the license (making much closer the analogy with "paying one's debt to society" by punishment). The choice between these two options could substantially affect the price at which licenses sell.

Let us consider the "pay later" option first. Where the penalty for two crimes is the same and the probability of suffering the penalty is also the same, it seems that (all else equal) the price of the two exempting licenses should be the same too. Suppose, for example, that two people are considering doing the same unlicensed harm, though one is considering murder and the other manslaughter. Neither will have to pay for the license until he is caught, tried, and convicted. Their market situation would, then, be exactly the same. Each is concerned with what he will have to pay when faced with the certainty of having to choose between paying for a license and suffering the penalty for poaching. So, under the "pay later" option, the relative price of a license to commit manslaughter should at least approach the price of a license to commit murder. The "pay later" option seems to be a variant of the "grace period" just discussed (and might seem to deserve to be rejected for that reason alone).

If, however, the criminal has to pay when he wins the bidding, the license becomes a kind of insurance. He may have a chance to use the license, but the possibility exists that he will not commit the crime, not be convicted, or for some other reason not need the license. The market price of the license should then be the value-if-used reduced by the likelihood that the license will not be used (and miscellaneous "transaction costs"). Since a potential murderer is much more likely to commit the crime she *intends* than the potential manslaughterer is to commit the crime he merely *risks*, the reduction for likelihood of use would, it seems, be much smaller for a murder license than for a manslaughter license. Adopting the "pay now" option would make proof of the relatively smaller unfair advantage of committing manslaughter easy.

That is worth noting. But, the very ease with which the pay-now option leads to the conclusion we expect makes the pay-later option more interesting. To avoid begging any questions, let us consider what would happen if payment were due only at time of use. Even though the "pay later" option seems to be a mere variant of the grace period discussed above, might it not still allow us to conclude that involuntary manslaughter deserves less punishment than murder? We cannot answer this question without first considering two other variations, one affecting the "shelf-life" of licenses, the other affecting their "liquidity." Let's begin with shelf-life.

There are two interesting options. One is to imagine our licenses to be like traveler's checks. Once issued, they would retain their usefulness until "spent." They could be saved indefinitely. The other option is to give licenses a relatively short life, perhaps a year or two (much like an option to buy real estate). Because we are now assuming the "pay later" option, adopting the "short-life option" seems to have some advantages for society. Licenses not used quickly would cease to exist. The society would not have to worry about a sudden wave of licensed crime should all the hoarders decide to cash in at once. The price of licenses would be more stable (or, at least, more closely related to the number society decided to issue in a given year). There would be little reason to buy licenses for long-term speculation, a serious possibility given that the "pay later" option makes hoarding cheap. For this reason, the "short-life" option seems the more plausible here.

There is no counterpart in criminal law as we know it to "shelf life" of licenses. That suggests that we ought to consider the "long-life option" a little more. There is another reason as well. The short-life option would tend to exaggerate any differences in the price of licenses because people would have to take into account the time (and other transaction costs) of obtaining a license and such costs would be relatively larger the less likely the license was to be used. The short-life option thus seems more likely than the long-life to give us the conclusion we want. Nonetheless, let us say no more about shelf-life for now. Once we consider liquidity, we shall see that we can adopt either short-life or long-life option without much effect.

Varying the Usefulness of a License

We must now consider whether we should allow licenses to be resold once "bought" (even if not yet paid for). Reselling would allow those who were lucky enough to win the bidding to sell off licenses they bought should it come to seem that they will not be able to use them in time or should they decide the price others would pay them more than makes up for the use that they might make of the licenses themselves. Allowing resale would make licenses into liquid assets.

Resale would also increase the efficiency of the market. People who wanted a license would no longer have to appear at the auction in person to bid for what they wanted. They could pay "jobbers" to do it for them, buying from the jobbers at the going rate. The jobbers could buy licenses in lots rather than singly, could use information about supply and demand the ordinary bidder is not likely to have time to use, and could otherwise reduce substantially the transaction costs of buying a license.

How far we want to carry resale is, I think, a matter of taste or theoretical economy. For our purposes, we might usefully imagine a particular kind of jobber, insurance companies. These jobbers would, for an annual premium, guarantee to provide a license if needed either at a set price or at a certain percentage of market price at time of purchase. Such an arrangement would allow the insured to share the risk of nonuse with all those similarly situated while assuring each exactly what he would have had if he had bought a license himself. If the policy set a price, then that price together with the annual fee would be a good index of the value of such a license to the person at the moment he acts (but before he knows that he will commit the crime). The market is not likely to let him get away with paying much less. And a rational person would not pay more. Similarly, if the policy only undertook to pay a certain percentage of the market price, then that market price (together with the part of the annual fee not used to pay for licenses) would be a good index of the license's value. Since the greater complexities of the percentage policy do not seem to signal any difference in likely ranking among licenses, let us hereafter imagine our insurance policies to promise a certain license at a set price when needed.

We can now return to our discussion of payment and "shelf life" options. These, it turns out, appeared to matter only because we were implicitly imagining a relatively inefficient market. Once we imagine (something like) our insurance companies among a society's institutions, the importance of the choice among such options disappears.

The importance of the choice between short-life and long-life options depended in part on the possibility of hoarding long-term licenses. To adopt the long-life option seemed to risk a build-up of unused licenses that might lead to a "crime wave" (for instance, because committing a certain crime suddenly came to seem easier). The importance of the choice between these two options also depended in part on the risk of short-term licenses being wasted because buyers (especially buyers of licenses to commit crimes like manslaughter) could be pretty sure they would *not* need the license before it expired.

The insurance companies both make hoarding of long-term options unnecessary and assure that short-term licenses are unlikely to go unused. The insurance companies make hoarding of long-term licenses unnecessary by assuring their customers a license when needed. (This means, of course, that insurance companies probably will *not* be able to insure all those who might want to be insured.) The insurance companies also make hoarding economically unwise.

Under the pay-now option, the hoarder would have to have his money tied up until he resold the license (losing the protection it gave him) or until he used the license (if indeed he ever did). Once he used (or resold) a license, he would have to take the trouble to buy another (taking as well the risk of failing to find one in time) or suffer reduction in his margin of safety. He would certainly be better off buying insurance. The insurance companies allow those they insure the use of most of their money while spreading the risk of license nonuse over such a large population that the risk (virtually) disappears. The return on money that would otherwise be tied up in licenses should pay for much of the insurance premium.

Under the pay-later option, the hoarder would, of course, not have to tie up any money until he had to use his license. But he would have to take the time to build up his hoard and, when the time came to use a license from it, would again have to take time to replace the license (or suffer reduction in his margin of safety). His hoard would represent a significant investment of time if not of money. Since insurance companies are relatively efficient jobbers, a hoarder would probably be better off, even under the pay-later option, if he bought insurance rather than hoarded. His annual premiums should cost him less than attending auctions would.

So, once we allow insurance companies, hoarding should cease being a significant factor in setting market price. Whether we choose the short-life or long-life option, insurance companies should come to dominate the auction. Because insurance companies would constantly be using the licenses they held and having to purchase new ones as they came up for auction, long-term licenses would in practice be very much like short-term licenses and pay-now like pay-later.

Reselling may seem very far from the criminal law as we know it, but it does have its counterpart. Someone considering the possibility that she may some day break a certain law should take into account the cost of *not* breaking it as part of deciding what to do. The cost of not breaking the law is the opportunity lost by abstaining from what she would otherwise do. For an intentional crime like murder, the opportunity cost would be the cost of abstaining from the single act constituting the crime (that cost being reduced by the net benefits of the best legal alternative). For a crime like involuntary manslaughter, however, the opportunity cost is the cost of abstaining from the whole range of conduct unreasonably risking someone's death (again reduced by the net benefits of the best alternative activity). Such costs must be set against something in any rational calculation of whether to undertake the activity in question. They cannot simply be set against the actual punishment-if-convicted because that would leave out of the calculation the probability of not being convicted. For crimes like manslaughter, there is also the very substantial probability that one will not even commit the crime. A rational person would have to take into account that probability in deciding how much to worry about punishment for the crime in question. Such calculations seem to be the counterpart of what our market registers.

Mention of opportunity costs may, however, suggest another objection to the conclusion we want to draw. Because avoiding an intentional crime means giving up only one act (and what would flow from it) while avoiding a crime like manslaughter means avoiding a range of activity (and what would flow from it), the opportunity costs associated with avoiding intentional crimes may seem likely to be *less* than those associated with avoiding the corresponding crime of recklessness or negligence. The potential murderer need only give up intentional killing to avoid committing murder but the potential manslaughterer must give up a range of activities like playing with a gun the firing chamber of which one has not carefully checked first. If we think of opportunity costs as providing the fund out of which a rational person would pay for any license he bought, a license to commit murder may seem likely to fetch less than a license to commit manslaughter.

That, however, is not so. The objection overlooks an important relation between murder and involuntary manslaughter. One who intends to kill need not worry that she may instead commit involuntary manslaughter. Her intention to kill so-and-so precludes any need to worry about killing him recklessly or negligently. This relation between murder and manslaughter assures a certain structure of opportunity costs. Before a potential criminal can face the opportunity costs of avoiding involuntary manslaughter, she must already have paid those of avoiding the corresponding murders. The opportunity costs of avoiding a crime of recklessness must be paid out of a fund already used to pay the costs of avoiding the corresponding intentional crime. So, for example, the question of showing reasonable care in the use of one's gun or paying for a license to commit manslaughter presupposes an activity already made relatively expensive by a deduction for certain opportunities to murder.

Now, if the fund out of which manslaughter's opportunity costs had to be paid were large, these consideration would provide only a weak argument for the claim that manslaughter licenses must sell for less than murder licenses. But the fund cannot in fact be large. As already explained, the principles of criminal legislation require crimes like manslaughter to be relatively easy to avoid. One should be able to avoid such a crime either by taking reasonable precautions or by avoiding activities peripheral to ordinary life. So, the fund out of which a manslaughter license would be paid cannot be larger than the cost of the relatively inexpensive alternative of giving up an activity like playing with a gun in the presence of others when one has not checked the firing chamber. Murder licenses, in contrast, are paid out of a fund the size of which is limited only by the value of the possible objectives murder might achieve.

Conclusion

We have now explained why murder deserves more punishment than involuntary manslaughter even though both do the same harm. We did that by relying upon certain uncontroversial facts (for example, the relatively higher probability of doing what one intends than of doing what one only risks). We have not had to rely upon such an opaque concept as culpability.[11] We have also shown that this result is far less dependent on the particular assumptions of our model than might have been supposed. Our result should be the same for any alternative assumptions — if they are just and plausible and generate a relatively efficient market. The *value* of the licenses by which, on my view, we should measure deserved punishment is not a mere artifact of any arbitrary assumption but as real as any economic fact can be. My rabbits come from an honest hat.

Notes

Work on this chapter was made possible in part by National Endowment for the Humanities Fellowship FB-22388-84. I should like to thank Paul Gomberg, Igor Primoratz, and Don Scheid for helpful comments on an earlier draft.

1. See, for example, Andrew von Hirsch, "Proportionality in the Philosophy of Punishment: From 'Why Punish?' to 'How Much?,'" *Criminal Law Forum* 1 (Winter 1990): 254-290, esp. pp. 266-67.

2. See, for example, Hyman Gross, "Fringe Liability, Unfair Advantage, and the Price of Crime," *Wayne Law Review* 33 (Summer 1987): 1395-1412, esp. pp. 1406-1409; and Jeremy Bentham, *The Principles of Morals and Legislation* (New York: Hafner Publishing Co., 1948), with his emphasis on making crime "unprofitable."

3. See, for example, R. A. Duff, "Auctions, Lotteries, and the Punishment of Attempts, *Law and Philosophy* 9 (February 1990): 2-37, esp. pp. 15-16.

4. For defense, see Chapter Two.

5. Barbara Wootton, *Crime and the Criminal Law* (London: Sweet and Maxwell Ltd, 1963).

6. The same would be true of both "individual restitutionists" such as Randy Barnett, "Restitution: A New Paradigm of Criminal Justice," *Ethics* 87 (July 1977): 279-301; and "systematic restitutionists" such as Margaret Holmgren, "Punishment as Restitution: The Rights of the Community," *Criminal Justice Ethics* 2 (Winter/Spring 1983): 36-49.

7. See, especially, von Hirsch, "Proportionality," pp. 268 and Don E. Scheid, "Davis and the Unfair-Advantage Theory of Punishment: A Critique," *Philosophical Topics* 18 (Spring 1990): 143-170, esp. pp. 162-163.

8. "How to Make the Punishment Fit the Crime," *Ethics* 93 (July 1983): 726-752, esp. pp. 744: "last (and most important), the seriousness of a crime would put a floor under the market price. The more people prefer not to risk something, the more they would pay a licensee not to use his license. The license would always be worth at least what they would pay." Note that I have omitted this from Chapter Four.

9. Though I have chosen the manslaughter-murder distinction more or less at random, the problem posed is by no means unworthy of attention in itself. I urge the reader to compare the treatment that follows with the corresponding discussion of "culpability" (or "blameworthiness") in, for example, Hyman Gross, *A Theory of Criminal Law* (New York: Oxford University Press, 1979), pp. 74-87; Andrew von Hirsch, *Past or Future Crimes* (New Brunswick, New Jersey: Rutgers University Press, 1985), pp. 71-75; or Sanford H. Kadish, "Excusing Crime," *California Law Review* 75 (January 1987): 257-289, esp. pp. 263-266. Where others offer an impenetrable black box ("culpability") or assume that legal culpability must mirror moral culpability (and then leave degrees of moral culpability unexplained), I offer an explanation.

10. For a fuller discussion of this point, see Chapter Seven.

11. For a similar substititon of "control" for "culpability," see Douglas N. Husak, *Philosophy of Criminal Law* (Totowa, New Jersey: Rowman and Littlefield, 1987), esp. 97-111.

Bibliography

Acton, H. B., ed. *The Philosophy of Punishment.* London: Macmillan, 1969.

Arneson, Richard J. "The Principle of Fairness and Free-Rider Problems." *Ethics* 92 (July 1982): 616–633.

Ashworth, Andrew. "Criminal Attempts and the Role of Resulting Harm Under the Code, and in the Common Law." *Rutgers Law Journal* 19 (Spring 1988): 725–772.

Barnett, Randy. "Restitution: A New Paradigm of Criminal Justice." *Ethics* 87 (July 1977): 279–301.

Bayles, Michael. "Punishment for Attempts." *Social Theory and Practices* 8 (Spring 1982): 19–29.

Beccaria, Cesaer. *Crimes and Punishments.* Translated by H. Paolucci. Indianapolis: Bobbs-Merrill, 1963.

Becker, Lawrence. "Criminal Attempt and the Theory of the Law of Crimes." *Philosophy and Public Affairs* 3 (Spring 1974): 262–294.

Bedau, Hugo Adam. "Classification-Based Sentencing: Some Conceptual and Ethical Problems." *NOMOS XXVII: Criminal Justice* (1985): 89–118.

Bedau, Hugo Adam. *Death is Different.* Boston: Northeastern University Press, 1987.

Bedau, Hugo Adam. "Retribution and the Theory of Punishment." *Journal of Philosophy* 75 (November 1978): 601–622.

Benn, S. I. and R. S. Peters. *The Principles of Political Thought.* New York: Free Press, 1965.

Benn, Stanley I. "An Approach to the Problem of Punishment." *Philosophy* 33 (October 1958): 334–337.

Bentham, Jeremy. *The Principles of Morals and Legislation.* New York: Hafner Publishing Co., 1948.

Bern, Walter. *For Capital Punishment: Crime and the Morality of the Death Penalty.* New York: Basic Books, 1979.

Bishop, Joel. *New Criminal Law.* 9th ed. Chicago: T. H. Flood and Company, 1923.

Blocker, H. G. and E. H. Smith. *John Rawls' Theory of Social Justice: An Introduction.* Athens, Ohio: Ohio University Press, 1980.

Bosanquet, B. "The Philosophical Theory of the State." 4th ed. London: Macmillan, 1965.

Bradley, F. H. *Ethical Studies.* 2nd ed. London: Oxford University Press, 1962.

Brady, James. "Strict Liability Offenses: A Justification." *Criminal Law Bulletin* 8 (April 1972): 217–227.

Braithwaite, John, & Pettit, Phillip. *Not Just Deserts: A Republican Theory of Criminal Justice.* Oxford: Clarendon Press, 1990.

Card, Claudia. "On Mercy." *Philosophical Review* 81 (April 1972): 182–207.

Carr, Charles R. "Punishing Attempts." *Pacific Philosophical Quarterly* 62 (January 1981): 61–68.

Clark, Michael. "The Moral Graduation of Punishment." *Philosophical Quarterly* 21 (April 1971): 132–140.

Davis, Michael. "Death, Deterrence, and the Method of Common Sense." *Social Theory and Practice* 7 (Summer 1981): 145–178.

Davis, Michael. "Guilty But Insane?" *Social Theory and Practice* 10 (Spring 1984): 1–23.

Davis, Michael. "Harm and Retribution." *Philosophy and Public Affairs* 15 (Summer 1986): 236–266.

Davis, Michael. "How to Make the Punishment Fit the Crime." *Ethics* 93 (July 1983): 726–752.

Davis, Michael. "Just Deserts for Recidivists." *Criminal Justice Ethics* 4 (Summer/Fall 1985): 29–50.

Davis, Michael. "Nozick's Argument for the Legitimacy of the Welfare State." *Ethics* 97 (April 1987): 576–594.

Davis, Michael. "Racial Quotas, Weights, and Real Possibilities." *Social Theory and Practice* 7 (Spring 1981): 49–84.

Davis, Michael. "The Relative Independence of Punishment Theory." *Law and Philosophy* 7 (December 1988): 321–350.

Davis, Michael. "Sentencing: Must Justice Be Even-Handed?" *Law and Philosophy* 1 (April 1982): 77–117.

Davis, Michael. "Setting Penalties: What Does Rape Deserve?" *Law and Philosophy* 3 (April 1984): 62–111.

Davis, Michael. "Smith, Gert, and Obligation to Obey the Law." *Southern Journal of Philosophy* 20 (Summer 1982): 139–152.

Davis, Michael. "Strict Liability: Deserved Punishment for Faultless Conduct." *Wayne Law Review* 33 (Summer 1987): 1363–1393.

Davis, Michael. "Using the Market to Measure Deserved Punishment." *Iyyun* 39 (July 1990): 295–319.

Day, J. P. "Retributive Punishment." *Mind* 87 (October 1987): 498–516.

Dennis, Ian. "The Criminal Attempts Act 1981." *Criminal Law Review* (January 1982): 5–16.

Devlin, Patrick. *The Enforcement of Morals.* London: Oxford University Press, 1965.

Dressler, Joshua. "Substantive Criminal Law through the Looking Glass of Rummel v. Estelle: Proportionality and Justice as Endangered Doctrines." *Southwest Law Journal* 34 (February 1981): 1063–1130.

Duff, R. A. "Auctions, Lotteries, and the Punishment of Attempts." *Law and Philosophy* 9 (February 1990): 1–37.

Duff, R. A. *Trials and Punishments.* Cambridge: Cambridge University Press, 1985.

Ellis, E. D. and C. S. Ellis. *Theories of Criminal Justice.* Wolfeboro, New Hampshire: Longwood Academic, 1989.

Fair and Certain Punishment: Report of the Twentieth Century Fund Task Force on Criminal Sentencing. New York: McGraw-Hill Book Company, 1976.

Feinberg, Joel. *Doing and Deserving.* Princeton: Princeton University Press, 1970.

Finnis, John. "The Restoration of Retribution." *Analysis* 32 (March 1972): 131–135.

Fletcher, George. "The Recidivist Premium." *Criminal Justice Ethics* I (Winter/Spring 1982): 54–49.

Fletcher, George. *Rethinking Criminal Law.* Boston: Little, Brown & Company, 1978.

Flew, Anthony. "The Justification of Punishment." *Philosophy* 29 (October 1954): 291–307.

Frankel, Marvin E. *Criminal Sentences: Law without Order.* New York: Hill and Wang, 1972.

Fuller, Lon. "Positivism and Fidelity to Law – A Reply to Professor Hart." *Harvard Law Review* 71 (February 1958): 630–672.

Gerwirth, Alan. *Reason and Morality.* Chicago: University of Chicago Press, 1978.

Gilchrist, Bruce W. "Note: Disproportionality in Sentences of Imprisonment." *Columbia Law Review* 79 (October 1979): 1119–1166.

Glueck, Sheldon. *Crime and Justice.* Cambridge, Mass.: Harvard University Press, 1945.

Goldberg, Steven. "On Capital Punishment." *Ethics* 85 (October 1974): 75–79.

Goldman, Alan. "The Paradox of Punishment." *Philosophy and Public Affairs* 9 (Fall 1979): 42–58.

Griffiths, A. Philips. *Philosophy and Practice.* Cambridge: Cambridge University Press, 1985.

Gross, Hyman. "Fringe Liability, Unfair Advantage, and the Price of Crime." *Wayne Law Review* 33 (Summer 1987): 1395–1412.

Gross, Hyman. *A Theory of Criminal Justice.* New York: Oxford University Press, 1979.

Hall, Jerome. *General Principles of Criminal Law.* Indianapolis: Bobbs-Merrill, 1947.

Hall, Jerome. *Principles of Criminal Law.* Indianapolis: Bobbs-Merrill, 1960.

Hamilton, V. Lee and Steve Rytina. "Social Consensus on Norms of Justice: Should the Punishment Fit the Crime?" *American Journal of Sociology* 85 (March 1980): 1117–1144.

Hampton, Jean. "The Moral Education Theory of Punishment." *Philosophy and Public Affairs* 13 (Summer 1984): 208–338.

Hart, H. L. A. *Law, Liberty, and Morality.* New York: Vintage Press, 1963.

Hart, H. L. A. "Positivism and the Separation of Law and Morals." *Harvard Law Review* 71 (February 1958): 593–629.

Hart, H. L. A. *Punishment and Responsibility: Essays in the Philosophy of Law.* New York: Oxford University Press, 1968.

Hegel, G.W.F. *Philosophy of Right.* 1821.

Hoekema, David. "The Right to Punish and the Right to be Punished." In *John Rawls' Theory of Social Justice: An Introduction* by H. G. Blocker and E. H. Smith. Athens, Ohio: Ohio University Press, 1980.

Holmgren, Margaret. "Punishment as Restitution: The Rights of the Community." *Criminal Justice Ethics* 2 (Winter\Spring 1983): 36–49.

Honderich, Ted. "Punishment, the New Retributivism, and Political Philosophy." In *Philosophy and Practice* by A. Philip Griffiths. Cambridge: Cambridge University Press, 1985.

Honderich, Ted. *Punishment: The Supposed Justifications.* Middlesex, England: Penguin Book, 1971.

Husak, Douglas. *Philosophy of Criminal Law.* Totowa, New Jersey: Rowman and Littlefield, 1987.

Illinois Annotated Statutes. St. Paul, Minn.: West Publishing Company, 1983.

Kadish, Sanford H. "Complicity, Cause and Blame: A Study in the Interpretation of Doctrine." *California Law Review* 73 (March 1985): 323–410.

Kadish, Sanford H. "Excusing Crime." *California Law Review* 75 (January 1987): 257–289.

Kant, Immanuel. *The Metaphysical Element of Justice.* Translated by John Ladd. Indianapolis: Liberal Arts Library, 1965.

Katkin, T. "Habitual Offender Laws: A Reconsideration." *Buffalo Law Review* 21 (Fall 1971): 99–120.

Kipnis, Kenneth. "Criminal Justice and the Negotiated Plea." *Ethics* 86 (January 1976): 93–106.

Kleinig, John. *Punishment and Desert.* The Hague: Marinus Nijhoff, 1973.

Kneale, William. *The Responsibility of Criminals.* Oxford: Oxford University Press, 1967.

Lacey, Nicola. *State Punishment.* London: Routledge, 1988.

LaFave, Wayne and Austin Scott. *Criminal Law.* St. Paul, Minn.: West Publishing Co., 1972.

Mabbott, J. D. "Professor Flew on Punishment." *Philosophy* 30 (July 1955): 256–265.

Mabbott, J. D. "Punishment." *Mind* 48 (April 1939): 152–167.

MacDonald, N. "A Critique of Habitual Criminal Legislation in Canada and England." *University of British Columbia Law Review* 4 (May 1969): 87–108.

Martinson, R. "New Findings, New Views: A Note of Caution Regarding Sentencing Reform." *Hofstra Law Review* 7 (Winter 1979): 243–258.

McAnany, Patrick. "Punishment: Current Survey of Philosophy and Law." *Saint Louis University Law Journal* 11 (Summer 1967): 491–535.

McCloskey, H. J. "Utilitarian and Retributive Punishment." *Journal of Philosophy* 66 (February 16, 1967): 91–110.

Menninger, Karl. *The Crime of Punishment.* New York: Viking Press, 1969.

Merry, George B. "Seeking Nationwide Sentence to Fit the Crime: States Move toward More Uniform System of Justice." *Christian Science Monitor* (June 1, 1981): 12.

Mitias, Michael H. "Is Retribution Inconsistent Without Lex Talionis?" *Rivista Internazionale di Filosofia del Diritto* 56 (Winter 1983): 211–230.

Montesquieu. *Spirit of Laws.* 1748.

Moore, Kathleen. *Pardons.* New York: Oxford University Press, 1989.

Morris, Herbert. *On Guilt and Innocence.* Berkeley: University of California Press, 1976.

Morris, Herbert. "A Paternalistic Theory of Punishment." *American Philosophical Quarterly* 18 (October 1981): 263–271.

Morris, Herbert. "Persons and Punishment." *Monist* 52 (October 1968): 475–501.

Murphy, Jeffrie. "Does Kant Have a Theory of Punishment?" *Columbia Law Review* 87 (April 1987): 509–532.

Murphy, Jeffrie. "Kant's Theory of Criminal Punishment." *Proceedings of the Third International Kant Congress.* 434–441. Dordrecht: D. Reidel, 1971.

Murphy, Jeffrie. "Marxism and Retribution." *Philosophy and Public Affairs* 2 (Spring 1973): 217–243.

Nagel, Ernest. *The Structure of Science.* New York: Harcourt, Brace, & World, 1961.

Nagel, Thomas. "Moral Luck." *Mortal Questions.* Cambridge: Cambridge University Press, 1979.

Note. "Constitutional Law – Criminal Law – Cruel and Unusual Punishment." *Cincinnati Law Review* 49 (1980): 725–737.

Note. "Constitutional Law – Texas Habitual Offender Statute Does Not Violate the Eighth Amendment." *American Journal of Criminal Law* 8 (July 1980): 209–216.

Note. "Constitutional Criminal Law – Eighth Amendment." *Tulane Law Review* 55 (February 1981): 560–576.

Note. "Criminal Liability Without Fault." *Columbia Law Review* 75 (December 1975): 1517–1577.

Note. "Rape, Recidivism, and Capital Punishment." *Ohio Northern University Law Review* 9 (January 1982): 99–119.

Note. "Recidivism and the Eighth Amendment." *Notre Dame Lawyer* 55 (December 1979): 305–315.

Note. "Recidivist Statutes — Application of Proportionality and Overbreadth Doctrines to Repeat Offenders." *Washington Law Review* 57 (July 1981): 573–598.

Note. "Rummel v. Estelle: Cruel and Unusual Punishment." *South Texas Law Journal* 19 (Fall 1978): 709–715.

Note. "Rummel v. Estelle: Sentencing without a Rational Basis." *Syracuse Law Review* 32 (Summer 1981): 803–840.

Note. "State v. Grant: Is Intent an Essential Element of Criminal Attempt in Maine?" *Maine Law Review* 34 (1982): 479–494.

Nozick, Robert. *Anarchy, State, and Utopia.* New York: Basic Books, 1974.

Nozick, Robert. *Philosophical Explanations.* Cambridge, Mass.: Harvard University Press, Belknap, 1981.

Packer, Herbert. *Limits of the Criminal Sanction.* Stanford, Calif.: Stanford University Press, 1968.

Packer, Herbert. "Making the Punishment Fit the Crime." *Harvard Law Review* 77 (April 1964): 1071–1082.

Packer, Herbert. "Mens Rea and the Supreme Court." *Supreme Court Review* 1 (1962): 107–152.

Perlman, Harvey S. and Carol G. Stebbins. "Implementing an Equitable Sentencing System: The Uniform Commissioners' Model Sentencing and Corrections Act." *Virginia Law Review* 65 (November 1979): 1175–1285.

Philips, Michael. "The Justification of Punishment and the Justification of Political Authority." *Law and Philosophy* 5 (December 1985): 393–416.

Pincoffs, Edmund L. *The Rationale of Legal Punishment.* New York: Humanities Press, 1966.

Plato. *Laws.*

Primoratz, Igor. "Punishment as Language." *Philosophy* 64 (April 1989): 187–205.

Rachels, James. *Moral Problems.* New York: Harper & Row, 1971.

Radcliffe-Brown, A. R. *Structure and Function in Primitive Society.* New York: Free Press, 1952.

Rawls, John. "Two Concepts of Rules." *Philosophical Review* 64 (January 1955): 3–32.

Reiman, Jeffrey H. "Justice, Civilization, and the Death Penalty: Answering van den Haag." *Philosophy and Public Affairs* 14 (Spring 1985): 115–148.

Ross, W. D. *The Right and The Good.* London: Oxford University Press, 1930.

Rossi, Peter H., et al. "The Seriousness of Crimes: Normative Structure and Individual Differences." *American Sociological Review* 39 (April 1974): 224–237.

Sadurski, Wojciech. *Giving Desert Its Due.* Dordrecht: D. Reidel Publishing Company, 1985.

Sadurski, Wojciech. "Theory of Punishment, Social Injustice, and Liberal Neutrality." *Law and Philosophy* 7 (December 1989): 351–374.

Sartorius, Rolf E. *Individual Conduct and Social Norms.* Encino, Calif.: Dickenson Publishing Co., 1975.

Scheid, Don E. "Davis and the Unfair-Advantage Theory of Punishment: A Critique." *Philosophical Topics* 18 (Spring 1990): 143–170.

Scher, George. *Desert.* Princeton: Princeton University Press, 1987.

Scott, Arthur P. *Criminal Law in Colonial Virginia.* Chicago: University of Chicago Press, 1930.

Sellin, Thorsten and Wolfgang, Marvin E. *The Measurement of Delinquency.* New York: Wiley, 1964.

Singer, Richard G. *Just Deserts: Sentencing Based on Equality and Desert.* Cambridge: Bollinger Publishing Co., 1979.

Smith, M. B. E. "Is There a Prima Facie Obligation to Obey the Law?" *Yale Law Review* 82 (April 1973): 950–976.

Sterba, James P. "Is There A Rationale For Punishment?" *American Journal of Jurisprudence* 29 (1984): 29–43.

Stevenson, Charles L. *Ethics and Language.* New Haven: Yale University Press, 1944.

Ten, C. L. *Crime, Guilt, and Punishment.* Oxford: Clarendon Press, 1987.

Twentieth Century Fund, Task Force on Criminal Sentencing. *Fair and Certain Punishment.* New York: McGraw-Hill Book Company, 1976.

Van den Haag, Ernest. "On Deterrence and the Death Penalty." *Ethics* 78 (July 1968): 280–289.

von Hirsch, Andrew. "Desert and Previous Convictions in Sentencing." *Minnesota Law Review* 65 (April 1981): 591–634.

von Hirsch, Andrew. *Doing Justice: The Choice of Punishment.* New York: Hill and Wang, 1976.

von Hirsch, Andrew. *Past or Future Crimes.* New Brunswick, New Jersey: Rutgers University Press, 1985.

von Hirsch, Andrew: "Prediction of Criminal Conduct and Preventative Confinement of Convicted Persons." *Buffalo Law Review* 21 (Spring 1972): 717–758.

von Hirsch, Andrew. "Proportionality in the Philosophy of Punishment: From 'Why Punish?' to How Much?" *Criminal law Forum* 1 (Winter 1990): 254–290.

von Hirsch, Andrew. "Punishments in the Community and the Principles of Desert." *Rutgers Law Review* 20 (Spring 1989): 595–618.

Wasserstrom, Richard. "Strict Liability in the Criminal Law." *Stanford Law Review* 12 (July 1960): 731–745.

Wertheimer, Alan. "Deterrence and Retribution." *Ethics* 86 (January 1976): 181–199.

Williams, Glanville. "Absolute Liability in Traffic Offenses." *Criminal Law Review* (April 1967): 194–208.

Williams, Glanville. "Problems of Reckless Attempts." *Criminal Law Review* (June 1983): 365–375.

Williams, Granville. *Criminal Law: The General Part.* British Publications: Stevens and Son, 1961.

Wootton, Barbara. *Crime and the Criminal Law.* London: Sweet and Maxwell Ltd., 1963.

Zalman, Marvin. "The Rise and Fall of the Indeterminate Sentence [Parts I and II]." *Wayne Law Review* 24 (November 1977): 45–94.

Index

About the Book and Author

While everyone may agree that the punishment should fit the crime, it is much harder to reach agreement on just what is called for in specific cases. Philosophical treatments of punishment, which tend to emphasize the nature or justification of punishment in general, are often of no help in dealing with practical questions of the appropriateness of specific punishments.

In this collection of often controversial essays, Michael Davis examines many of the practical problems of punishment. Among the issues discussed are how recidivism should be punished, how unsuccessful attempts at crimes should be punished, and how courts should deal with crimes of strict liability. Davis, a long-time contributor to the literature on punishment, also discusses problems of sentencing, and he responds to his earlier critics, including Hyman Gross, Andrew von Hirsch, and R. A. Duff.

To Make the Punishment Fit the Crime is written in the rigorous, accessible, and iconoclastic style Davis's readers have come to expect. It is an essential book for philosophers, lawyers, criminologists, and others concerned about the future of criminal justice.

Michael Davis is senior research associate at the Center for Study of Ethics in the Professions and adjunct professor of philosophy at the Illinois Institute of Technology.

BGSU Libraries

A11320018168

K 5103 .D38 1992

Davis, Michael.

To make the punishment fit
 the crime